SATISFACTION
GUARANTEED

Also by Linda West Eckhardt:
The New West Coast Cuisine
The Only Texas Cookbook
An American Gumbo

SATISFACTION GUARANTEED

Simply Sumptuous Mail-Order Foods
with Recipes and Menus for Fast
and Fabulous Meals

LINDA WEST ECKHARDT

JEREMY P. TARCHER, INC.
Los Angeles

Distributed by St. Martin's Press
New York

Library of Congress Cataloging in Publication Data

Eckhardt, Linda West, 1939-
    Satisfaction guaranteed.

    Includes index.
    1. Food—Catalogs. 2. Cookery. 3. Menus. I. Title.
TX354.5.E25   1986   641.5′029′473   86–6036
ISBN 0-87477-387-3

Jeremy P. Tarcher, Inc.
9110 Sunset Blvd.
Los Angeles, CA 90069

Design by Mike Yazzolino

Illustrations by Valerie Deo

Manufactured in the United States of America
10 9 8 7 6 5 4 3 2 1

First Edition

for Shirley Barr,
the best in the business

Thanks to Janice Gallagher, who edited this book with such good judgment and such good grace. Thanks also to Jeremy Tarcher, who liked the idea, and to the rest of the staff who turned to, to produce a great-looking book.

Thanks also to the food purveyors in this book, without whose cooperation this book would not have been possible. You're doing a great job, guys. Keep stirrin' and choppin'.

Many thanks to Kathy Parson, who believes and who cheers me up when I get down.

SATISFACTION GUARANTEED

Table of Contents

I tell you what, it's just like Christmas, your birthday, and Valentine's Day all rolled into one. You order something, and before you know it, the doorbell rings, the Federal Express man stands there, package in hand, a smile on his face, and there's your present. A package that came overnight, cloaked in a portable styrofoam refrigerator, fresh, just-made. Say a fresh pâté and a jar of cornichons. Open it up. Cold. Aromatic with the scent of peppers and herbs. What more do you need? A fresh baguette . . . a bottle of wine . . . a piece of fruit . . . your best friend. It's a picnic you won't soon forget.

Thanks to the overnight shippers, the availability of products in America is changing fast, and an entire food business has developed as a result. Up on Cape Cod, for example, you can call Linda Louis and order an authentic clambake with everything from live lobsters, clams, and mussels to corn on the cob and sweet sausage. Linda will pack a big can with live seaweed, place everything in the proper layers, and next day the whole thing will appear at your door, before noon. The clambake comes to you. And you don't have to live in Short Hills, New Jersey, to get this, I might add. With overnight shipping, Linda can send it just as fast to your door in La Jolla, California.

In the last three or four years UPS, Federal Express, and all their cousins have blossomed and made it possible to have delivered to you fine, fresh regional specialties grown and made in far-flung locations. Live crawfish and the Cajun specialties to go with them. Blue corn from New Mexico, with

How to Use This Book

Within each chapter of this book, you'll find subdivisions that contain listings for particular food items—cheeses, for example—with full descriptions of the food products and complete addresses for where to get them. Some companies sell more than one kind of product, in which case I've given you a full listing with their primary product and a reference with their secondary products that says, *"See also: (company name)."*

You won't find exact prices in this book. They change too fast. Call or write to the companies for a current quotation of prices. I have tried to advise you if prices creep toward the national debt.

I have listed the credit cards accepted by each company. Ae designates American Express, while v stands for Visa and mc for Mastercard. Diner's Club and Carte Blanche are listed as dc and cb, respectively.

At the beginning of every chapter, you'll find a quick rundown of what is contained in that chapter. If you want a particular product, check the general index at the back of the book under the product name, generic name, brand name, and company name. I've tried to cross-reference this book everyway from Sunday to help you track down your favorite foods.

CONTINUED ON PAGE XI

peppers and salsas besides. Tiger prawns from Malaysia, shipped live to your door. Small-batch jams, made with local wild berries and fruits, maybe sweetened with fruit juices and no sugar at all. Handmade cheeses of a quality you may have thought you'd have to go to the countryside of France to get. Family-made ethnic sauces and spice blends, so that you don't have to go to Bombay or to an Indian restaurant to taste authentic Indian cuisine. All these indigenous ethnic foods are yours with a phone call.

It actually started in the new American restaurants with the young chefs who got interested in presenting freshly grown local specialties. Food co-ops began to develop between growers and restaurant operators so that new and greater varieties of fresh foods were grown and presented to enthusiastic restaurant goers. It was a short step for those people to ask the waiter, "Where can I get this? I want to serve it at home."

This new generation of farmers and cooks have rejected mass production; they've taken a great leap backward, to pure, fresh, unadulterated local foods, grown carefully, prepared without chemicals, and presented promptly to a growing population of devotees who care enough to insist on the very best. Purity, goodness, and small-batch cooking are the principles that guide today's new food purveyors. The principles guarantee that what you receive from the UPS man, sight unseen—a pig in a poke, as they say—will, in fact, provide Satisfaction Guaranteed.

Look in this book and you will find the same sources for fresh foods that the most current restaurants have. You can get everything of the superior quality demanded by the most discriminating chefs.

Because, right this very minute, real people in real kitchens are stirring together real food to package and ship out today to really discriminating diners who are sophisticated about food, interested in regional specialties, health conscious, and may eat out two or three times a week. If that describes you, then you'll probably get as excited as I did, trying for the first time the best foods that America has to offer.

You don't have to be Charles Kurault to find America. You can find it yourself, and through the back door—through the food America grows and prepares to feed itself. Thanks to UPS, we're all one big neighborhood now. The wonderful individuality that our country prizes can be seen clearly in the people who reject corporate life, who take risks and put everything they have on the line to start a business making cheese, or raising lambs, or growing baby vegetables. I wish you could know these people as I've come to know them. Restaurant owners who live above the store, who finally begin selling their sauces because the customers demand it. Breadmakers who start by milling their own flour—between stones. Vegetable and herb growers who'd never consider using a pesticide or herbicide and who are sophisticated enough to prevent the accidental introduction of any contaminant into their product. The food producers presented in this book began with a philosophy that says, "I want food that tastes great and is good for me besides."

Begin ordering from these people, and you'll find, as I have, that you have a group of new friends. People who make their living feeding people are, in my experience, generous and giving. Getting to know them is almost as rewarding as eating the food they prepare.

CONTINUED FROM PAGE X

You will find recipes and serving suggestions alongside some listings. These represent good ways to use the various products.

In the Mail-Order Menus chapter, you'll find complete menus that refer you back to the body of the book, where you'll find the sources for the products, and recipes where appropriate.

All recipes that appear in the book are listed in the recipe index.

In case you're wondering who "we" are in these pages, we are the taste panel employed to test the food products that passed through this kitchen. To begin with, my husband, Joe; my son, Jay; and various and sundry passing-through friends were rounded up to taste-test everything from vinegars to sun-dried tomatoes. It wasn't hard to gather a panel to try out the fresh pâtés, or the live lobsters. (I did begin to believe that if I saw another jar of mustard, I would throw myself on my sword.)

In deciding what went into the book, we used these criteria: First of all, did it taste good? Did it arrive in safe condition? Was it free of chemical adulteration? Did the maker know how to ship things? Last, but not really least, did the package look good?

All you need besides this book is a telephone, a credit card, a fork, and an appetite. Then, I can assure you, you'll have Satisfaction Guaranteed.

CHAPTER 1

BREAD AND BREAKFAST

When we say bread and breakfast, we're thinking of the Continental breakfast, consisting of cheese and bread and fine jam. You'll find a good bit of crossover between the items in this and other chapters, so be flexible. Bacons and sausages are in the Protein Purveyors chapter. These cheeses work as well for dinner as for breakfast. But here you'll find the best breads, cheeses, jams, honey, and maple syrup for your pancakes. And the pancake fixings too. Good morning!

MAKING CHEESE IN SMALL BATCHES

Small-batch cheeses are among the most intriguing products of American farms and kitchens. You simply cannot buy in a store cheeses that are this interesting. Order five of them and I'll guarantee you'll never be happy again buying cheese only at the deli. Even the most expensive imported cheeses you can buy in stores are mass produced. But by shopping directly with cheesemakers, you have access to handmade cheeses as fine as any you'd find, say, in the countryside of France, where cheesemaking is part of the farmwife's repertoire. And by cutting out the middleman, you will be getting a real bargain, for all of these cheeses are priced competi-

<u>1</u>

tively with mass-produced ones, whether imported or domestic.

Not only that, but there's no chemical inducement, no "better living through chemistry," but rather all natural, all handmade products wherein the cheesemaker controls everything, often beginning with the grass and grain that the cow or goat eats.

In my research, I noted a couple of interesting facts about cheesemaking in America. First of all, the cheesemakers seem to live in clusters. You'll find more cheeses made in the Northwest, Northeast, and Wisconsin. And in these cases, the predominant country of origin of the area's original settlers has an impact on the kinds of cheese made. New England, as its name suggests, is big on cheddar. More German and Scandinavian types of cheese are made in the Midwest. In the Northwest, where numerous city names mimic the Northeast—Portland, for example— the cheeses seem to spring from English roots again. Then there are the academic cheesemakers who are professionally trained, and they seem to favor the French farmhouse cheeses—chèvre, brie, the American blues.

We have in America a good sampling of cheeses from the best European cultures. I will say this: We as a family have been totally spoiled and know now that we cannot live ever again without wheels of these splendid cheeses sitting in our cool cellar. Already we've had to reorder that most incredible of cheeses made by the Trappists, who—defying all convention—are located in Kentucky. They call their cheese semisoft mild, but in our experience it has the authority of the Pope. As the best example of American-made cheese, this is served in the White House to foreign dignitaries.

Other outstanding cheeses are made in this country as well: Sadie Kendall's goat cheese, combining the best of dairy science and the French farmwife. The Herkimer New York cheddars made by the Basloe family, who practically invented cheese balls after Sheldon began stopping by the supermarket for a sack of nuts, then drafting his wife and children to crack them as they sat around the television at night. Is that American or what? Oregon's Blue Heron brie, made in the shadow of a famous cheddar maker but creating an exquisite fresh dessert cheese that is truly handmade . . . as opposed to those crafty imports you see in the delicatessens.

These are just a few examples of the fabulous cheeses made in America. You'll have to read the section to begin to grasp what's happening in American cheesemaking today. Who knows? At the rate we're going, if another decade produces an equal number of new cottage kitchen cheesemakers, perhaps we'll get to be like France. You've heard what Churchill said, eh? "A country with 365 cheeses cannot be governed."

Goat and Sheep Cheeses

Goat and sheep cheeses come in many guises. We've offered a good range—from the fresh cream cheese types from Sadie Kendall, all the way to deep, aged cheeses such as Tome from Laura Chenel, suitable for grating.

FRESH GOAT CHEESE, CRÈME FRAÎCHE, AND BUTTER

Kendall Cheese Co.   phone orders: yes
PO Box 686   805-466-7252
Atascadero, CA 93423

Sadie Kendall is the kind of food expert you can trust. She's a trained dairy scientist, with an interest in and respect for traditional methods of her craft as well. She's blended art and science to raise fresh goat cheeses to new heights. She also makes the finest butter in America and a crème fraîche you cannot duplicate at home.

Sadie Kendall's chèvrefeuille is as good as any in France. It is hand-dipped and double cream, making it delightful when young and even more complex when mature. Her pure goat's-milk Camembert, chèvre sec, chèvre frais, and chèvredoux, made with half goat's milk and half cow's milk, are equally subtle and authoritative.

For the serious cook, chocolatier, and baker, Sadie Kendall's butter, always in short supply and big demand, is the only unsalted ripened-cream butter available in the United States that isn't imported. Her crème fraîche is thick enough to float a silver spoon. You can't lose with Kendall's products.

Jim Demeter's Suggestions for a Successful Wine and Cheese Party

■ Figure on about 3 ounces of cheese and/or meat per person.

■ Variety is the key to success.

■ Separate soft-ripened and strong-flavored cheeses to prevent strong flavors from overwhelming the more delicate varieties.

■ Serve cold cuts on a separate tray from cheese.

■ Garnish cheese with fruits—slices of apple or pear, or grapes. Douse apple and pear slices in acidulated water to prevent darkening before arranging on the tray.

■ Serve soft cheeses such as brie or Old Heidelberg alone on a separate tray along with a butter knife for spreading.

■ Unflavored crackers such as Vermont common crackers or Valley lahvosh, along with cubes of French bread, make good backers. Good black breads, pumpernickel, rye, and other dark breads work well with strong cheeses. Avoid flavored crackers that will fight the cheese.

■ If you are serving a variety of cheeses, it is advisable to have on hand the three basic wine types: a robust red, a dry white, and a rosé. There are no hard-and-fast rules for matching cheese to wines. Best to let the guests make their own decisions about what goes with what.

Here's a suggestion from Kolb-Lena. For the holidays, make a "Brie Torte." Decorate the top of a brie round with nuts, herbs, or fruits—almonds, walnuts, and raisins, for example. Remember that brie is temperamental and will quickly pick up "off" tastes, so be sure your decorations are absolutely fresh.

Mama Demeter's Scrambled Eggs with Feta Crumbles

For each person:

   2 eggs
   1 teaspoon cooking oil
   2 tablespoons crumbled
      feta cheese
      Freshly ground coarse
      black pepper

Soft-scramble eggs in oil over medium heat, then remove from heat. Toss feta and pepper into eggs. Keep tossing and mixing until cheese blends. The trick is not to overheat the feta, which creates a soggy mess. Just warm the crumbles. Mama says this is a lunch that comes in under 200 calories and over the top in satisfaction. Light, zesty, and delicious.

ILLINOIS FETA, CHÈVRE, AND BABY SWISS

Kolb-Lena Cheese Co.   phone orders: yes
301 W. Railroad St.   815-369-4577
Lena, IL 61048   ae/visa/mc

Just before the turn of the century, Frederick Kolb came to the United States from Wachtersbach, Germany, to join his cousin in a venture known as the French Cheese Company. His cousin, homesick for Germany, soon sold out to Fred and went home. Then, literally following the milk cows, Fred Kolb moved his cheese factory around until, in 1925, he settled in the little pastoral town of Lena, Illinois.

Now, through two generations of family cheesemakers, and adhering to the premise on which Fred began his business—to produce cheeses the public wants—the Kolb-Lena Cheese Company offers cheeses reliably made by hand that meet the demands of the 1980s. They produce a low-sodium, low-cholesterol Swiss for those on restricted diets. The Swiss-Lo they sent me was laced with vegetables and was bright and tasty. If you need to know caloric output, sodium count, or any of a dozen other pieces of nutritional information, you'll find them all printed on the Kolb-Lena label.

Drawing on his Greek background, Jim Demeter, Mr. Kolb's grandson-in-law, has developed a feta so tangy and bright-sour that it is in great demand by Greek restaurants in the Chicago area. Equally popular is the baby Swiss, developed by Kolb-Lena and the Aggies at Ames, Iowa State's School of Agriculture. New but gaining in popularity is the Illinois chèvre, a snow-white fresh goat cheese.

Under the guidance of Demeter and his wife, Dorothy, both of whom have degrees in dairy sciences from the Iowa State School of Agriculture, the Kolb-Lena cheese line has expanded to include an American brie proclaimed by James Beard to be the best in the United States; an Old Heidelberg with the authority of Limburger; Sno-Belle, their own double-cream variation of brie; and Port Salut, cheddar, Jack, Havarti, and—to my mind their very best product—Alpendeler Swiss, three-time grand champion at the Illinois State Fair. Almost 20 cheese varieties in all. Write for a current price list. You'll be pleasantly surprised at their modest rates. These people are reliable, dedicated cheesemakers.

SWISS STYLE RAW GOAT'S-MILK CHEESES

Briar Hills Dairy, Inc.   phone orders: yes
279 S.W. 9th St.   206-748-4224
Chehalis, WA 98532

For a mild, white, firm goat's-milk cheese particularly suited to cooking, Briar Hills makes an elastic-curd cheese they call Cascadian and a more crumbly, dry, sharp type they call Briar Hills Natural. The latter comes with or without caraway seeds.

Most interesting is their own version of gjetost, known as Viking Brown Whey Cheese. This cheese is a rich caramel brown in color, melts on the tongue, and has the complex taste of caramels, but without sugar. Popular with runners, it is high in potassium, phosphorus, and carbohydrates. It is made from skim milk and is low in fats. Long popular with Scandinavians, this type of cheese is gaining popularity in this country with every Boston-type marathon. Taste it and you'll see why. Its rich caramel taste is wonderfully satisfying and you just know it makes itself available to you. Keep running.

CUSTOM-MADE CHEESES: SHEEP, GOAT, AND COW'S MILK

Sally Jackson Cheese Co.   phone orders: no phone
Star Rte., Box 106
Oroville, WA 98844

Sally and Roger Jackson produce sheep's cheeses of extreme delicacy and subtlety. They grow their own hay. They care for their animals' needs with the care most

---

Pheasant in Gjetost Cream Sauce

Serve with cranberry sauce and boiled red potatoes. This sweet-sour sauce has a hint of burnt sugar from the addition of caramel-like gjetost to the sauce.

Serves 4 in 2 hours

1	3-pound pheasant (or chicken)
	Salt, pepper, and paprika to taste
¼	cup sweet butter
1	cup whipping cream
1	tablespoon flour
1	cup milk
¼	cup gjetost cheese, shredded
1	tablespoon cider vinegar

Season bird with salt, pepper, and paprika, then sauté in hot butter until golden on all sides. Reduce to a simmer, then add cream. Cover and cook until bird is tender, at least an hour, turning pieces from time to time. Remove bird to a warmed plate. Combine flour and milk into a smooth paste, then add to sauce. Cook to a smooth sauce, stirring and adjusting seasonings as necessary. Just before serving, stir in cheese and vinegar. Serve sauce on the side with cooked bird.

Fresh Pasta with Sheep's Cheese and Bacon

Serve this pasta in springtime with a salad of dandelion, tender baby radish leaves, baby turnips, and spinach.

Serves 4 in 20 minutes

¾	pound fresh pasta
3	strips bacon, cooked and crumbled
4	ounces feta cheese, crumbled
4	ounces sheep's or goat cheese
½	cup sour cream

Cook pasta al dente. Meanwhile, cook bacon. Once pasta is cooked, drain and add to skillet in which you cooked bacon. Toss to coat with bacon grease. Combine crumbled bacon, cheeses, and sour cream and toss with pasta. Serve immediately.

people reserve for children. In addition to fresh sheep's cheeses, they carefully make soft and semihard goat cheeses plain or with herbs, semihard cow cheeses plain or with herbs, and a soft sheep's cheese packed in olive oil. The Jacksons will even custom-make a 5-pound wheel of cheese for you, even marbling goat and cow cheeses with your choice of herbs. Their prices are amazing. From about $3 a pound you'll get these fine handmade cheeses, free from any impurities—right down to the hay and grain the Jacksons grow.

CALIFORNIA CHÈVRE

Laura Chenel   phone orders: yes
1908 Innes St.   415-648-5252
San Francisco, CA 94124

Laura Chenel has gained a national following for her fresh goat cheeses. She has also written a cookbook on the subject. You can choose from nine fresh cheeses, beginning with the simplest fromage blanc, chabis, discs, logs, pyramids, and up through cabecou—small, dense, buttonlike discs with a nutty flavor marinated in California olive oil and herbs. Recently she's added an aged hard goat cheese she calls Tome, suitable for grating.

The American Blues

According to legend, a French shepherd boy who forgot his lunch of bread and curds in a limestone cave invented blue cheese. It seems the boy rediscovered his lunch weeks later and found the curds had acquired a blue blush and a delicate flavor. He showed the cheese to monks in a nearby monastery, and they were as intrigued as our budding gourmand. They soon began making a sheep's cheese and using the caves to create the same effect the shepherd boy had stumbled onto. You know where these caves are: Roquefort. Later the blue mold powder came to be called *Penicillium roqueforti*.

Only cheese from this region can be called Roquefort, but other places also make blue-veined cheeses. The English have their Stiltons and the Italians their Gorgonzola. Here we just call them the American blues. And we make them from the milk of Holstein cows. Their differences are substantial, but what these cheeses have in common is *Penicillium roqueforti.*

We have three outstanding cheesemakers in different parts of the country, each making a cheese that, taken alone, may seem like any other blue you ever tasted, but when taste-tested against the famous foreign relatives, stands on its own two feet. And, in our typical American fashion, two of the three began with university research. Good old Iowa State with its dairy sciences department developed and patented the system now in use by Maytag and Nauvoo. Only the Oregon cheesemaker is a maverick, and he makes a fine, eccentric, yellow-hued blue.

OREGON BLUE

Rogue River Valley Creamery
311 N. Front
Central Point, OR 97505

phone orders: no
503-664-2233

This unimposing creamery on the main street of a little town just up the road apiece from where I live makes an interesting Girl Scout outing, provided you don't blink and miss it. Big signs they don't have. But a cheesemaking operation behind a glass wall, in all its pristine, creamy cleanliness for the curious to watch, they do have. Oregon blue is highly prized by West Coast gourmands. It is a creamy color, has a sharp greenish-blue mold, and ages well. They sell it after 90 days of aging, and it becomes more graceful if you keep it awhile at home. Their minimum order is 5 pounds, but it keeps. They also make cheddars, Jacks, colbys, and the best butter this side of the Mississippi. Unfortunately, I can't talk them into shipping the butter, at any price. Maybe you could try.

MAYTAG BLUE

Maytag Dairy Farms   phone orders: yes
Box 806   800-247-2458
Newton, IA 50208   ae/visa/mc

All those jokes about separating the curds from the whey in the Maytag aside, yes, this is the same family, and no, they don't slosh the cheese in the washer. The Maytag farm was originally the plaything of a washing machine heir who took to cows more than to laundry. But once he was out of the picture, the grandchildren said, "Well, we either make this thing pay off or we dump it." They decided to make cheese.

At various times, Maytag cheese has been called the best American blue. At other times it has been called the world's best blue. So much for excess. This is a good, reliable product that comes to you with the same kind of backing as the washer that never needs repairs. You won't complain about this cheese. It's the real thing. Maytag cheese is aged a full six months, and this gives character to its taste. Maytag melts on the tongue and is assertive, full, and piquant. With a Comice pear and port for dessert, it's to die for.

NAUVOO BLUE

Nauvoo Blue Cheese Co.   phone orders: yes
PO Box 188   800-358-9143
Nauvoo, IL 62354   visa/mc

Bill Scully and the cheesemakers at Nauvoo seem to come the closest to that little French shepherd boy in their system for making blue cheese. The name, Nauvoo, begins to tell why. Nauvoo is the name of the town, and Scully's father-in-law, Oscar Rohde, chose this site because of the limestone caves here that are similar to those in France. Rohde, like other well-trained American cheesemakers from Iowa State, built a business on scientifically controlled cheesemaking that utilizes the best from Old World techniques as well.

Nauvoo Quick Serving Ideas

Blueburgers: Top almost-done hamburgers with blue cheese, then fold into a sourdough bun along with grilled onions and mayo.

Top BLTs with crumbled blue.

Top homemade pizza with crumbled blue along with two other milder American cheeses for an All-American Cheese Pizza (I'd suggest Sonoma Jack and Trappist cheese from Kentucky).

Add 2 tablespoons Nauvoo blue to pastry when making crust for an apple pie.

At the 1984 World's Natural Cheese Championship, sponsored by the Wisconsin Cheese Makers Association, Nauvoo won first place in the "Blue, Gorgonzola, Stilton, and Roquefort" category. Not only was it the first time Nauvoo had won this honor, it was the first time *any* American blue cheese maker had taken this prize. Nauvoo blue is good. We like it because it has a creamy texture and is more pungent than harsh.

The Cheddars

Cheddars were first made in England in the late 17th century in a Somerset town that was named—you guessed it—Cheddar. Americans have embraced cheddar with a vigor that has practically made it *the* American cheese. When I was a kid I thought all cheese *was* cheddar. The part of the cheesemaking process that distinguishes cheddars from other cheeses comes after the rennet is poured into the warm milk and after the curds have formed. The curds are then cut into small cubes, heated to 102° F., and held at that temperature for an hour. They "knit" together to form one huge piece. The cheesemaker cuts these into slabs, which are stacked three high and turned—by hand—every 10 minutes for an hour. This is the "cheddaring" process, which expels excess whey. Some cheesemakers handle the slabs gently and others knock them around, but this step is what differentiates cheddars from their other cheese cousins.

Vermont, a state once known for having more cows than people, still has fewer than a million people, lush green mountain pastures, and herds and herds of dairy cattle. The English stock that settled the state created a cheddar industry that is known worldwide.

A good Vermont cheddar should be a pale gold color or white (that reddish hue you see in the supermarket is dye); moist but not oily; crumbly; clean and sharp without being bitter—on a scale that goes from mild as Clark Kent all the way up to a cheese that bursts forth with the authority of Superman landing in the living room.

CABOT CHEDDARS

Cabot Farmers	phone orders: yes
Cooperative Creamery	802-563-2231
Cabot, VT 05647	visa/mc

The farmers around the tiny town of Cabot banded together in an attempt to stabilize their individual economic situations. At first they produced only milk and high-quality butter. Later, like others in the dairy industry, they began making cheese because the demand for milk is not stable throughout the year. The result has been a pooling of not only the best-quality milk but also information and skills, so that Cabot says cheddar to many lovers of Vermont cheeses. Cabot makes all cheeses naturally, by hand, with no chemicals or preservatives. The cheeses are aged to a variety of flavor levels: the longer the aging, the sharper the cheese. There are five grades—from young, mild cheddar aged two to three months, up through the Private Stock cheese aged at least two years, which is extraordinarily fine and clean flavored, hand-picked by the cheesemakers for this distinction.

COLBY FROM CROWLEY

Crowley Cheese	phone orders: yes
Healdville, VT 05758	802-259-2340
	visa/mc

In case you're wondering why there's no street address for Crowley, the town only has 71 residents, and any one of them can point the way to the "factory." If that's what you care to call it—a pure two-story New England box house more than a hundred years old, with a brown wood hide that looks like it has lived every year of its life. As indeed it has. This designated National Historic Place is the oldest continuously operated cheese factory in the United States.

Still using hand methods and no artificial ingredients or chemical shortcuts, the Crowleys produce cheese that Mimi Sheraton has called "my favorite far and away . . . technically a colby and a first cousin to cheddar, but softer, moister, and less acidic."

Colbys are not "cheddared" but instead are hand-kneaded at the curd stage to express whey from the curds. As a result they "come up" more quickly, being mild in two to three months and fully sharp within six. The cheese is softer, more moist, and less acidic than cheddars. There's no aftertaste with a Crowley cheese. With a crisp Jonathan apple, it's lunch.

PURE NEW ENGLAND DELICACIES

Harman's Cheese &
   Country Store
Sugar Hill, NH 03585

phone orders: yes
603-823-8000

In the far north country of New Hampshire sits Harman's, in a town so small you don't need directions to find the store. The owners live upstairs. The products they sell are few, carefully chosen, and as pure as a New England winter. For example, a two-year-old cheddar that is rich, crumbly, looks like butter, and is sharp but never bitter. This same cheddar is folded into Sandeman Oporto port wine and laced with Courvoisier Napoleon brandy to make a cocktail spread with a light texture and a sharp aftertaste. You can shop by mail from this little country store for a small collection of hard-to-find, pure, top-quality New England delicacies. Ask for Maxine. That's Maxine Aldrich, who started working here in 1974 and bought the business from the estate of the Harmans when they died—both at the age of 89—in 1981.

Following the food philosophy of the Harmans, Maxine stocks best-quality maple syrup, Atlantic blue crab claws, dried soldier beans, local honeys, kipper fillets, and New England common crackers. Write for a free catalog.

Harman's Store Cheese Balls

You'll have to make the cheese balls yourself. Maxine's are made for her locally by an elderly lady, who makes eight double batches a week, and they are usually gone the day after Maxine gets them. Do try them yourself, but be sure to use Maxine's cheese or an equally sharp cheddar. Don't turn up your nose at the Rice Krispies. They make the texture really nice.

Cream 1 cup grated Harman's Aged Cheddar with ½ cup butter. Add 1 cup flour, ½ teaspoon Tabasco, ⅛ teaspoon salt, and 1 cup Rice Krispies. Shape into marble-sized balls. Bake on baking sheet in a 350° F. oven 12–15 minutes or until lightly browned. Keep in tightly closed container in refrigerator.

Maxine's Cheddarful Hints

Cheddar should keep several weeks in the refrigerator if wrapped in plastic or foil to keep it from drying out. Mold is harmless; just scrape it off. Dry cheddar grates easily. You can freeze less than pound pieces, which will keep about six months. It will get crumbly, but the flavor will remain about the same. Cook cheddar only until melted—if longer it tends to toughen. One-quarter pound equals 1 cup grated cheese.

Maple syrup: Keeps indefinitely. After opening, keep the can in the refrigerator. For longer periods, store in freezer; the syrup will not freeze, but holds its flavor. If a coating (known in the trade as mother) ever forms, simply boil the syrup, skim it, and let cool. Continue to refrigerate. Try heating syrup before pouring on pancakes.

The designation "farmhouse" means that all the milk for a particular cheese comes from that farm and is not purchased from outside vendors.

REAL RAT-TRAP CHEESE

The Plymouth Cheese Corp.
PO Box 1
Plymouth, VT 05056

phone orders: yes
802-672-5129

A true, old-fashioned Vermont granular curd cheese, less densely textured than cheddar, this sharp, tangy cheese is fine for toasted cheese sandwiches, for eating out of hand, or for cooking. The cheese factory began in 1890 under the part ownership of Colonel John Calvin Coolidge, whose son Calvin went on to become president and whose grandson John reopened the business because "I hated to see the building running down right next to the family homestead, so I finally started it up again." With his cheesemaker, John Butler, he makes a small amount of cheese each year—about 75 tons. And now you know it must be good for something besides baiting mousetraps.

You can order the waxed rounds anywhere from mild (aged three months) up to extra strong (which may be over three years old). When the box comes—with your address written in Mr. Coolidge's own crabbed script, your cheese wrapped in tinfoil and a plastic bag—you really do feel like you just got a present from your favorite uncle, handmade by him just for you. The prices Mr. Coolidge charges are about a third lower than comparable ones I know about, and their quality is second to none. Mr. Coolidge will also sell you a bottle of maple syrup. Call and order. He is not one for a lot of palaver. It won't take long on the phone.

FARMHOUSE CHEDDAR

Shelburne Farms
Shelburne, VT 05482

phone orders: yes
802-985-8686
visa/mc

The Shelburne Farms cheesemakers keep a herd of Brown Swiss cows exclusively for their milk to go into Shelburne cheddar. The cows are fed only grain and silage organically grown on the place. This cheese is distinguished from others by being aged at least a year and by being less dry. Those Brown Swiss cows must have a higher butterfat content than their spotted cousins. When you receive a brick of this cheese, hand-dipped in brown wax and stamped with the date, you are receiving a product that's been handmade and controlled from the ground up.

The Shelburne Farms were the utopian dream of a Dr. William Seward, who bought up 30 small farms, hired Frederick Law Olmstead—who designed Central Park—to do the grounds. He employed New York architect Robert Robertson to design buildings that resemble an English country house or castle. Of course, these days, the whole thing is a nonprofit institution and a research center for farm and garden concerns. Open daily from 10–5, it's a worthwhile stop for tourists.

MAPLE-SMOKED VERMONT CHEDDARS

Sugarbush Farm　　　phone orders: yes
High Pastures Rd.　　　802-457-1757
Woodstock, VT 05091　　ae/visa/mc/dc

Betsy Luce's daddy, Jack Ayres, made a good business aging and smoking cheddars from small producers in Vermont. He is knowledgeable about cheeses beyond many university-trained dairy scientists. Today Betsy carries on, naturally aging and smoking cheddars in what *Gourmet* magazine called "one of the most dependable places in America in which to find assertive yet richly mellow cheddar." In addition to a well-aged medium-sharp wheel, you can get a sage cheese, a sharp cheddar, or the famous smoked bar, which is the best of Vermont.

The Ayres-Luce family also tap their trees and make maple syrup, maple sugar, maple cream, and a melt-in-your-mouth maple sugar bonbon in the shape of a maple leaf. These people have some of the most attractive prices available and good, personal service besides.

Vermont Cheese Pudding

Yankee ingenuity combines the best qualities of the collapsible soufflé, the flammable fondue, and the impossible raclette into a dish as easy as the proverbial pie. Serves eight people who have been skiing. Recipe can be cut in half, placed in a smaller dish, and cooked in half the time for four.

8　slices French bread
¼　pound butter, melted
3　cups half-and-half
3　eggs
¼　cup port
1　teaspoon Worcestershire
1　teaspoon Dijon mustard
½　pound sharp cheddar, grated
½　teaspoon salt
¼　teaspoon pepper
¼　teaspoon Hungarian paprika

Preheat oven to 325° F. Remove crusts from bread and dip bread in melted butter. Completely line a 2-quart soufflé dish with buttered bread. Whisk together remaining ingredients. Pour into ovenproof dish and place dish in a pan of hot water that comes up three-quarters of the way to the top of the dish. Bake about an hour, or until top puffs and is brown. Pudding is done if a knife blade inserted in it comes out clean. Remove from water bath and let stand 10–15 minutes before serving.

Vermont Cheddar Pastry Shells

Flaky, sharp pastry makes a fine do-ahead hors d'oeuvre base. Simply mix, cook, and freeze the shells—double-wrapped and in a box so they won't be crushed —then fill at serving time with whatever filling you like: smoked salmon, Cowboy Caviar (see index), even something as simple as avocado blended with lemon juice and cilantro. Or with good Vermont apples and cinnamon sugar. Try making the pastry with other cheeses, too. Parmesan with an extra shot of cayenne pepper is bright and tasty under various antipasti. Jack with a bit of pepper flakes makes a good base for soft scrambled eggs at midnight.

Makes 40 shells in 40 minutes

1	cup flour
½	teaspoon salt
¼	teaspoon cayenne pepper
⅓	cup butter
½	cup shredded cheddar
1	tablespoon sesame seeds
2–3	tablespoons water

Preheat oven to 450° F. In food processor bowl, combine ingredients in order listed to make a short ball of dough. Roll out thin (⅛ inch), handling as little as possible. Cut into 2½-inch circles. Pat circles into bottom of small muffin pans (1½ inches across bottom). Bake until lightly browned, 6–8 minutes.

TILLAMOOK CHEDDARS

Tillamook County
  Creamery Association
PO Box 313
Tillamook, OR 97141

phone orders: yes
503-842-4481
visa/mc

I include The Tillamook co-op here because, if you live outside the distribution area, you may not be able to buy at the supermarket (as I can) one of the three best cheddars in America—Tillamook (the other two being Vermont and New York's Herkimer).

Virtually all the milk produced around Tillamook, Oregon, is delivered to Association headquarters for processing into cheese. Can you imagine 319 million pounds a year? And from that they get a mere 27 million pounds of cheese. Such is the popularity on the West Coast of Tillamook cheddar.

In response to the wishes of the public, the Tillamook cheesemakers have developed a low-sodium cheese. They point out that it is very fragile (salt does preserve things), and one can tell from the tone of their notices that they don't like it very well, but there it is. Actually it tastes quite good, and for those on low-sodium diets, it does make it possible to include cheese. Tillamook also makes a Monterey Jack that is nothing to write home about. Stick with the cheddar. It's really good.

COUGAR CHEESES

WSU Creamery
Troy Hall 101
Pullman, WA 99164

phone orders: no
509-335-7516
must receive check to ship

WSU Cheddar, Cougar Gold, Viking, and Hot Pepper Viking are cheeses made and marketed by Washington State University Creamery, Department of Food Science and Human Nutrition. Each 30-ounce cheese is vacuum-packed in a tin. The cheddar is aged a full 12 months, while the Viking—a mild, white cheese with or without peppers—is ready in 4 months. At last report the tins were $7.75 each for any variety.

Cougar Gold is the most popular of the WSU cheeses, having the texture and taste of a fine Gouda. The cheese was developed at this creamery about 30 years ago by Dr. N. S. Golding and his students, who named the cheese after—you guessed it—the school mascot. Sis, boom, bah.

The cheese is good, but I do wish they'd institute some modern marketing practices up there. You have to send them a check up front to get the cheese, and you have to call or write for an order form before you can even write the check. If you have a friend or neighbor who has taken advanced courses in accounting, invite him/her over to help you figure out the chart with the shipping charges. Luckily, they sent me a sample. I'd never have figured this stuff out.

HERKIMER COUNTY NEW YORK CHEDDARS

Herkimer Family Treasure House
RD 2, Box 261
Ilion, NY 13357

phone orders: yes
315-895-7832
must receive check to ship

The elements in Herkimer County are pure serendipity: the climate, the soil, the grass, the cattle herds, the English immigrants who settled the county, bringing their cheddar craft along. All combine to make it possible to produce a cheddar that is in my opinion the best made in America.

The owner of Herkimer's trademark and plant is a guy named Sheldon Basloe. In 1949, after coming out of the army and looking for a business suitable for a family operation, Basloe decided to put out a product with the trademark his farsighted father had registered during the heart of the Depression. Herkimer County had been selling cheddar to barge operators on the Erie Canal since early in the 19th century. But Sheldon Basloe's dad, riding the back roads of the county during the Depression,

bored enough to look up records in the county courthouse, discovered that the well-known name "Herkimer
County Cheddar" had never been registered. He did so
and kept the trademark active without actually manufac-
turing a product.

Sheldon Basloe was the first commercial cheesemaker to perfect the now familiar "cheese ball." He tells
of the first winter his family made them. He'd stop by the
grocery store and pick up a sack of 15 pounds or so of
nuts. Then the whole family would sit around, watching
television and cracking nuts. The next morning they'd
have enough cracked nuts to roll out the cheese ball
orders for the day. The nut-covered cheeseballs were
what put Basloe's business on the map. People loved
them.

Now, I have had a knee-jerk reaction to cold-pack
cheese food ever since I graduated from my mother's
favorite, Velveeta. When my foodie friends began asking
me if I had Herkimer for this book, I assumed they were
referring to the original Herkimer cheddar. Well! Little did
I know that Herkimer cold-pack cheese foods are about as
good as their original cheddar, and for that very reason
they begin with superior cheese.

A 3-pound, black-waxed cheddar—white, rich, full-
bodied, smoother than its Vermont cousins, sharp but
never bitter, aged at least nine months and able to stand
a longer period of maturation at home—is still only about
$20. Combine that with a cheese ball, or one of Basloe's
special flavored cheeses—I like the one called "root cellar," which is smooth and pink lemonade colored but
bright and tart with the taste of horseradish and beets.
They also make a product called "chutter," a blend of
cheddar and cream that makes a smooth spread with a
nice balance between cheddar and butter.

Place an order and get on Mrs. Sheldon Basloe's
mailing list. She sends letters to the customers that are as
friendly as a note from your Aunt Martha. You'll like the
Basloes and all their cheeses. They're made in small
batches. The cheese balls are hand-rolled. Everything is
hand-cut and hand-wrapped. The Basloes put all four children to work. They've made a business of togetherness.
It works.

CHEESEMAKER'S SUPPLIES

New England Cheese-
  making Supply Co.
Box 85
Ashfield, MA 01330

phone orders: yes
413-628-4568
visa/mc

If you have available to you a goodly supply of fresh
milk and a hankering to make cheese yourself, help is
on the way. From their home in Massachusetts, Bob
and Ricki Carroll offer kits for the home or farm cheesemaker. For beginners, they'll tell you everything you
need to know about fromage blanc. You can move up-
ward via bacterial cultures and molds to ripened cheeses
of sophistication and difficulty. The Carrolls have also
written a book, *Cheesemaking Made Easy,* and are
quoted in many other cheese books. They also publish a
newsletter and journal to keep you current. They'll even
tell you how to milk a ewe—in case you've always wondered.

Specialty Cheeses

Here are the one-of-a-kind cheeses made by hand by
America's cheesemakers, who are giving their European
counterparts a run for their money. Blue Heron brie. Guilford fromages blanc. Our favorite, the Trappists' cheese.
Each of these is so individual, you'll never forget it.

FRENCH FARMSTEAD
COW'S-MILK CHEESE

The Guilford Cheese Co.
RD 2, Box 182
Guilford, VT 05301

phone orders: yes
802-254-9182

While all the rest of Vermont was turning to cheddar, Ann
Dixon looked over the backs of her 15 Jersey cows to
France and the delicate, white, mounded fresh farmstead
cheeses. Ann, her surgeon husband, John, and their two
sons, Peter and Sam, studied the French system and de-

Trappist Cheese Bisque

With all due credit to Helen Corbitt, who first brought Canadian cheese soup to the South, here's a version using this splendid and authoritative Kentucky cheese made lovingly in God's service by the Trappists of Gethsemani. Delicious with blue corn bread (see index: Blue Corn Connection) and a winter fruit salad of grapefruit, orange, banana, and pomegranate with poppyseed dressing.

Serves 8 in 45 minutes

- ¼ pound butter
- ½ cup *each* coarsely grated onion, carrot, and celery
- 1 finely cut green onion and top
- ¼ cup flour
- 1 quart rich chicken broth
- 3 cups milk
- 1 cup heavy cream
- 1 cup grated Trappist cheese
  Salt and cayenne pepper to taste

In heavy soup pot over medium heat, melt butter, then add vegetables. Cook and stir until soft (10 minutes). Sprinkle flour over vegetables, cook and stir 3 minutes. Add broth, milk, and cream. Raise to gentle boil and cook 15 minutes. Remove from heat. Stir in cheese until melted. Adjust seasonings to taste with salt and a whiff of cayenne pepper. Serve immediately. You may reheat the soup, but *never* boil it. It will curdle.

cided it was for them. Their cheeses are fresh, soft, and less salty than the original French version, rather like a frothy, light cream cheese. Ann calls her cheese Verde-Mont and makes one plain and one with herbs—sage, dill, garlic, and pepper. Mixed with vinegar, oil, and milk, the latter makes an outstanding salad dressing.

The thing that's surprising about these smooth, spreadable, rich-tasting cheese mounds is that they're low in fat, with a butterfat content ranging from only 18 to 22 percent. It's that rich-tasting Jersey milk that gives the cheese its taste.

This French-inspired cheese is in short supply and rare as a small vineyard wine. It only lasts about three to four weeks, but it's so precious, it's worth it. You'll love the way it looks. It comes wrapped in a French provincial–looking paper so charming I'd like to wallpaper the kitchen with it.

WISCONSIN PORT SALUT

Stallman's Cheese phone orders: yes
35990 Mapleton Rd. 414-474-7142
Oconomowoc, WI 53066 visa/mc

Howard Stallman calls his cheese Bon Bree, which means happy cheese. Don't confuse this creamy cheese with brie, however, for it has more authority than brie.

This Swiss-style cheese comes in three grades from mild to sharp. As with other cheeses, the grades translate directly into age. Young, mild cheese is often sold just after wrapping, but the cheese ripens into its full sharpness within three months. Howard Stallman makes this cheese by hand, using no chemical shortcuts, and welcomes visitors to his old cheese factory to watch.

TRAPPIST CHEESE

Gethsemani Farms phone orders: no
Trappist, KY 40051

The Trappists have operated this farm in Kentucky since 1848 and support themselves by the manufacture of cheese and fruitcakes. This cheese, a semisoft cow's-milk in the same family with Havarti, is one of the most enticing I have tasted out of literally hundreds of wheels that rolled across my desk. This is no pale, sissy cheese but an iron fist in a velvet glove. The mild (young) cheese has an identity, while the aged version has enough authority to tell you to sit down and button your lip. I love these cheeses. This is the cheese they serve at the White House when they want to impress the foreign dignitaries. Try it and you'll see why. It is one cheese that can be used from beginning to end of a meal.

The Trappists have this mail-order thing down pat. Their very reasonable prices are postpaid, and they have a brochure and mail-order form that is a breeze to fill out.

HAWTHORNE VALLEY'S ALPENKAESE

Hawthorne Valley Farm   phone orders: yes
RD 2, Box 225A,   518-672-7500
Harlemville   visa/mc
Ghent, NY 12075

Handmade Swiss-style cheese from Hawthorne Valley Farm is strong enough to make you pay attention, and their dense loaf of sourdough rye is as good as any *bauerbrots* (farm bread) from Switzerland or Germany. This is honest food, prepared in an honest way, and from an outfit whose philosophy even extends to shipping their fine products with a bill, "confident you will pay promptly." Did you know there were such people left in the world?

Christoph Meier is the visionary farmer who operates this combination farm/school under the aegis of the Rudolf Steiner Farming and Gardening Association. He uses biodynamic farming methods that guarantee that this raw-milk cheese is perfectly pure. It's graded from mild to sharp, but the mild is sharp enough to satisfy an American sissy. He taught Edi Griffiths to make the cheese, and she's developed a love for the rhythms of rural life and a substantial forearm from hoisting the heavy slabs of cheese in the painstaking labor-intensive method demanded by this Swiss process.

Twice-Baked Hawthorne Valley Alpenkaese Potatoes with Green Onions and American Golden Caviar

---

Serve with fresh fruit of the season, dark bread and sweet butter, and a cup of tea for a satisfying light supper.

Serves 2 in 1½ hours

- 2 large russet potatoes, scrubbed, skin pierced with fork
  Salt and pepper to taste
- 1 tablespoon caviar, preferably American Golden, plus additional dabs for garnish
- ¼ cup finely cut green onion and top
- 1 tablespoon butter
- 2 tablespoons heavy cream
- ¼ cup grated Alpenkaese, plus 2 tablespoons for toppings

Bake potatoes in 375° F. oven until tender (1 hour). Remove from oven and cool slightly. Cut off top horizontal quarter. Scoop out cooked potato flesh, leaving a sturdy shell. Salt and pepper shells and reserve. Combine potato flesh with caviar, green onions and tops, butter, cream, and cheese. Taste and adjust seasonings. Stuff potato mixture into shells. Sprinkle with additional grated cheese. Bake at 400° F. until bubbly and brown (15 minutes). Garnish with additional caviar and serve immediately.

Blue Heron Brie with Pecans

Suitable and equally delicious at either end of a meal: fore and aft. Calls for a ripe, juicy pear.

Serves 4 in 1 hour

- ¼ cup soft butter
- ¼ cup pecans, finely chopped
  Few drops Tabasco
- 2 tablespoons lemon juice
  8-ounce wheel of brie, cold
  Armenian cracker bread

Blend nuts, Tabasco, and lemon juice into soft butter. Cut cheese in half horizontally and spread with butter mixture. Chill. A half hour before serving, cut into mini-pie wedges, place on crackers, and bring to room temperature. Garnish with additional pecans.

Orb Weaver Cheese Linguine

Delicious with escarole and cherry tomatoes, crisp green apples for dessert, biscotti, and a glass of port.

Serves 4 in 30 minutes

- 1 tablespoon light salad oil
- 2 cups fresh broccoli flowerets

CONTINUED ON PAGE 21

Susan Riley bakes sourdough rye and wheat-rye daily. Phone and ask what's coming out of the oven today. You might just get lucky and catch Susan on a day when she's baking a special, like fruit-rye, and they'll ship that too. Order three or four loaves. This pure bread, made from only stone-ground flour, water, and sourdough starter, keeps beautifully and freezes well. Besides the bread and the three grades of cheese from mild to sharp, you can also order cob-smoked or caraway-studded cheese as well as granola, honey or maple.

I swear the prices are the same as the grocery store. For the quality you get, this place is a godsend. If you're in the New York area, drive up and see this real working farm. It's only 120 miles north of the city and worth every mile just for the chance to have lunch in their lunchroom. Good, honest food and cheap besides.

OREGON BRIE

Blue Heron French Cheese Co.

2001 Blue Heron Dr.
Tillamook, OR 97141

phone orders: yes
503-842-8281
ae/visa/mc

Tillamook says cheddar to West Coast cheese eaters, but quietly for six years, on a street whose name they took as their own, Lou Minisce and friends have been making a brie to rival anything from France. Working on a scale no larger than a French farmer and using the same fine milk that goes into the cheddar just down the road, these cheesemakers have found that everything comes together properly here—the climate, the grass, the milk, the imported mold *(Penicillium candidum)*, to produce a delicate, all-natural dessert cheese.

Cheese connoisseurs say that brie has one perfect day in its lifetime. When you buy Blue Heron you can find that day, because the date the cheese was made is stamped on the package. Blue Heron recommends you buy the cheese about 10 days old, then decide how you like your brie: second to third week, firm and fresh; fourth to fifth week, partially ripened; sixth to seventh week, fully ripened. Remember to refrigerate brie for storing but serve at room temperature for maximum taste.

VERMONT FARMHOUSE CHEESE

Orb Weaver Farm phone orders: yes
RD 1, Box 75 802-877-3755
New Haven, VT 05472

In the first place, Orb Weaver is not the name of some crusty New Englander, smoking a corncob pipe and telling pithy stories. No, it is the name of the large spotted garden spider who spins those big round webs you see if you visit the countryside. The farm was named for the spider by its two new owners, Marjorie Susman and Marian Pollack, who have delighted the community for the last five years by their success with Jersey cows and cheese.

Their cheese is not cheddar but is more in the Gouda family, being a semihard slicing cheese with a very creamy consistency and a smooth, pale, buttery-rich Jersey milk taste. They make it two or three times a week, in small batches of 50–100 pounds only from the milk of their own cows (thus the label "farmhouse").

Every step is done by hand, then the cheese is aged at least 60 days. You can buy either a 2- or 5-pound wheel. This cheese sharpens as it ages and keeps well. I am once again amazed that you can purchase such a high-quality cheese for a price that is completely in line with what you'd pay for some mass-produced grocery store cheese that isn't half the quality. This cheese is a winner.

GOUDA AND FARMSTEAD CHEESE

Pleasant Valley Dairy, Inc. phone orders: yes
6804 Kickerville Rd. 206-366-5398
Ferndale, WA 98248 won't ship in hot weather;
minimum order:
2-pound wheel

Dutch-style Gouda—smooth, subtle, and nutlike—makes a fine beginning or ending to a meal with fresh fruit. George and Dolores Train, who have been in the dairy

CONTINUED FROM PAGE 20

1 medium red pepper, cut into thin strips
½ cup toasted whole almonds, plus 2 tablespoons for garnish
2 tablespoons butter
2 tablespoons flour
2 cups milk
2 cups grated Orb Weaver Farmhouse cheese
2 tablespoons grated Parmesan cheese
¾ pound fresh pasta

In a 10-inch skillet over medium-high heat, in hot oil, stir-fry broccoli, red pepper, and almonds. Add 2 tablespoons of water; cover and cook until broccoli is crisp-tender (5 minutes). Remove from heat and reserve.

In a heavy saucepan, make a white sauce. First melt butter, then stir in flour. Cook 2 minutes. Stir in milk; cook, stirring constantly, until mixture boils and thickens. Remove from heat and stir in cheeses until melted. (You may reheat sauce, but don't boil it.)

Meanwhile, in a pot of boiling water, cook fresh pasta al dente.

Drain pasta and place in serving bowl. Toss vegetables with pasta, cover with sauce, and garnish with additional toasted almonds. Serve immediately.

business a good while, make a Gouda from their own cows' milk. They control every step of the procedure and do not bleach, color, or chemically treat the milk or cheese. Each wheel is hand-dipped in wax, dated by hand, and left to age at least 60 days. The cheese is made with natural calf rennet (they make a few batches of rennetless cheese each season; call for availability). They also have a new cheese out, Farmstead, that is pale, sharp, smooth—a cousin to cheddar.

If you are in the state of Washington, on I-5 between Blaine and Bellingham, and would like to see a bucolic scene more vivid than any calendar—dazzling green, undulating hills, spotted cows, brilliant blue sky, clean air, barn—stop by any day but Sunday and the Trains will show you around. They'll also sell you raw milk and cheese right on the spot.

SONOMA JACK

Sonoma Cheese Factory
2 Spain St.
Sonoma, CA 95476

phone orders: yes
707-938-JACK
ae/visa/mc

The Viviani family can thank the oil embargo of 1973 for their jump in popularity. That was when the San Francisco hordes, who were used to fanning out as far away as Tahoe, began to find Sonoma, a mere half tank away, and to discover this quaint cheese store on the square.

Real Sonoma Jack, literally handmade on the spot, bears little resemblance to that poor imitation they sell in the grocery store. It is more like a first-quality mozzarella. We are particularly fond of Sonoma Jack laced with garlic. I mean, how California can you get? Most Jack is made into soft, high-moisture wheels, but some is made drier by cutting the curd into smaller pieces, thus expelling more whey. Dry Jack is used for grating (see Vella Cheese of California). The Vivianis make mostly high-moisture Jack with a number of additions including onions, garlic, and red peppers.

Monterey Jack was first made on farms in Monterey County, California, during the 19th century. The cheese was derived from a type made at the Carmel Mission. A Scotsman named David Jacks first saw its commercial potential and named it for himself: Monterey Jack's. Later it was shortened to Jack's and finally Jack. The cheese of California . . . no matter what county it's made in.

DRY GRATING JACK CHEESE

Vella Cheese of California   phone orders: yes
315 Second St. E   707-938-3232
PO Box 191
Sonoma, CA 95476

Dry Jack is a hand-labor–intensive cheese defying mechanization. From its forming in muslin sacks, brining, coating, oiling, and re-oiling—plus the skill necessary to achieve the nutty-sweet, medium-cure, Parmesanlike taste, it is made rarely. But Ignazio Vella still produces this California original in his cheese factory just two blocks off the plaza in sleepy little Sonoma. He also makes Bear Flag Brand high-moisture Jack and sells a variety of other cheeses for your Wine Country picnic . . . even if you're having that picnic outside Baltimore. His prices are astonishingly low for the quality you get. And the keeping qualities of the dry Jack are superb. Good local dry Jack is better than questionable-quality imported Parmesan or Romano, and can stand in their place in any recipe.

BREADS, FLOURS, MEALS, AND MIXES

Here you'll find the whole grains, the regional specialties that can make your breakfast in bread. Blue corn, beignets, and buckwheat. Sourdough from start to bread. The best breads and bread makings I could find.

SOURDOUGH WHOLE WHEAT BREAD

Baldwin Hill Bakery   phone orders: yes
Baldwin Hill Rd.   617-249-4691
Phillipston, MA 01331   minimum order: 12 loaves

If there was ever a case where technique is all, traditional European country bread is it. What could you do with a sack of organic whole wheat berries, a little sea salt, and a good water well? Hy Lerner, of Phillipston, Massachu-

In the spring of 1915, grocer D. F. DeBernardi ordered his usual fresh Monterey Jack supply from local sources, and from Italy he ordered the Romano and Parmesan necessary to satisfy the needs of San Francisco's Italian community. Two things happened. Italy entered World War I and withheld all food orders so they could feed their soldiers. And—mysteries of the market—the fresh Jack didn't sell. So what happened? The Jack dried out, and DeBernardi made a discovery. It developed a Parmesan–Romano-like sweet, nutty flavor. He decided to offer this "dry" Jack as a wartime substitute to the imports. Following the tradition of the Italian cheeses, he coated the dry Jack with oil, pepper, and lampblack. This cheese became so popular that by the middle of the Depression, more than 60 cheese factories made it. But today it's about as rare as World War I Parmesan, because of the expense of the process. Thank goodness for the Vellas.

Baldwin Hill Pâté
Kathleen Bellicchi

Makes 2 standard loaves in
2 hours

2	cups dry lentils
4½	cups water
½	teaspoon sea salt
1	bay leaf
1	pound Baldwin Hill whole wheat bread
1	tablespoon vegetable oil
1	cup diced onion
½	cup diced celery
1	cup minced parsley
½	cup tahini
3	tablespoons miso
1	teaspoon dried thyme

Cook lentils, water, salt, and bay leaf together until soft. Trim off bread crusts, cut bread into eight pieces and soak in water to cover until soft, about 15 minutes.

Heat a large, heavy pot; add oil, onion, celery, and parsley and cook until onion is soft, about 10 minutes. Add tahini, miso, and thyme. Cook and stir 2 minutes.

Squeeze out excess water from bread, break into small pieces, and add to vegetables. Add lentils. Stir to mix thoroughly. If you want a perfectly smooth pâté, run it through a food processor now.

Bake in two foil-lined bread pans 45 minutes at 350° F. Remove from pans to cool, leaving foil in place. Then cover completely and refrigerate. Keeps two weeks refrigerated and is best after at least a week.

setts, knew what to do. He apprenticed himself to the LIMA bakery in Belgium and learned to bake honest bread.

This may be the best bread made in America today, and it's nothing but whole wheat, pure well water, and sea salt. A dark, round 1¾-pound loaf, it feels substantial when you lift it from the box. Open the wrapper and take a deep breath. The aroma of caramelized wheat berries, hint of hardwood smoke, and bite of natural sourdough combine to produce a bread as complex and mysterious as the most exotic perfume.

Just today I had the most satisfying lunch of a slice of Hy's bread, some Trappist cheese from Kentucky, the last of my own sun-ripened yellow plum tomatoes, a glass of Oregon Pinot Noir, and for dessert just a little dollop of honey from Utah. That, my friends, is lunch.

This bread keeps about a week in the pantry and up to six months in the freezer. You can get a mixed lot that includes not only rounds of the original whole wheat sourdough but also the stupendous raisin bread (which has ¾ pound of raisins per loaf), rye, sesame wheat, and salt-free whole wheat. The lagniappe is that Hy Lerner charges about the same as you'd pay for a loaf of decent bread in your local bakery, and you know when you buy his breads that he's controlled everything from the ground up in his self-sufficient farm operation.

ARMENIAN CRACKER BREAD

Valley Bakery   phone orders: yes
502 M St.   209-485-2700
Fresno, CA 93721   visa/mc

Janet Saghatelian, second-generation Armenian baker, has made her reputation with flat cracker bread known as lahvosh. This is the most amazing stuff. She sent me a case of it when I was writing my last book, and even a year later the last pack tasted as good as the first. Made from Montana spring wheat flour, water, cane sugar, vegetable shortening, salt, yeast, malt, sesame seeds, and dry milk, this ancient type of bread is rolled thin, sprayed with a milk wash, and sprinkled with sesame seeds before baking. Once it enters the special 30-foot oven that Janet's father devised, the batter develops surface bubbles that give the bread its special crisp, light texture. It comes in 15-inch rounds and in Janet's own cracker-sized hearts. You can use it for cheese, as a palate cleanser at a wine tasting, or you can moisten the big rounds, as Janet's mother did, and use them in a variety of ways that Janet calls Valley wraps.

NEW ORLEANS BEIGNETS

Community Coffee Co.   phone orders: yes
PO Box 3378   800-535-9901
Baton Rouge, LA 70821   ae/visa/mc

I've never quite figured out whether these Louisiana-style doughnuts—square, hot, light, and delicious, like puffy fritter pillows dipped in confectioners' sugar—were supposed to be eaten for breakfast when you got up, or after you'd stayed up all night, just to kind of steady you until you got back to the hotel after a night of revelry in the French Quarter. Served alongside New Orleans–style coffee laced with chicory, this is the breakfast that made New Orleans famous, served at standup bakeries throughout the city. Using the Community Coffee mix, you can close your eyes and almost hear the Mississippi lapping at the banks, if you try. Don't forget you can order the right kind of coffee here, too (see Chapter 6 listing for Community Coffee).

KANSAS CITY ENGLISH MUFFINS

Wolferman's   phone orders: yes
2820 W. 53rd St.   913-432-6131
Fairway, KS 66205   ae/visa/mc
    minimum order: ½ case

Imagine the usual container of English muffins, except instead of six, you find four 2-inch high, wide, and handsome heart-of-America English muffins. The Wolfermans have been making and offering their famous muffins since

---

Janet Saghatelian's Sunday Brunch Wrap

Makes 4 sandwich servings or 12–16 appetizers

- 1   15-inch cracker bread
- 8   slices bacon, cooked crisp, crumbled
- 6   hard-cooked eggs, chopped
- ½   cup thinly sliced green onions
- 1   tablespoon Dijon mustard
- ⅓   cup mayonnaise
-    Salt, pepper to taste
- 1   cup chopped watercress

Wet cracker bread under cold running water about 10 to 30 seconds on each side. Place between damp towels. Set aside about an hour to soften.

In a bowl, mix cooked crumbled bacon, eggs, green onions, mustard, and mayonnaise. Season to taste with salt and pepper. Spread mixture evenly over softened cracker bread. Cover with watercress. Roll up tightly, jelly roll fashion, enclosing all ingredients. Wrap tightly in plastic wrap and chill at least an hour. Slice thin with a very sharp knife.

Simple Hollandaise

One of the best breakfasts I know combines a Wolferman's muffin, a poached egg, cold smoked lox from Josephson's (see index), and just made hollandaise. Call it Eggs Oregon.

  2   egg yolks
  1   tablespoon lemon juice
  1   tablespoon hot water
       Pinch of salt and
       cayenne
 ¼ pound butter, melted

Whip together the egg yolks, lemon juice, hot water, salt, and cayenne pepper (easiest in a processor, but OK with wire whisk). Melt butter and heat to bubbly. Dribble butter into egg mixture, beating constantly, until you have a perfect emulsion. Heat until mixture thickens. This is easiest in a microwave set on medium/low in 15-second increments—heat 15 seconds, stir and turn, repeat until mixture is thick as pudding. Old-fashioned method is to heat mixture in double boiler. It works but is slow. Use those new tools. Simple.

1888. These muffins are so generous, I fear the English would find them quite profligate. But never mind, break them open with a fork, toast, slather them with butter, and you're on your way to a fast and fabulous breakfast. Cheese, piece of fruit, cup of tea. Good enough for any time of day.

The Wolferman family has operated a grocery store in this Kansas City suburb so long that third- and fourth-generation Kansas Citians still do their shopping here. If Calvin Trillin would get his mug out of the barbecue long enough to find a place for breakfast, I'm sure he'd head straight for Wolferman's.

In addition to the original flavor English muffins, Wolferman's has cinnamon-raisin, cheddar cheese, light wheat, and blueberry.

THE CRUMPET EXPRESS

The English Tea Shop   phone orders: no
511 Irving St.   415-564-2255
San Francisco, CA 94122 minimum order: 12 crumpets

Walk along Irving Street and peer into the window of a quaint little bakery and you're liable to see an energetic baker, toque and all, busily making crumpets. These English cousins to the so-called English muffin have much the same ingredients and texture of the more familiar muffin but are cooked on a grill and, properly done, have a crisp, golden, hot-griddle shine to their skin. James Beard, in his bread book, gave instructions for making them at home, pouring the batter into tuna fish can rings, but I could never make anything that didn't seem more suited to catfish bait. Enter the Crumpet Express. They'll jet the crumpets to you with your choice of traditional Triptree preserves, Vermont maple syrup, or—my favorite—Deer Mountain preserves from Washington . . . full of fruit and fresh as a kid in junior high.

The crumpets are shipped the day they're baked and are good for special breakfasts (you should see the line around this bakery in the morning before work) as well as for tea. Call them and they'll help you put together a great packet. Only hitch is, you have to plan in advance because, for some reason, they ask you to allow three weeks for delivery.

BLUE CORN PANCAKES AND WAFFLES

Blue Corn Connection
Natural Specialties of the
   Southwest
8812 4th St. NW
Alameda, NM 87144

phone orders: yes
505-897-2412

Ross Edwards, who owns this outfit, calls blue corn pancakes "Blue Heaven." Actually, the first time you see blue corn products you may be a little disappointed. The corn kernels themselves are a deep bluish purple, and the ground corn flour is a lovely shade of lavender, but the cooked cakes are golden outside but shirt flannel gray inside. . . . Oh, well. You get used to it. And with that out of the way, we can get to the important stuff, how they taste: Great. Sweet. Corny—in the best sense of the word.

The Hopi Indians have been growing, grinding, and eating blue corn for centuries. Highest in protein and minerals, it also has a superior taste to white and yellow cornmeal, even if it does look like your old gray suit run through the processor. Blue cornmeal boiled with water and sweetener into a cream-of-wheat consistency is called atole and is, according to Indian lore, a "strong food," Indian chicken soup, Pueblo penicillin. At a hospital in Gallup, atole is given to patients who have refused to eat anything else.

Ross's blue corn is organically grown. Choose from whole-kernel, regular-grind, and fine-grind cornmeal; corn flour; pancake and waffle mix; or a gift pack that even includes some dried blue corn on the cob. Gorgeous. Try Ross's Blue Heaven pancakes topped with sweet butter and a dab of pure maple syrup from Vermont. That, my friends, is a natural gourmet breakfast from the U.S. of A.

Ross Edwards's Blue Corn Crêpes

We sometimes bread pan-sized trout that our son pulls from the downtown stream with blue cornmeal for a nutty, crunchy crust.

Ross will send you recipes for polenta, hush puppies, a carrot cake, the traditional atole, and other blue corn dishes. This is one we particularly liked.

Serves 4 in 20 minutes

¼	cup blue cornmeal (roasted fine-grind)
½	cup unbleached white flour
1	cup milk
2	eggs
1½	teaspoons cooking oil

Filling:
    Sour cream
    Jalapeño jelly
    Piñon nuts (optional)

Combine meal, flour, milk, eggs, and oil. Stir to mix thoroughly. Heat an 8-inch crêpe pan over medium heat. Moisten with oil. Drop about 3 tablespoons of batter into hot pan and roll the batter around so it coats the pan. Cook until edges are brown, then flip crêpe and cook other side (about 40 seconds). Remove to warmed plate. Place waxed paper between crêpes as you cook them, and cover. To serve, mix sour cream, jalapeño jelly, and piñon nuts. Place a dollop inside each crêpe, roll up, and serve, two to the plate.

Windsor Court Crumpet Flambé

Down in New Orleans, the lowly English crumpet has been given star billing by Arizona native Marlin Shipley, who twice a week makes flaming crumpet desserts in a pricey English restaurant known as LeSalon in the Windsor Court. Shipley told UPI's John DeMers: "I wouldn't advise the average Joe to create blazes in his living room." But what the heck? Sometimes the fire is half the fun.

Serves 2 in 10 minutes

2	tablespoons sugar
4	tablespoons butter
3	tablespoons raspberry preserves
	Juice of half a lemon
1½	ounces Chambord (raspberry liqueur)
2	lightly toasted crumpets
2	ounces cognac
2	scoops vanilla ice cream
2	teaspoons lemon curd
	Zest of lemon rind

Combine sugar, butter, raspberry preserves, lemon juice, and Chambord in a crêpe pan over a flame, allowing mixture to thicken into a sauce (2 minutes). Add crumpets face down and swirl; turn them and swirl once more.

Away from the flame, push crumpets and sauce to rear of the pan and add half of cognac to the crumpets and other half to

CONTINUED ON PAGE 29

BREAKFAST IN BREAD: STOLLEN

New Glarus Bakery and Tearoom
534 First St.
New Glarus, WI 53574

phone orders: yes
608-527-2916
visa/mc

Howard Weber is a classically trained baker who just happened onto this 65-year-old bakery located in a restored Swiss town of 1,700 people. Like other independent craftsmen, he opted for life in the slow lane and the chance to perfect his craft. He employs local talent and has trained them in the procedure for making fine Swiss pastries, including the stollen, which he'll mail to you from November 10 through December 20.

Not only is the bread laced with marzipan, light and dark raisins, and almonds, with a buttery yellow crumb, but the instant these loaves come from the oven, the New Glarus bakers form a mini-assembly line. First they dip each hot, pungent loaf into pure melted butter, then pass it on to be rolled in powdered sugar. It is set aside to cool, then shrink-wrapped, tied with a bow, boxed, and put in the mail. They'll even put in a gift card for you. Each loaf is enough to serve eight, for about $13.50. Once you get it, store in a tin. Cut in thin slices, toast, and slather with sweet butter. This must be what they had in mind when they spoke about the Continental breakfast. Great.

SAN FRANCISCO SOURDOUGH

Boudin Bakery
1995 Evans St.
San Francisco, CA 94124

phone orders: yes
415-854-9090
visa/mc

The sourdough culture that goes into San Francisco's famous bread was started about the time of the Gold Rush. Although many people have tried, they can't transport the temperamental stuff any farther than Oakland or the bread tastes different. If you're traveling out of San Francisco, you can always grab a loaf or two at the airport. But if only your heart is there, just pick up the phone.

On Tuesdays, Boudin ships six-loaf-minimum orders via UPS blue label second-day air, guaranteed to reach you no later than Thursday, and you can freeze what you don't use that day. You will have to admit that the bread doesn't taste quite as good as it does when you're sitting in the sunshine on Fisherman's Wharf, tearing into the loaf and a just-cooked Dungeness crab you bought from a sidewalk fishmonger, washing it down with Anchor Steam beer—but it's close.

SAN FRANCISCO SOURDOUGH STARTER AND BREAD MIXES

Goldrush Enterprises   phone orders: yes
122 E. Grand Ave.   800-531-2039
S. San Francisco, CA   visa/mc
  94080

If all those miners and camp cooks who spent half their lives nursing sourdough through bad weather had known what the Goldrush folks know, they'd have said yahoo and gone on to their card games a good bit sooner. After a bunch of money and a lot of heartache, the Goldrush boys have figured out how to dehydrate the natural sourdough starter so that it will hold and spring to life with the addition of water.

You can purchase a packet of sourdough starter along with recipes for San Francisco–style sourdough French bread, biscuits, and pancakes. Better yet, you can purchase instant mixes for pancakes, waffles, biscuits, and cornbread, all tangy and sour as a camp cook's disposition. If you're tired of your pet rock and bored with taking care of your Cabbage Patch doll, you can even purchase a Baby Sourdough, complete with a parent manual that explains the care and feeding of sourdough, a registration form, starter, flour, pans, baking labels, instructions, and recipes.

CONTINUED FROM PAGE 28

the front of pan. Return pan to flame and ignite, swirling slowly throughout. Remove to plates, top with ice cream, lemon curd, and zest. Serve at once.

Lemon Curd

Once you see how easy lemon curd is to make, you may make it routinely. A genuine comfort food, and delicious on English muffins and crumpets.

Makes 3 cups in 10 minutes

- 3 eggs, slightly beaten
- 6 tablespoons unsalted butter
- ⅞ cup sugar
- ½ teaspoon pure vanilla
  Juice and zest from 2 lemons
  Few grains salt

Combine ingredients. Cook and stir until thick and smooth, but do not allow mixture to boil or it will curdle. This is easiest in a microwave set on medium/low, stirring every 30 seconds, or it can be done in a double boiler. Cook about 15 minutes; mixture should be as thick as pudding. Pour into three sterilized 8-ounce jars, seal, and refrigerate. Keeps for two weeks. Give one jar to your neighbor.

New Orleans Oyster Loaf Sandwich

Serves 4 in 30 minutes

 1 loaf day-old French
   bread
   Butter to spread
 1 pint oysters, drained
   Cornmeal
   Cooking oil
   Dill pickles, thinly sliced

For dressing: Use either Cajun catsup or an ad-lib mixture of catsup and mayonnaise with a hint of mustard and horseradish, and a shot of Worcestershire, Tabasco, and lemon juice.

Slice loaf of bread horizontally and place on a cookie sheet. Remove most of the insides and spread the hollowed-out loaf with butter. Place loaf and bread crumbs in 300° F. oven and toast while you fry oysters.

Drain oysters, dredge in cornmeal, then fry in hot oil until golden on both sides (no more than 3 minutes).

Place cooked oysters in toasted bread cavity. Top with dill pickle slices. Cover with dressing. Sprinkle with toasted bread crumbs until contents form a mound. Now replace top of loaf and warm in oven thoroughly. Slice loaf into four pieces and serve.

NEW ORLEANS–STYLE FRENCH BREAD

Gazin's	phone orders: yes
PO Box 19221	504-482-0302
New Orleans, LA 70119	visa/mc

For a reasonable fee you can have a dozen loaves of New Orleans–style French bread. Properly double-wrapped, it will keep in the freezer until your next event. This is the bread they mean when they talk about oyster loaf sandwiches. You can also order "Cajun catsup" for the sandwich as well as a lot of other Cajun necessities from Gazin's ("Gahzhahhh" is what they say when they answer the phone).

IOWA STONE-GROUND FLOURS, MEALS, AND MIXES

Brumwell Flour Mill	phone orders: yes
South Amana, IA 52333	319-622-3455

When the "Doonesbury" comic strip lampooned Sen. Charles Grassley, Republican of Iowa, about the senator's posture toward the plight of the Midwestern farmer, a mythical senator in the strip suggested this requirement for federal farm loans: "Well, first they must prove they still make their own cornbread." "From scratch?"

The real-life senator sent cartoonist Garry Trudeau two bags of Brumwell's cornmeal and a recipe for cornbread. The Brumwells do make their cornmeal from scratch, by the ancient method of stone-grinding without discarding any of the natural oils, minerals, or vitamins. This cornmeal is known as "unbolted" and will do the senator and the Trudeau babies a lot of good made into cornbread.

The Brumwell brothers, Norman and Vernon, learned their trade from their daddy. Until recently they powered their grinding stones with a 1949 Buick engine. But business has been brisk and now they've been able to replace it with a nice, quiet electric motor. Brumwell's prices are modest and you can order whole-grain goodness in the form of cornmeal, corn flour and cornbread mix; whole wheat flour; graham flour; rye meal and flour; barley grits; soy flour; unbleached white flour; rolled wheat; steel-cut oats; cracked wheat and wheat bran; and fine mixes for pancakes and waffles from unbleached white flour, buckwheat, or whole wheat.

We are simply wild about Brumwell's buckwheat pancake mix. It produces light, flavorful, nutty cakes that don't bear any resemblance to the slate roofing tiles usually palmed off as buckwheat cakes. The Brumwell's oatmeal cookie mix will make your kids dash home from school. The main point is, the Brumwell brothers ship directly to you without warehousing the stock, so you get fresh whole-grain, stone-ground products with all their nutritive value intact.

STONE-GROUND FLOURS, MEALS, CEREALS, AND MIXES

Butte Creek Mill   phone orders: yes
402 Royal Ave. N, Box 561   503-826-3531
Eagle Point, OR 97524

Using a method developed by the Egyptians 5,000 years ago, Peter and Cora Crandall stone-grind a dozen different grains using waterpower from Little Butte Creek diverted through a millrace that activates a turbine that turns the wheels that slowly turn the 1,400-pound millstones against one another to grind the whole grains into flour.

In addition to flours, meals, and cracked grains, you can order outstanding 10-grain cereal, Scottish oatmeal, and grain and nut cereals. One product line the Crandalls seem to have perfected is mixes. Their bran muffin mix makes a dense, sweet, nutty, dark muffin aromatic with the scent of whole grains. This muffin mix is used by many bed-and-breakfast places on the West Coast. They also have a fine cornbread mix that begins with their germ-in stone-ground cornmeal.

Write for a complete price list, and if you're in the area, do drop in. The mill has been in continuous opera-

---

Company-Best Whole Wheat Rolls

Cora Crandall perfected this recipe. The resulting rolls are a miracle. Solid nutrition in a light, aromatic roll as airy as one made with white flour.

Makes 48 rolls in 8 hours with less than 1 hour's work

-   2   tablespoons dry yeast
-   2   tablespoons brown sugar
-   ½   cup warm water (110° F.)
-   1   pound butter
-   2   cups cold milk
-   4   large eggs, beaten
-   ¾   cup brown sugar
-   2   teaspoons salt
-   8   cups 100 percent stone-ground whole wheat flour

Dissolve yeast and 2 tablespoons brown sugar in warm water. Set aside to proof. Melt butter. Pour cold milk into melted butter. Add yeast mixture, eggs, ¾ cup brown sugar, and salt. Slowly work in flour. No kneading required. Refrigerate at least 8 hours. Now dough can be shaped into your favorite roll.

Let rolls rise 1–2 hours. The test is: Will a dent remain when the dough is lightly touched? When it does, the rolls are ready to bake. Bake at 350° F. for 12 minutes, or until golden.

Eleanor Smith's Pumpernickel Bread

Makes 4 loaves

¾ cup Falling Waters
    cornmeal
1½ cups cold water
1½ cups boiling water
1½ teaspoons salt
1   tablespoon sugar
2   tablespoons shortening
1   tablespoon caraway
    seed
2   cups mashed potatoes
1   tablespoon dry yeast
¼   cup lukewarm water
6   cups Falling Waters rye
    flour
2   cups Falling Waters
    unbleached flour

Stir cold water into cornmeal until smooth. Place over heat and add boiling water. Cook and stir 2 minutes or until it forms a mush. Add salt, sugar, and shortening and cool to luke-warm. Add caraway seed, mashed potatoes, and yeast dissolved in warm water. Add flours.

Knead to a smooth, stiff dough, then cover and set aside in a warm, draft-free place to rise until double in bulk, about an hour. Punch down, shape into four standard loaves, and place in greased baking pans. Let rise over tops of pans, about 40 minutes, then bake about an hour in a 350° F. oven. Will keep about a week. Freezes well for up to six months.

tion since the late 19th century and is quite a step back into our own pioneer period. It is listed on the National Register of Historic Places. Their country store has an interesting combination of natural food products and collectibles.

FALLING WATERS STONE-GROUND FLOURS AND MEALS

1788 Tuthilltown Grist Mill   phone orders: yes
Albany Post Rd.   914-255-5695
Gardiner, NY 12525

If you live in the eastern half of the country, this is probably the mill of choice for you to get stone-ground flours and meals. Located just north of New York City, this grist mill has been in constant operation since 1788 and is a must-see for foodie tourists to the area. Using only the waters of the Shawangunk River for power, the mill grinds whole grains of wheat, corn, rye, soy, and buckwheat. They also stock a good selection of what they refer to as "old-fashioned health foods": Rumford baking powder, which contains no sodium aluminum sulfate; spices; medicinal teas; cereals; dried fruits; nuts; seeds; and sprouts. Write for a price list. Prices are more than reasonable.

JAMS, MARMALADES, PRESERVES, AND JELLIES

The criterion we used in selecting jams, jellies, conserves, and preserves was this: Does it taste like the fruit or berry it's made from, or does it just taste sweet? You will only find jams here that have a greater proportion of fruit than sweetener. I particularly call your attention to Beginnings, Endings, Etc. These jams are made without sugar at all. And boy, are they good. Aside from this splendid no-sugar jam, we found that the best jams are made right where the berry or fruit grows. These jam makers can let the fruit vine-ripen for maximum taste. Then the quicker the fruit hits the jar, the better the jam. These are regional specialties par excellence.

THE CHERRY ORCHARD

Rocky Top Farms   phone orders: no
Rte. 1, Essex RD   616-599-2251
Ellsworth, MI 49729

The branch doesn't fall far from the tree, and when vacationing salesman Tom Cooper saw a corn patch overlooking Lake Michigan about eight years ago, he thought about his daddy. Tom grew up helping his father in a plant nursery, and something in that piece of rocky ground—he now calls it his soul—spoke to him that day. He drove his wife, Ruth, out to one spot that had a spectacular sunset view of Leelanau Peninsula and the Manitou islands. He asked her if she thought it was as beautiful as he did. When she said yes, he pulled out a hidden bottle of champagne, popped the cork, and said, "Good! Guess what I just bought today."

Today, after planing off the rocky surface and filling in with topsoil, Tom Cooper has planted some 60 acres in fruit: row on row of perfectly manicured trees, tart and sweet cherries, apricots, plums, and peaches—the very varieties that do best in the high country bordering Lake Michigan. He's also put in 40 acres of red raspberries. And that is the backdoor through which Tom Cooper moved into the preserve business.

The second year he had a bumper crop of raspberries, more than he could sell fresh, but not enough to tempt a packer. Not being ones to waste things, Tom and Ruth got out a cookbook, looked up a recipe, and made 240 pounds of raspberry preserves. Now, some six years later, Tom and his staff put up 16 varieties of jams, preserves, and toppings, all made from their own fruit and berries in their farm kitchen in a gleaming copper cauldron.

In the nine preserves, seven toppings, four butters, and six croissant fillings, the same philosophy prevails. Fruit, not sugar, is the predominant taste. Every jar contains more fruit than sweetener or water. We particularly like the cherry-berry preserves, the berry blossom honey, and the cherry almondine topping, which cloaks a roast duck as admirably as it does ice cream.

The bonus you get when ordering from Tom is the package. He discovered that one of his pickers, George Muto, a retired GM employee, was also an expert woodworker. George first developed a packing box that doubles as a wren house once you get it home. All you have to do is punch out the holes, drive in the dowel perches, leave the cedar shavings the jam was packed in, and soon you'll have wrens nesting in the backyard, in their own little home with the woodburned logo "Rocky Top Farms" emblazoned on the side. That is the kind of bonus and care that comes from Rocky Top. Write for a brochure and choose which group of three to six jars you want and what handmade wooden container you'd prefer: birdhouse, truck, wheelbarrow, or sleigh.

ALASKA KITCHEN

Alaska Wild Berry
   Products
528 E. Pioneer Ave.
Homer, AK 99603

phone orders: yes
907-235-8858
visa/mc

Forty years ago, Hazel Heath began picking berries ripened by the midnight sun, and turning them into jams she then shipped to the lower 48. The business is still housed in a wooden structure that looks like Santa's workshop, complete with not-for-special-effects snow on the ground. If you're in Homer, Alaska, stop by the famous kitchen and taster's table. In back you'll find a Wild Berry picnic park complete with wildflowers and berries of Alaska, an old-fashioned food cache, a working sluice box where you can pan for real Alaskan gold, and the log cabin that served as the original post office for pioneers in Homer.

Owners Peter Eden and Richard Countryman (we'll try to resist the pure Herb Caenism of their names and their location) set up stations in September and buy all the wild berries that pickers can pick. Rosehips, lingonberries, highbush and lowbush cranberries, wild raspberries, mossberries, and salmonberries. And from these they make a variety of pure jellies, jams, and sauces. One of their most interesting products is called sourdough sauce, made from Alaskan wild cranberries. The original camp cooks, of necessity, mixed the berries with salt and pepper as a meat sauce to stand in the place of catsup. Beginning thus, and adding herbs and spices, they've come up with a smooth, tangy meat and fowl sauce.

You can write for a list of all the combination packages they have. One of the most interesting is called Brooks Range. For less than $50 you get the sourdough sauce, rosehip jelly, lingonberry jam, wild highbush cranberry jelly, a couple of cans of Alaskan salmon, some reindeer Polish sausage, smoked salmon strips, and even smoked cheddar cheese. That is truly a taste of Alaska.

OLD-FASHIONED SUN-COOKED JAMS

Greenbriar Jam Kitchen   phone orders: yes
6 Discovery Hill Rd.   617-888-6870
E. Sandwich, MA 02537   visa/mc

In the old days, when the ripening of fruit and berries coincided with the hottest days when the home cook was least likely to wish to stoke the wood cookstove all day, sun cooking was a practical solution. Today, in the face of electric stoves, vents, and air conditioners, sun cooking is almost a lost art. Almost, however, save for the good ladies of the Thornton Burgess Society, who still use the hot summer New England sun to cook the strawberry jam they make to support their nature center.

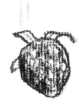

Jam made thusly begins by barely heating berries with sugar syrup on the stove, then pouring them into wide, flat enamel pans, which are then placed on wooden racks to catch the hot southern exposure for two or three days. What you get is whole fruit suspended in clear, ruby-colored syrup so perfect you'll want to spoon it over gelato for dessert. The berries taste fresh and are crisp, never turning to mush as they do in conventional preserves. The only ingredients in this product are strawberries and sugar, and the preserves are as aromatic as an afternoon in the berry patch.

Sun-cooked brandied peaches from Greenbriar are to die for. Firm, aromatic peaches suspended in a clear, thick, orange syrup with a brandy kick to it. I dare you to offer these to anybody else. Believe me—order these and you'll hide them in the pantry for your very own. Let others in your household content themselves with damson plum

jelly, an excellent soft jelly made only with the juice of plums and sugar. No pectin, no corn sweeteners, nothing else. Good as homemade.

Last but not least, the good ladies of the Burgess put up a grandma's-type relish of sweet peppers, onions, vinegar, sugar, and salt. A carrot color with that sweet, salty taste and a pepper-bitter undercast that Grandma thought was terrific. Of all the jams and preserves I tested, the Greenbriar products are in a class by themselves. And the price they charge is more than reasonable. These are each and all one of a kind.

EASTERN BERRY JAMS

Berry Best Farms phone orders: yes
Box 444, Barry Rd. 609-397-0748
Lambertville, NJ 08530

Best known at Bloomingdale's under the Coryell's Crossing label, these pure berry preserves are made in small batches from the homegrown berries of Gilles Carter and Rob French. This extremely small company only makes raspberry, blackberry, blueberry, and strawberry. If you yearn for berry jam as good as homemade but don't want to do it yourself, this is the jam for you. If you live in the area and want fresh berries, call up Gilles and Rob and find out exactly when the berries will peak. Remember, the season is short, but you can get berries picked not a moment too soon from the Berry Best Farms.

PACIFIC NORTHWEST BERRY JAMS

Deer Mountain Berry Farm phone orders: yes
PO Box 257 206-691-7586
Granite Falls, WA 98252

Gooseberries, raspberries, boysenberries, loganberries, strawberries, blueberries. All grown in the fog-shrouded green hills of Washington and turned into sumptuous preserves noted for their fresh taste and mostly-berry ratio of fruit to sweetener. John and Barb Graham are berry grow-ers first, jam makers second. They use their own well-tended berries and their grandmothers' recipes. They don't pick the berries until they're fully ripe, dripping with sweet, tart juice, and they put them up in small batches. You can order these singly or in combination at a price that is so reasonable you'd think your grandmother just asked you to provide the sugar and jars for a batch of homemade preserves.

PUGET SOUND BERRY PRESERVES

The Maury Island   phone orders: yes
  Farming Co.   206-463-5617
Rte. 3, Box 238   visa/mc
Vashon, WA 98070

Not only can you buy the best-quality red currant jelly you ever tried from these berry farmers, but they're always coming up with new flavors. This year, with great success, they've combined red currants and raspberries into a pre-serve that is deep and rich and glazes a lamb to perfec-tion. An example of small-batch slow cooking, with the freshest, ripest berries they can grow, and no corn sweet-eners, these products (including an outstanding blue-berry) are first rate. Write for a catalog.

CALIFORNIA BERRY JAMS, VINEGARS, AND WINE JELLIES

Kozlowski Farms   phone orders: yes
5566 Gravenstein Hwy.   707–887–2104
Forestville, CA 95436   visa/mc

Carmen Kozlowski has turned her farm into a regular food factory and tourist stop. In a gleaming farm kitchen she makes preserves good enough to have warranted a visit from Julia Child for a "Good Morning America" slot. Be-ginning with a red raspberry that lingers in my memory a full year after I saw or tasted it, the Kozlowskis go on to make a range of berry jams, wine jellies using their berries and local vineyards' wines, vinegars, and an outstanding mustard. The list changes with the season. Write for a current listing of what's being put up at the moment.

LOW-SUGAR JAMS

Linn's Fruit Bin   phone orders: yes
RR 1, Box 600   805–927–8134
Cambria, CA 93428   visa/mc

John and Renee Linn operate a working farm just down the road from Hearst Castle. Renee began offering her low-sugar jams just because she believed in the principle of a spread for bread that was more berry than sugar. Before long, the Linns had a nice little country fruit stand going. If you're in the area, stop by. Renee makes a great chicken pie you can get if you're out at the farm.

You can order 10-ounce jars of jams and preserves the Linns grew in their orchard, then put up in their own farm kitchen. Refrigerate after opening. Apple butter, olallieberry, boysenberry, raspberry, strawberry, blueberry, kiwi, peach, and peach pecan are among the choices. Minimum order is three 10-ounce jars.

TOTALLY FRUIT PRESERVES

Beginnings, Endings, Etc.   phone orders: yes
14524 Benefit St., #100   818–340–2801
Sherman Oaks, CA 91403

I didn't think it was possible to have a sugar-free preserve that tasted like anything. That was before I tried Judy and Toby's Totally Fruit Preserves. These taste more fruity than any other and there's a good reason for it. All these preserves utilize apple and/or pear juice so that you get a complex, high-acid preserve that tastes superior to any preserve put up with sugar. Why not? Apple juice tastes better than sugar water. To my mind this is one of those *Eureka* ideas. Why didn't somebody do this before?

Even diabetics can enjoy these preserves. Each teaspoon has 16 calories and is ½ a fruit exchange on the Weight Watcher's diet. So, you can see that you can't just wantonly ravage a jar and get away with it, but you can enhance foods, diet or not. Flavors include Concord grape, strawberry, raspberry, boysenberry, and orange-cranberry marmalade. Apple butter and apricot butter complete the choices. Three-jar minimum order at about $12.

WILD HUCKLEBERRIES

Wilds of Idaho
1308 W. Boone
Spokane, WA 99201

phone orders: yes
509–326–0197
visa/mc

If you ever tasted homemade huckleberry jam once, you'll want more. If you have ever tried picking the elusive wild huckleberry, you may just figure nothing could be worth what it takes to get these berries. They grow in the remotest woods, on low bushes; they are as small as pyracantha berries but never in clumps; and, as if the backbreaking work of finding and gathering a bucketful weren't difficult enough, you'll have to compete with wild bears, who are particularly fond of these berries. And if that's not enough to scare you back to the safety of the urban wilds, remember they ripen just as sow bears are out teaching their cubs to forage. Forget it.

Louise Sevier didn't give up. Not even after she discovered that Huckleberry Hound wasn't just some Saturday morning cartoon character, but was in fact her own black Lab, who managed to eat—with gusto—at least half of the first batch of berries she and her daughters had picked. But now Louise has found pickers, a secret resource she guards as carefully as the keys to Fort Knox, and she gets sufficient quantities to make her award-winning jam, syrup, topping, and—this year—Hucklebears. These are beguiling candies in the shape of the infamous bears, made from Guittard milk chocolate with whole huckleberries inside.

Wilds of Idaho Huckleberry Dumplings

Serves 6 in 20 minutes

- 1½ cups flour
- ⅓ cup sugar
- 1½ teaspoons baking powder
- ¼ teaspoon salt
- ¼ cup soft butter
- ⅓ cup milk
- 1 12-ounce jar huckleberry topping
  Sour cream

Combine dry ingredients. Cut in butter, then add milk. Mix quickly with a fork.

Spoon the huckleberry topping into a 10-inch skillet. Thin the topping with one jar (12 ounces) of water. Place the skillet over medium heat. Drop dumpling batter by tablespoonfuls into the topping. Cover skillet and simmer 15 minutes. Serve with sour cream.

HAWAIIAN JAMS AND SALAD DRESSINGS

Tropical Temptations   phone orders: yes
333 Cobalt Way, Ste. 107   408–733–8017
Sunnyvale, CA 94086

Pamela Hildebrand is importing Hawaiian fruits to create some of the newest jams on the Pacific Rim. Kiwi; a blend of pineapple and blueberry; a really great one blending papaya and macadamia nuts. The most amazing of all is a golden mango jam set off by a burst of ruby pomegranate jelly rising from the bottom of the jar. Looks great wrapped with a gold foil top and tastes even better.

Pamela also makes salad dressings. They have silly names like Opiate of the Gods, Sweet Passions, and Pele's Offering, but what they are respectively are a good, reliable poppy-seed dressing, a passion fruit-honey salad dressing, and a Hawaiian barbecue sauce.

IN A JAM

Sarabeth Preserves   phone orders: yes
423 Amsterdam Ave.   212–496–6280
New York, NY 10024   ae/visa/mc

A little over five years ago, Sarabeth Levine inveigled her aunt into giving her a 200-year-old family recipe for orange-apricot marmalade, invested $100 in fruit, sugar, and jars, and began making jam in her New York apartment. It was an easy sell to Bloomingdale's, Macy's, and New York's leading gourmet shops. All it took was a taste. Once you taste it you'll see what all the excitement is about. Colored like a good Tequila Sunrise, sweet and sharp with citrus shards, this puts both orange marmalade and apricot jam in the shade.

Today, Sarabeth Levine owns two (going on three) restaurants and a bakery. In a commercial canning kitchen, she makes 10 jam flavors, punningly named: Plum Loco, Apricadabra, Rosy Cheeks, Cranberry Relish, Miss Figgy, Beau Pear, Chunky Apple Butter, Fruit Fantasy, Lemon-Pear Butter, and the original Orange-Apricot.

Sarabeth's Chicken Breasts with Marmalade

Good with Wild Pecan Rice from Louisiana (see index), steamed asparagus, a loaf of French bread, and ice cream for dessert. Easy. You could even use the marmalade over the ice cream.

Serves 4 in 1 hour

    4   large mushrooms
    ½   cup chopped onion
    1   tablespoon butter
        Salt and pepper to taste
    ¼   cup teriyaki sauce
    ¼   cup water
    ⅛   cup Sarabeth's
        Orange-Apricot
        Marmalade
    2   whole chicken breasts

Sauté mushrooms and onion in butter. Season with salt and pepper and set aside. Combine teriyaki sauce, water, and marmalade and set aside. Cut chicken breasts in half and place, skin side down, in electric skillet or frying pan. Pour liquid ingredients over chicken, cover, and cook at 325° F. (medium heat), turning from time to time, until done (about 20 minutes). Add vegetables, cover, and heat for 10 minutes. Serve over rice.

Each comes in a mason jar with flat and lid and is as carefully made as if it were done in your own kitchen. Sarabeth once sent back 10 shipments of plums before she got ones with just the right blush for the preserves. That's how the name plum loco came about. Whether or not the plum packer called her that goes unrecorded. Never mind, Sarabeth's preserves contain no additives, fillers, or preservatives. Only the finest pure ingredients and handmade. No wonder she wins "best of show" at National Association of the Specialty Food Trade shows.

SEVILLE ORANGE MARMALADE

Corti Brothers   phone orders: yes
5770 Freeport Blvd. #66   916-391-0300
Sacramento, CA 94822   visa/mc

Using Mrs. Beeton's hundred-year-old recipe for marmalade, and sour Seville oranges that were planted in California's capital just for the blossoms, Darrell Corti has created a new/old classic, an orange marmalade he calls "A Capital Vintage Marmalade." Supplies of this jam are extremely limited—there aren't a whole lot of those trees in Sacramento—but this is a rare and exotic product. Every jar is put up by hand and aged a year before it's sold. Mixed with bouillon and sherry, it makes the most mysterious, complex poultry glaze you ever had. A product for the real gourmands.

BRANDIED FRUIT, PRESERVES, AND FRUIT CAKES

Running Deer Ranch   phone orders: yes
Creston Star Rte.   805-239-1784
Paso Robles, CA 93445

Arthur and Anneliese Katz call their blue-ribbon products pure delight. Pure, yes. Delight, indeed. All handmade, in small batches, without preservatives, additives, or dyes. On their 70-acre ranch they have what they call VIP, vertically integrated production. They grow their own

fruits, nuts, berries, grapes, and vegetables. Then Anneliese turns this carefully tended, field-ripened, freshly
picked produce into fine homemade food products right
in her own ranch-canning kitchen.

Anneliese comes from a small town in the Black Forest
region of southern Germany and learned to can on her
grandparents' farm. The German influence is so predominant in her products that they almost made my German
husband cry. The Germans do know one secret to good
taste: A tad of sugar in things makes them taste better.
Anneliese's barbecue sauce is bright red, laced with fresh
cracked pepper, lemon-tart, sweet, and pungent. Even
her salsa, which she calls "Español," might better be de-
scribed as "Aleman." Hot, sweet, and more complex than
any Mexican-style salsa. And those brandied pears! Bracing and—as my husband would quickly tell you—just like
mother used to make.

At this moment Running Deer offers 20 products, including a splendid sun-started strawberry preserve, various berry preserves, as well as fig, orange, and plum. And
their pomegranate jelly—oh, my god, is it gorgeous!
Deep, clear ruby-colored and as pure as the gem. Marmalades—pear, citrus, cherry-orange. And more wonderful brandied apricots, cherries, and pears. Their brandy
and sherry fruitcakes are moist, rich, and delicious for tea.
Anneliese Katz has won many blue ribbons at county fairs
for her preserved fruits. Getting a package from the Running Deer is like getting a present from your favorite
grandmother. This woman knows how to can.

PURE CALIFORNIA PRESERVES AND SPREADS

Thatched Cottage
PO Box 5593
Carmel, CA 93921

phone orders: yes
Tuck Box
408-624-6365
visa/mc

Apricots and citrus fruits. Two of California's best products that are surprisingly hard to get out of the state in any
form that tastes as good as it does to the lucky native.
Peggy Greco, a schoolteacher with six children under the

age of fourteen, has solved the problem. Her Lemon Spred is similar to England's lemon curd but better tasting because of the superiority of California's lemons, and her Fresh Apricot Jam really lives up to its name, having the aroma and taste of fully ripe apricots. Here is California, captured in a jar.

Peggy Greco is particular. Her standards are high. Only fresh squeezed lemons from Ventura blended with real whole eggs and real butter go into the lemon spred. The apricots she buys from just one ranch, carefully waiting for just the right moment when the "cots" are ripe but still have enough natural pectin so she won't have to add more. These are old-fashioned runny preserves. The best. She also makes a boysenberry and a gooseberry as tart as cranberries. These are good as homemade and available at Carmel's famous tearoom, the Tuck Box, to be taken at tea or shipped out in custom orders.

Line the bottom and sides of a freshly baked pie shell with a generous amount of Peggy Greco's Lemon Spred using a knife to smooth. Fill with fresh strawberries and top with freshly whipped cream.

For holidays: Spoon lemon spred atop mincemeat pie, steamed puddings, gingerbread, pumpkin bread, and all nut breads.

For breakfast, spoon lemon spread onto bagels, scones, or English muffins with a dollop of fresh cream cheese.

SOUTHERN TRADITIONAL JELLIES

Bainbridge Corp. phone orders: yes
PO Box 150805   615-383-5157
Nashville, TN 37215 visa/mc

Tom Bainbridge is an insurance man in Nashville who's always been interested in cooking. Preserving traditional recipes and presenting them to a national audience is his new passion. When you receive his four-pack in the mail, it's like a raid on the family cellar. Put up in Kerr jars with flats and lids, the flavors are as traditional as the packaging: black walnut, fig, blackberry, apple pie, lemon honey, kiwi mint. Kiwis? How did kiwis get in here? Because Tom Bainbridge is also an innovative cook and discovered that California's kiwi, when blended with the mint he grows out by the water hydrant in his hot Tennessee backyard, makes a super jelly alongside a country ham. To that end he also makes a golden garlic-with-parsley jelly and a spring onion jelly. Red hot pepper and green mild pepper jellies complete the array. If you've never tried Southern spiced crisp sweet pickles—they're usually only available out of somebody's fruit cellar—ask Tom to send you some.

Ginger-Buttered Fruit Kebabs

Makes 10 kebabs in 20 minutes

A brunch to remember begins with hot, spicy fruit on a stick. For each serving, skewer an orange segment, red apple wedge, thick diagonal slice of banana, slice of mango or papaya, and a chunk of pineapple onto a bamboo skewer. Grill 5–10 minutes until lightly browned, turning and basting frequently with ginger butter: made from ½ cup melted butter and ¼ cup ginger jelly. Makes enough ginger butter to baste 10 kebabs.

Hot Gingered Papaya

Good for breakfast, for dessert, or as a meat accompaniment.

Serves 4

  2 firm, ripe papayas
  ¼ cup butter
  2 tablespoons lime juice
  2 tablespoons ginger jelly
     Dash cayenne

Cut papayas in half, scooping out seeds. Arrange papayas in baking pan. Melt butter with lime juice and ginger jelly. Spoon jelly mixture into the papaya cavities. Bake at 350° F. for 30 minutes, basting several times.

CONTINUED ON PAGE 45

GINGER AND PEPPER JELLIES

Judyth's Mountain, Inc.   phone orders: yes
1737 Lorenzen Dr.   707-944-8802
San Jose, CA 95124   (Oakville Grocery)
  ae/visa/mc

For those of us who grew up on jalapeño jelly, this is the real item. The only one to buy. Mona Onstead's jelly comes in two strengths: hot and hotter. No artificial ingredients. No dye. Just a blast furnace of pleasure. Another jelly of hers that is a favorite of our family is ginger jelly, known around here as "gj" and as much a staple at our house as coffee beans. No well-stocked larder should be without either of these. And ask for Mona's cookbook, which will tell you ways to use these jellies in every course.

HONEY

I had no idea when I began this project that there were so many choices in honeys. To the honey connoisseur, the subtle variations in taste make not-so-subtle differences in desirability. It depends on what you want to use the honey for. A strong, deep-colored honey is inappropriate, for example, in cooking because it will overwhelm other tastes. A pale, mild, bland honey, the standard grocery store offering, is boring as corn syrup when used on a biscuit.

Everybody and his brother is putting up honey. We narrowed our choices down to just a few purveyors who had something special to offer. These honeys have in common the fact that they are unpasteurized, unfiltered honeys, sometimes called "raw," and they are labeled for the nectar of origin. I have always wondered, I will confess, how they can get the bee to tell them just where he's been poking around all day.

WILD AND RAW HONEYS

Oregon Apiaries   phone orders: yes
1118 N. College   503-538-8546
Newberg, OR 97132

Beyond the five flavors of honeys that entomologist Marita Truck gathers, the most interesting product she has is known as honey butter. She blends this smooth-as-creamery butter from honey and nuts, either Oregon filberts or almonds. The result is a spread that exceeds both honeys and nut butters in taste and texture. The delicious wild honey flavors are fireweed, blackberry, clover, star thistle, and wildflower, in a range that grades from light to dark and from mild to strong in taste.

WASHINGTON BERRY HONEYS AND BEEKEEPERS' SUPPLIES

Heidi Honey   phone orders: yes
2210 E. Pioneer   206-841-7245
Puyallup, WA 98371

Wayne and Carla Robinson have been keeping bees for 15 years in the verdant Washington valleys where the berry industry thrives. Setting out hives in the berry thickets serves both the berry growers and the honey business. The bees pollinate the berry vines, and the berry blossoms provide the necessary nectar to make honey. By careful placement of their portable hives, the Robinsons can offer raspberry, strawberry, and blackberry honeys as well as wild Cascade Mountain fireweed honey. If you like the comb, you can purchase the honey of choice and the comb from the Robinsons.

These experienced beekeepers still retain their enthusiasm for the occupation that began for them strictly as a hobby. They sell beekeepers' supplies and will give instructions to would-be keepers who call or stop by their retail business called The Bee Barn.

CONTINUED FROM PAGE 44

Remove from oven and add a dash of cayenne.

Other serving suggestions:

Simons Restaurant Brandied Peaches:
Heat fresh peach halves in brandy. Fill centers with hot pepper jelly and serve with roast lamb or pork.

Ginger Applesauce:
Combine 1 cup unsweetened applesauce, ¼ cup ginger jelly, and ½ teaspoon cinnamon. Heat and serve.

Broiled Grapefruit:
Top prepared grapefruit with a spoonful of ginger jelly and broil. Good for breakfast, brunch, or dessert.

FLAVORED HONEYS

Trappist Creamed Honey   phone orders: yes
Abbey of the Holy Trinity   801-745-3784
Huntsville, UT 84317

"When they live by the labor of their hands, as our fathers and the apostles did, then they are really monks" (Rule of St. Benedict, Chapter 48). The Cistercian monks in Utah are an outgrowth of the Kentucky abbey (see Trappist Cheese). By the labor of their hands they process honey into a smooth-flavored cream, which they offer by mail order; make stone-ground whole wheat bread; raise chickens for eggs and cattle for milk and beef, which they sell only at their abbey high in the dramatic mountains of Utah.

Creamed honey is made by combining pure liquid honey with a precise amount of granulated honey, then whipping it so that it will retain a butterlike texture and spreadability at room temperature. Honey is a natural preservative and when creamed and blended with fresh nuts, natural fruits, spices, and spirits, what you get is a product that retains the maximum taste of the fruit or nut in a honey suspension.

The Trappists sell more than 20 flavors of blended honeys in half-pound containers. Toasted almond is their best seller, and with good reason. Suspending freshly toasted almond slivers in honey cream keeps them as fresh-tasting as if you'd just pulled them out of the oven, and their honey base is a mild yet distinctive wildflower flavor. For bakers and sweet-roll makers, these honeys could become the secret weapon in the cinnamon roll wars. Currently offered in the fruit flavors are lemon, orange, apricot, cherry, strawberry, and raspberry. Nuts include almond, date pecan, peanut butter, and black walnut. Maple cinnamon, brandy, and rum make up the final category. As we go to press, the monks are experimenting with real liqueurs. By the time you are reading this, they've probably got that ready for market. Ask.

As of press time, they sell six half-pound containers—flavors of your choice—for under $10 postpaid, which makes their product a bargain as well as a flavorful addition to the larder. And does this honey keep. Six months after the honey arrived, the almonds taste as fresh as if they'd been roasted yesterday.

HONEYS, BEESWAX, ROYAL JELLY, AND BEE POLLEN

Honey Heaven   phone orders: yes
949 Pearl St.   503-344-5939
Eugene, OR 97401

As the name implies, this store sells everything from the bee, including more than 25 varieties of local, unpasteurized raw honeys in flavors you might never have even imagined. They sent me some poison oak honey—guaranteed to desensitize one to the plant. I didn't roll around in the plentiful stuff to test, I might add. You can get honey, pollen for your health, royal jelly for your youth, honeycombs for fun. If it's honey, they have it.

GOURMET HONEY BUTTERS AND SPREADS

Moonshine Trading Co.   phone orders: yes
PO Box 896   916-795-2092
Winters, CA 95694

The honeys put out by the Moonshine Trading Company look so enticing, you may just want to feast your eyes on the labels. But do open the jars. They choose honeys flavored from yellow star thistle, sweet clover, sunflower, orange blossom, eucalyptus, black button sage, and Christmasberry. Each honey is distinctive in taste—going, as honeys do, from light to dark in strength and intensity. My favorite is the eucalyptus. Moonshine also packages splendid almond nut butter to go with the honey on your best biscuit. One of their more interesting packages is a snuff-sized can of honeycomb from mountain wildflower honey. Remember how you used to chew that stuff as a kid? Honeycomb, I'm talking about, not snuff.

THE FRENCH CONNECTION: HONEY

Schoonmaker-Lynn
  Enterprises
4619 N.W. Barnes Rd.
Portland, OR 97210

phone orders: yes
503-222-5435

Dottie Schoonmaker is lucky. She has her own French connection. Her daughter Karen married Frenchman Peter Lynn and moved with him to the south of France, where they keep bees. Setting their hives in remote fields of flowers, far from the pollution of cities and towns, the Lynns collect honeys of exquisite quality.

In the early spring, they set their hives on the hills below Donadei Domaine and collect honey from the white heather and from wild sea lavender that grows only in view of the sea. Lavender honey is one of the rarest honeys and most treasured by Frenchmen. Later, they move the hives up to the high, wide valleys of the subalpine mountains and get a medium honey they call Montagne. In July, they split the hives between French orange groves and sunflower fields. Come autumn they set the hives in acacia and chestnut groves and get stronger, slightly bitter honey they add to stews. Finally, the hives go to the pine forest to collect the clear, dark amber liquid honey that Europeans believe has medicinal properties.

Dottie imports eight honeys from her daughter and son-in-law. She'll send any pair of these 8-ounce treasures anywhere for under $10. This honey is valuable. The Lynns call it Domaine de Donadei, Gift from God. It's the best I know.

MAPLE SYRUP DOESN'T GROW ON TREES

The women of local American Indian tribes taught the European settlers how to derive sweeteners from the trunks of trees. Sinzibukweed ("drawn from the wood") was the name the Indians gave to what we now know as maple syrup. Squaws hacked the maple trees with tomahawks, inserted reeds to run the sap into vessels of clay, hollowed-out wood, or birch bark, then boiled the syrup by dropping hot stones into the brew. At the end of the short spring season, during the "sugar moon," the Indians celebrated a rite of spring that thanked the gods for the maple tree, the never-ending source of food and life.

The process is essentially unchanged. Today's maple syrup maker may use a power drill to tap the trees, he may create a maze of plastic tubing that funnels the sap into holding tanks, he may use an oil burner and a fancy retort cooker to evaporate the sap into syrup, he may host hordes of city tourists who make a festive "rite of spring" pilgrimage to New England during the annual sugaring-off time—but this maple sugar maker may be the only American left who makes his living gathering, just as the original Indians did.

And that, perhaps, is the cause for what one maple sugar maker calls the "disease" that afflicts those who have gone through the process of making maple syrup. It gets in the blood, they say. Once you've done it, you want to do it again. Perhaps it's the rhythm of the seasons, becoming so in tune with nature that you can—as Everett Palmer says he can sometime along about March—smell it in the air when it's time to tap the trees. Maybe it's the measurement of time in decades rather than days—it takes 40 years for a maple to grow big enough to tap— the very real notion that you are creating something to pass on to your children. Whatever the elements, the American maple syrup makers are among the most contented people I met in researching this book.

The work involved in making one gallon of maple syrup is rather astounding. They call a group of maple trees the "sugarbush," and it takes four maple trees, at least 40 years old, growing in this mountain "sugarbush," to yield enough sap in six weeks to produce a single gallon of maple syrup. Forty gallons of sap it takes. Forty gallons hauled from the tree to the stove. Forty gallons of sap that weigh in at 8 pounds per gallon must be gathered every single day, through knee-deep snow, through wet spring storms in the high, steep green mountains, to make that single gallon of syrup. It takes the equivalent of a four-foot long sawed, split, dried, and burned in a raging fire under a cauldron of merrily bubbling sap for every gallon you get. It takes a whole crew—usually the sugarmaker's family—to gather the sap, fire the stove, sterilize, filter, grade, and pack each gallon of syrup. Now you know why it costs so damn much.

Maple Nut Brittle

Makes 1 lb. in 45 minutes

- 1 cup nut pieces (pecans, walnuts, or hazelnuts)
- 1 cup maple sugar
- 1 cup light corn syrup
- ½ cup water
- 2 tablespoons butter

Preheat oven to 350° F. Heat nuts in oven until crisp and golden, about 10 minutes. Meanwhile, cook and stir maple sugar, corn syrup, and water until sugar dissolves. Then cook without stirring until candy thermometer reads 240° F., or until mixture becomes slightly brittle when dropped into cold water. Stir in butter and toasted nuts, then pour into a prebuttered cookie sheet to cool. When cool, break into pieces with knife handle. Store in a tin. If there is any to store, that is. Gads! This stuff is delicious.

The Vermont Shake

For each shake, use ¾ cup cold milk, 2 tablespoons dark maple syrup, and a scoop of vanilla ice cream. Shake well and serve.

There are hundreds of small maple syrup makers in Vermont and New Hampshire. I have chosen just a few representative ones who produce top-quality, Grade A maple syrup products, who have added new elements to the basic process, and who have created interesting uses for this most American of products.

FANCY GRADE A LIGHT AMBER SYRUP

Everett and Kathryn
  Palmer
Waisfield, VT 05673

phone orders: yes
802-496-3696

Everett Palmer, pushing 80, and his wife, Kathryn, a couple of years younger, have been making maple syrup the artful old-fashioned way for all of the 55-plus years of their marriage. According to Everett, who has made a living tapping trees on his 34-acre farm his entire life, they're "too old" to buy the new scientific equipment. This means that Everett Palmer, by himself, cuts, loads, hauls, and stacks 45 cords of wood every year. Have you ever tried to stack even one cord of wood? In the spring, when he can smell it in the air, Everett Palmer straps on snowshoes and slogs through knee-deep snow every day for six weeks, collecting sap from the same trees his grandfather and father before him tapped. For this part of the job, at least, he has the help of his son and three hired hands.

Everett Palmer uses his century-old wood-fired evaporator in a sugarhouse that he's never quite gotten around to even electrifying. His wife, Kathryn, stands and stirs the boiling sap, holding a spoon up until the golden syrup sheets off just to suit her. Then the two of them pack 800 gallons of syrup—by hand. Much of it they sell right out of the sugarhouse.

Their product is the purest ginger ale color, the highest grade. All made by hand in a way that blends art, experience, and craft so subtly it probably never can be passed on to another generation.

Kathryn Palmer has just lately taken to making a maple cream, the color of cow's cream, smooth and crystal-free as velvet, as thick as fine nut butter, the absolute essence of maple to spread on a bagel or English muffin. The lucky visitors to the Palmer place will no doubt be treated to one of Kathryn's famous doughnuts. She arises daily at 5 to prepare what usually runs to hundreds of dozens before the season ends. She'll even teach the kids how to make "sugar on snow," a Vermont tradition, wherein boiling syrup is poured onto snow and then pulled up, forming a soft, waxy taffy. It's served with—you won't believe this—unsweetened doughnuts, sour pickles, deviled eggs, milk and coffee.

Customers of Everett and Kathryn Palmer are fanatic in their devotion. They know the product is in short supply and only available as long as the Palmers can keep up the pace of this vigorous, outdoor life.

NEW HAMPSHIRE HANDMADE SYRUPS

Dan Johnson's Sugar House
Rte. 1, Box 265
Jaffrey, NH 03452

phone orders: yes
603-532-7379

Dan Johnson was a city schoolteacher when he was bitten by the maple-sugaring bug about 15 years ago. He has been gainfully employed sugaring ever since, doing 97 percent of the work himself, but with a different slant than Everett Palmer. Dan Johnson is the true amateur, a man who does it for love.

He turned his academic mind to the study of sugaring and now has a picture-book sugaring house, rigged so that he can do almost all the work without help, which keeps him free, he says. He begins setting out tubing in trees in November, before the snow gets too deep, and from then until May, he works outdoors almost every day. Beginning in February (despite the conventional wisdom that says wait until March), he uses a gravity and vacuum system to draw sap from the trees into tubes that feed into holding tanks. This way Johnson gets the first, pure run. He boils the sap and stores it until summer, when he reheats and packages it. With this system, he can almost single-handedly produce 800 gallons of Grade A syrup,

Old-Fashioned Vermont Yellow-Eye Beans

Butternut Mountain Farm's Donald Campbell went to his local supermarket to get me some yellow-eye beans when I told him they don't sell them on the West Coast. They look most like big black-eyed peas and can be exchanged with either those or navy beans for this traditional winter dish. Serve with steamed brown bread and additional maple syrup for the true Vermont supper.

Serves 8. Cooks all day.

    1   pound dried yellow-eye
        beans (or black-eyed
        peas or navy beans)
    ½   pound salt pork or ham
        hock, rinsed
    1   medium onion, peeled
        and sliced
    ½   teaspoon baking soda
    2   teaspoons salt
    1   teaspoon dry mustard
    ½   to 1 cup pure maple
        syrup, to taste

Parboil beans in water to cover until skins wrinkle. Then, into a bean pot or crock pot, place pork, onion, and remaining ingredients. Add beans and water to cover. Cook covered in oven at 325° F. for 8 hours, or in crock pot set on low for an equal period of time. Check from time to time and add hot water if beans seem to be drying out. Remove cover for last 30 minutes to thicken the juice.

most of which he sells through his private mailing list of 15,000. He welcomes visitors, those who dare brave the car-swallowing mud of a New England spring, and says that anybody who makes it up to the house gets a big welcome.

SCIENCE AND SUGAR

Butternut Mountain Farm phone orders: yes
Johnson, VT 05656   802-635-7483

David Marvin holds a degree in forestry from the University of Vermont. His father was a famous botanist and maple researcher there, who purchased the first segment of the Butternut Farm and planted the sugarbush with specimen maples beginning in the 1950s. David Marvin now shepherds his 600 acres making maple syrup and sugar, growing Christmas trees, cutting spruce for wreaths, and cutting sawlogs, firewood, and pulpwood. In 1983, he was named National Outstanding Tree Farmer of the Year.

You won't see the picturesque buckets on trees here, but rather an unnatural spider web of plastic tubing that by gravity and vacuum draws the sap to holding tanks, a system that turns 144,000 gallons of sap into 3,600 gallons of pure maple syrup. It comes in three grades: fancy, the light amber, delicate-flavored syrup; Grade A medium amber, the most popular; and Grade A dark amber, the hearty, robust syrup that comes at the end of the season. Marvin also makes and sells pure granulated maple sugar, a product with more uses than you might ever imagine.

CHAPTER 2

FARMER'S MARKET

I. Mushrooms and truffles
II. Fresh herbs, exotic vegetables, flowers, and seeds
III. Onions and garlic
IV. Rices
V. Fruits and nuts, fresh and dried

Just now, I was eating a Comice pear. These are a fairly exotic variety: sweet and aromatic, dripping with juice, mostly grown in the neighborhood in which I live, in such short supply they are shipped only to a small radius of grocery stores—say, within 500 miles. But the Comice pear is well known in the United States, largely through the offices of Harry and David, just down the road a piece from where I live. Under the trade name "Royal Riviera," Harry and David have virtually built a business by mail-ordering this pear directly to eager pearo-philes.

People come back to Harry and David year after year for this pear because they cannot get it locally. In this chapter, I'm going to tell you where you can buy the regional specialties that usually can't be purchased in your neighborhood super-market. The avocado, for example, is widely disseminated. But the Bliss avocado, from Santa Barbara, hand-picked for you and weighing over a pound apiece—bigger than a grapefruit if not a breadbox—is only available by mail, unless you happen to live down the block from the Bliss family.

The farmers, growers, gleaners, and orchardists who make up the purveyors in this chapter must indeed promise *Satisfaction Guaranteed,* because they of all people have the fresh produce markets with which to compete. I have only included items in this chapter that are better than what you can buy locally, and this means no matter where you live—even the largest city. Unless, of course, you live in the neighborhood where the product grows.

Maybe you can buy walnuts for a song . . . or maybe you have a lemon tree in your backyard. The point I am trying to make in this chapter is that by developing your own sources, you can have the absolute best, the freshest, Grade A, extra-large, perfectly ripe whatever, from every locale. The whole country becomes, for you, one big neighborhood, courtesy of UPS. And just as soon as I finish my own work this morning, I'm calling that Texas pecan grower, because we miss these pecans every fall.

MUSHROOMS AND TRUFFLES

In the last few years, our mushroom IQ has gone up dramatically. Not only do we know about button mushrooms, but we are conversant about wild chanterelles, morels, matsutakis, enokis, oysters, truffles, and shiitakes. We see ever-increasing numbers of these in the grocery stores. But each mushroom has a short season and its availability fresh is limited by time and place. I am listing here for you sources of fresh mushrooms and truffles in season and for dried mushrooms year-round.

WOODLAND PANTRY DRIED MUSHROOMS

Forest Foods, Inc.
PO Box 373
River Forest, IL 60305

phone orders: yes
312-848-3144

This company was formed to service the so-called New American chefs and *au courant* restaurants. But when home cooks demanded the same varieties they'd enjoyed in restaurant preparations, Forest Foods began putting the mushrooms up in attractive boxes complete with directions for rehydration, menu suggestions, a little spoon-fed mycological information about the species and recipes. You can buy Michigan morels, Italian porcini, Japanese shiitake, and native oyster mushrooms in ⅝-ounce boxes from these people.

OYSTER AND SHIITAKE MUSHROOMS

Full Moon Mushroom Co.   phone orders: yes
PO Box 6138   206-866-9362
Olympia, WA 98502   visa/mc

Barbara and Mike Maki grow both oyster and shiitake mushrooms and offer them for sale every Saturday at Seattle's Pike Place Market. They will ship to you not only these two varieties but also special custom-grown mushrooms, like the Garden Giant. They also will help you get started in the mushroom-growing business yourself with information and will provide mushroom spawn, quality hardwood sawdust and chips, pasteurized straw, and other proper bedding products.

MATSUTAKIS, CHANTERELLES, AND MORELS IN SEASON

Hasson Brothers Fruit and   phone orders: yes
   Produce   206-622-1370
1527 Pike Place Market
Seattle, WA 98101

Peter Hasson employs pickers to bring in bushels of the apricot-colored chanterelle during its September-October growing season. At the same time, the pickers see a few matsutakis, which are valuable for Japanese preparations. In the spring, Washington morels are available through this open-air vegetable stand, located in the heart of Pike Place Market. Because Pike Place is a regular stop for tourists, the merchants here are accustomed to shipping their products, and you can count on things being done in an orderly way.

Pâté Morels

The rich, meaty taste of morels combined with bacon, onion, and tomatoes creates a smoky forest pâté to begin a fine dinner.

Makes 2 cups

1¼	ounces dried morels
4	tablespoons butter
1	small onion, chopped
2	strips bacon, chopped
1	cup tomatoes, chopped
½	pound fresh mushrooms, sliced
2	eggs, beaten
	Salt to taste
	Whiff of cayenne

Soak morels in warm water or broth to cover until soft (about 15 minutes), then drain and slice. In half the butter, brown onion. Add remaining butter and stir in bacon, tomatoes, and all mushrooms. Cook 10 minutes over medium heat, then puree in food processor or blender. Put into saucepan. Add eggs and stir over low heat until mixture thickens (do not boil). Season to taste. Pour into crock, cover, and refrigerate. Serve chilled. Good with water biscuits.

You can call up Peter Hasson for a price and availability quote on any Washington produce item that strikes your fancy: mushrooms, Walla Walla onions, exotic varieties of apples, berries, blue potatoes. If it grows in Washington, is in season, and didn't get rained out, Peter Hasson has it.

OREGON WHITE TRUFFLES

White Truffle Foods, Inc.   phone orders: yes
829 7th St.   503-635-6444
Lake Oswego, OR 97034

The canned truffle—imported, costly, and taste-diminished—pales by comparison to fresh domestic truffles picked in Oregon. Although food snobs assure me this truffle is inferior to the black truffle from France, all I can say is, you have to figure compared to what? . . . Remember that truffles are fragile and should be slivered, then added to a dish at the last moment and barely heated through for maximum flavor.

FRESH AND DRIED MICHIGAN MORELS

See also: American Spoon Foods.

DRIED CHINESE MUSHROOMS

See also: Chinese Kitchen.

ENOKIS, SHIITAKES, AND MORELS

See also: Frieda's Finest.

OYSTER MUSHROOM GROWING KIT

Kurtzman's Mushroom
Specialties
c/o Harvest Glow
Systems, Inc.
32 E. Filmore Ave.
St. Paul, MN 55107

phone orders: yes
415-233-0555
visa/mc

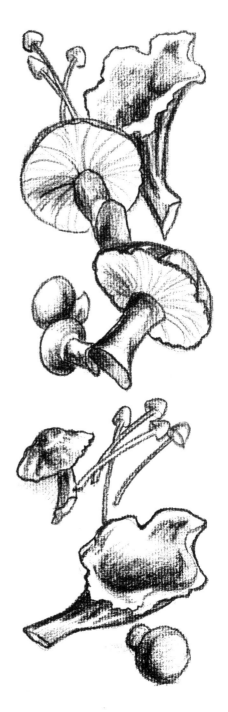

Dr. Ralph Kurtzman, plant pathologist, biochemist, and world-famous mushroom expert, first got into the mail-order business of supplying spawn (seed) for oyster mushrooms to amateur and commercial growers. But after answering the same questions over and over, he solved everybody's problems by creating a kit. This kit will give you up to six pounds of oyster mushrooms over a three-month period. Then, you can just phone Dr. Kurtzman and he'll send you more spawn.

If you have never tried the oyster variety, you're in for a treat. Called the shellfish of the forest, it is a lovely, creamy, flute-shaped mushroom with overtones of oyster. We have grown these mushrooms successfully at our house. My only word of warning is that, for obvious reasons, you have to keep the moist, dark, inviting box away from the cat.

If you get into mushroom growing, Dr. Kurtzman can also supply you with spawn for six exotic varieties. He'll send directions.

FRESH HERBS AND WHERE TO GET THEM

One of the most recent innovations in American cooking is the use of fresh herbs. We are beginning to accept what the fine chefs of France, Italy, and China have always known: Some herbs just plain lose it if dried. And the longer an herb is separated from the plant, the more of its aroma is likely to be lost. Therefore, if you really want top-notch herbs, grow your own. Here are sources for every herb seed you might ever imagine. If, however, you don't wish to grow your own, the next best thing is to buy potted herbs. We offer sources for those as well as for cut herbs.

What herbs don't dry well? Basil is a prime example. There is simply no comparison between fresh and dried basil. Tarragon, savory, chervil, sorrel, cilantro, and lemon grass are others that pale when dried. Thyme, rosemary, sage, and oregano dry well but lose their pungency after a year. If you want to dry your own herbs, simply cut and tie them and hang them upside down in a cool, dark place until dry, then store in a sealed jar.

SOUTH BRONX BASIL AND EVERY EXOTIC FRESH HERB

GLIE Farms
1600 Bathgate
Bronx, NY 10457

phone orders: yes
212-731-2130

When Gary Waldron, founder of GLIE Farms, begins to tell a group of gourmands about his place, a profound hush comes over the audience. Not only does he operate a lush, bountiful farm that supplies the finest restaurants from New York City to Montreal with every conceivable fresh herb, he operates his farm in a bombed-out area of the South Bronx that has produced little but slums in the past 50 years. His fellow farmers are the would-be subway hustlers, house burglars, West Side Story gang-members-without-the-music that usually spring from this soil. GLIE means Group Live-In Experience, and the farm has been a shelter for runaway youths since 1980, when Bronx 2000 Local Development wrote its first contract with GLIE to grow vegetables and flowers for community gardens.

Under the auspices of Waldron, the project has matured into a bona fide business with an impeccable reputation among the most persnickety chefs. Lemon thyme, bay, hyssop, pineapple sage, lemon geranium, rose geranium, fuzzy yarrow, oregano, orange mint, lemon verbena, tarragon, chervil—you name it and GLIE probably grows it. As we go to press, GLIE is looking into growing mushrooms; so when you call, ask if they've got the mushrooms growing yet. GLIE ships anywhere by Emery second-day air, has a $15 minimum, and the shipping costs usually run about four bucks—herbs are light.

If you want something really exotic, or if you operate a restaurant and need a reliable source for greenhouse-grown herbs year-round, call GLIE Farms. Not only do the plants thrive here but the planters as well.

SAGE ADVICE FROM HEARTLAND HERBALIST

Herb Gathering, Inc.   phone orders: yes
5742 Kenwood   816-523-2653
Kansas City, MO 64110

Paula Winchester majored in botany and journalism at the University of Kansas and after graduation joined the St. Louis Herb Society. Her backyard herb garden evolved into lessons and finally, in 1979, to a restaurant call requesting 100 pounds of fresh herbs a week. "I didn't even know what 100 pounds of herbs looked like," she says now. She phoned up herb-growing friends and began a collective that now supplies fresh herbs, exotic seeds, kits, and blends of herbs for many uses.

Paula admits to being an herb junkie, enraptured with the folkloric history of both culinary and medicinal herbs. If you are, as I am, an information junkie, ordering from Paula is a thrill. Just today I received, along with nasturtium seeds, a mimeographed sheet giving me a little tasteful history, major uses, cooking hints, and six recipes for using the nasturtium leaf and flower.

Paula has put together seed groupings that will make the gardener's heart swell with joy. For example, The French Gourmet: nine packets for under $9—celeriac, cornichon, corn salad, endive, *haricots verts,* leek, Kagraner Sommer lettuce, French melon, and *petits pois.* There are other groupings. This is only the beginning.

Paula grows gourmet baby vegetables, including carrots thin as a lady's pinkie; ruby, green, and golden globe beets; scallopini squash . . . no telling what all by this season. Call and ask. You can get herbal teas; blends for gingerbread boys complete with cookie cutter and spices; catnip animals; flea-repelling dog collars drenched with pennyroyal, eucalyptus, and rosemary; bath potpourri; spice samplers including Madagascar vanilla bean, saffron threads, *herbes de Provence,* and pickling spices. All this in addition to a reliable assortment of fresh herbs that

Nasturtium Sandwiches from *Herbs for Health and Cookery*

Finely chop nasturtium leaves and place on buttered slice of whole wheat bread. Cut into triangles and serve.

Nasturtium Fruit Salad from *Herbs, a Cookbook and More*

Add ⅓ cup finely chopped nasturtium leaves and blossoms to ¾ cup French dressing, along with 2 tablespoons honey and 1 tablespoon dry white wine. In large bowl, combine oranges, pineapple chunks, grapes, strawberries, and a tablespoon finely chopped ginger. Pour dressing on fruit. Garnish with nasturtium blossoms.

Paula Winchester's Herb Vinegar or Herbal Oil

Use either cider vinegar, white or red wine vinegar, or rice vinegar. Soak herb sprigs to soften before inserting in bottle. It takes at least 10 days to extract the best flavor. Be creative: Add red nasturtium flowers, chive blossoms, opal basil to impart color. Do the same to make herbal oil. Use peanut, safflower, or olive oil. Set bottle in sun. Leave at least 15 days for best flavoring. Use on salads or to fry chicken.

she'll express to you. If you live nearer to the center of the country than to either coast, this is your source. Fresh herbs begin to lose their potency soon after being cut, and the closer you are to the source, the better the herbs will be. It may be best to get the seeds from Paula and grow your own.

THE CALIFORNIA CONNECTION

California Sunshine Fine
  Foods
144 King St.
San Francisco, CA 94107

phone orders: yes
415-543-3007
visa/mc

Acting primarily as a source to fine restaurants and as an outlet for specialty growers, California Sunshine becomes the West Coast express for fresh, seasonal items including edible blossoms (one week alone they offered nasturtiums, chervil, borage, basil flowers, and blooming oregano), salad greens including radicchio, arugula, baby yellow plum tomatoes, *haricots verts,* mâche, mixed baby lettuces, and baby Blue Lake beans. They carry every imaginable mushroom. Try them for American Southwest specialties including all fresh and dried chile varieties, corn husks, tomatilloes, baby corn, blue corn tortillas, chayote, nopales. From Hawaii they garner exotica including dragon's-eyes, sea beans, ogo, and pokpoklo. They also sell fresh golden American caviar from West Coast fishes. Call for price and availability quotations.

EXOTIC FRUITS AND VEGETABLES

Frieda's Finest
PO Box 58488
Los Angeles, CA 90058

phone orders: yes
(wholesale and
information only)
213-627-2981

Although Frieda is a wholesaler, call Carol Bowman-Williams in her office and she'll tell you where you can find exotic fresh produce close by. These people sell everything in exotic produce.

Cindy's Lima Beans Santa Barbara

Serves 4 in 20 minutes

- 1   medium onion, chopped
- ¼   cup butter
- ¼   pound fresh tomatilloes, chopped
- 1   cup chicken broth
- 1   4-ounce can green chiles
      Salt and pepper to taste
- 1   pound lima beans (frozen o.k.)

In a 10-inch skillet over medium heat, sauté onion in butter until golden. Add tomatilloes and cook another 5 minutes. Now add chicken broth and green chiles. Cook and reduce by half. Puree in processor or blender. Adjust seasonings to taste with salt and pepper. Return sauce to skillet; cook and stir until thick as catsup. Meanwhile, cook lima beans in salted boiling water until tender. Drain beans and serve with sauce on top.

SALADS IN THE MAIL

Fresh Northwest   phone orders: yes
13217 Mattson Rd.   206-435-4648
Arlington, WA 98223

Aside from growing and gathering a remarkable array of Northwest salad greens, these growers have made their reputation by concocting and shipping fresh salads that include at least 12 ingredients, some grown and some gathered, perhaps including mâche, arugula, or cattail shoots. All come garnished with edible flowers. The salads, designed for restaurant use, come single-service and prepped. Minimum order is for eight. Shipping is not too costly, since salads are light, and Fresh Northwest will ship anywhere in the country between the months of March and October.

THE GOURMET'S GARDENER

Le Jardin du Gourmet   phone orders: no
W. Danville, VT 05873

When Frenchman Raymond Saufroy moved from New Jersey to Vermont, he took with him an educated palate and years of experience cooking in fine restaurants. He began a mail-order business for fancy foods and shallots, a business he really invented, Saufroy says, because he claims he introduced shallots commercially to the United States after his restaurant customers asked about ingredients in his sauces. Sometime later he expanded his wares to seeds and has become famous as "the 20-cent seed man."

Saufroy sells more than 200 varieties of American and French vegetable, herb, and flower seeds at a bargain price because his thrifty French nature abhors the idea of selling you enough seed to plant a hundred-foot row. For 22 cents (inflation struck this year), you get enough seed with instructions to plant, harvest, and cook a decent amount of everything from angelica to basil to woodruff. His plain and simple eight-page catalog offers 200 kinds of best-quality seeds, herb plants, several kinds of shallots, garlic, leeks, Egyptian onions, rocambole,

Raymond Saufroy's Sauce Augusta

Makes 2 cups in 10 minutes

Raymond named this sauce for his first cooking instructor, and suggests using it with warm or cold meats. He particularly likes it with calf's head or tongue. Sometimes they eat it by the spoonful, he says, just for the heck of it.

Make a mayonnaiselike emulsion by combining 2 egg yolks, salt, pepper, $\frac{1}{3}$ teaspoon prepared Dijon mustard, and 1 teaspoon lemon juice. Then add, drop by drop, 1½ cups safflower oil, beating vigorously until you have a mayonnaise. Now, still beating, add 2 tablespoons finely chopped shallots, 1 tablespoon chopped parsley, 1 tablespoon chopped sour gherkins, and 1 tablespoon white wine vinegar. Will keep, covered in the refrigerator, up to a week.

Raymond Saufroy's Shallot Omelet for Two

Here's a great brunch with crusty French bread, sweet butter, champagne, and fresh fruit of the season.

In 3 tablespoons of butter, sauté a cup of chopped shallots until golden brown. Then add 6 eggs that have been slightly beaten. Cook over medium-low heat to desired doneness without stirring.

Tips from Raymond's Kitchen

Prepare Jerusalem artichokes the same way you prepare potatoes. The most ancient way is baking them under the embers; today you can simply bake them in the oven. When cooked, serve with a vinaigrette sauce, or make them into fritters. When a recipe calls for artichoke bottoms, substitute Jerusalem artichokes. Very good in a potato puree, about 30 percent Jerusalem artichoke and 70 percent potatoes.

Leeks, often used in soups, are also good prepared and served like asparagus or braised.

The shallot is originally from Syria and got its name from Ascalon in ancient Palestine.

wreaths of bay and balsam made by his daughter, and books—Rodale, Elizabeth David, Food Preservation—whatever he's interested in. He offers bulbs that will produce shallots three times the diameter of a quarter. Ask him to send you his recipe flyer. Raymond Saufroy really knows how to use fresh herbs.

VERMONT FARM AND GREENHOUSES

Hickins Mountain Mowings Farm
RFD 1, Black Mountain Rd.
Brattleboro, VT 05301

phone orders: yes
802-254-2146

Frank Hickin, according to the *Brattleboro Reformer,* can "work up a missionary zeal about a carrot." Frank and his wife, Mary, love to grow things. They generally produce more than 100 varieties, from traditional garden offerings and fresh herbs to the new gourmet baby vegetables. If you're looking for radishetta or lemon cucumbers or any one of 25 varieties of lettuce, call up Frank Hickin. He's probably got it in the ground. In addition, they make their own maple syrup, sell Vermont cheeses, salami, Vermont apples, raspberries (both red and black), jams, jellies, and a dazzling array of pickles—dill, maple icicle, maple mustard crock pickles, splendid dilly snow peas, dilled fiddleheads, and dilled asparagus tips. If you're traveling through New England, the Hickins's farm is a good stop for picnic supplies and a taste of the beautiful Vermont countryside.

STALKING THE BEST ASPARAGUS

Mr. Spear
PO Box 1528
Stockton, CA 95201

phone orders: yes
209-464-5365
visa/mc

From mid-April through early June, you can order 7½ pounds of extra-plump asparagus (¾-inch thick at least) either white or green. According to Chip Arnett, who is one of the Misters' Spear, pencil-thin asparagus comes from old, depleted plants and is not, as we've all been told, better.

Each box contains about 50 spears. When you get it, rinse in ice water, drain, place in plastic bags, and refrigerate for up to ten days. For the ultimate luxury, serve lunch that is nothing but a mound of perfectly steamed asparagus with a choice of sauces: hollandaise, melted butter with pine nuts, light lemon vinaigrette. A loaf of perfect bread. Skip the wine, it tastes funny with asparagus. Gelato for dessert. That's a lovely lunch.

HERB GARDENS

Halcyon Gardens, Inc.   phone orders: yes
PO Box 124   412-443-5544
Gibsonia, PA 15044   visa/mc

For more than 10 years the gardeners at Halcyon Gardens have been searching out rare and common herb seeds. You can buy herb kits in eight different groupings. Halcyon has everything from the culinary herbs—French basil, curly chervil, Greek oregano, sweet marjoram, garlic chives, and French thyme—to gourmet salad herbs including burnet, watercress, dill, cilantro, French sorrel, and roquette. Then there are the herb teas; a Shakespeare garden herb collection, and even wonderful wildflowers. You'll get everything you need—seeds, decorative pots, soil, and instructions.

If you haven't tried cooking with fresh herbs yet, you have missed something. French sorrel folded into an omelet makes a meal to remember. Pizza made with fresh basil and oregano is a new taste experience.

ONIONS AND GARLIC

Errol Flynn, playing General Custer in the 1941 film "They Died with Their Boots On" (thank you, Janice, and film trivia expert Joe McBride), ate an onion as if it were an apple. Although this may have looked like a macho stunt, it actually might have been a hint about the location of the movie, for there are only three places in the United States where water, soil, and climate combine to produce

Fresh Herbed Pizza

In this pizza, the herbs go not only in the sauce but in the dough as well. Once you try this, you'll never want plain crust again.

Serves 4 in 45 minutes

1	tablespoon dry yeast
½	teaspoon sugar
¾	cup warm water
1	egg
2	tablespoons olive oil
1	teaspoon salt
2+	cups flour
¼	cup chopped fresh basil
1	tablespoon fresh oregano
2	cloves garlic, pressed
¼	teaspoon pepper

Dissolve yeast and sugar in warm water. Add egg and oil and combine with proofed yeast (mixture should bubble readily). Stir in salt. Combine flour with herbs. Add flour mixture to liquids until it loses stickiness. Knead about 5 minutes, then cover and set in a warm place to

CONTINUED ON PAGE 64

CONTINUED FROM PAGE 63

rise until doubled in bulk—about 20 minutes.

Now preheat oven to 400° F. Coat your hands and a cookie sheet with oil, and free-form the dough into a rough 12-inch diameter. Set dough aside to rise for 10–15 minutes.

Top with your favorite tomato sauce and toppings: sun-dried tomatoes; red and green pepper rings; Niçoise olives and anchovies; dry Jack cheese and San Francisco dry salami. Don't forget to add some additional chopped fresh basil to the tomato sauce. People will fall out of their chairs, it's so good.

onions so sweet you can eat them like apples: Walla Walla, Washington; Vidalia County, Georgia; and Maui, Hawaii. In all three places they usually grow the same hybrid, yellow granex type F, and when put down into the soil of any one of these places, the hybrid produces a sweet, succulent onion. If you planted it in your garden, I fear you'd probably just get a plain old make-your-eyes-water onion.

These onions are short-lived, do not store well, and are best used within a month or so of when you get them. Beverly Conner Cole, of Conner Farms, says you can store them in a cool, dry area if you place them in the legs of old panty hose with a knot tied between each onion. (Can't you just imagine the look on the furnace repairman's face if he found all those knotty legs in the basement?) Or, she says, you can store them on an old window screen or air-conditioner filter, being careful that they don't touch. In my experience, you're better off buying just what you can use during the mid-May to early July harvest time, then look forward to them the next year.

WALLA WALLA ONIONS

CHS
405 Denny Bldg.
Walla Walla, WA 99362

phone orders: yes
800-223-7519 (national)
509-529-2130 (WA)
visa/mc

Order 20 pounds of Walla Walla sweets from the Children's Home Society of Washington before August 1 and not only do you get a box of good onions but you have donated to a worthwhile charity that aids family support and foster care programs in the Northwest. Under $20.

Walla Walla Gardeners'
   Association
210 N. Eleventh St.
Walla Walla, WA 99362

phone orders: yes
800-553-5014 (national)
509-525-7070 (WA)
visa/mc

Twenty-pound boxes of Walla Walla onions are processed by the farmers themselves. First quality.

MAUI SWEET ONIONS

Ili Farms   phone orders: yes
Box 150-C   800-367-8004
Kula, HA 96790

Not only can you order Kulasweet Maui onions here but other of Hawaii's finest fancy foods and exotic flowers: macadamia nut butter, authentic Hawaiian teas, honey, and protea. Call for free catalog.

VIDALIA ONIONS

Conner Farms, Inc.   phone orders: yes
PO Box 1566   404-226-5674
Dalton, GA 30722   visa/mc

Beverly Conner Cole has taken onions from her brother's patch and put them up using traditional Georgia recipes so that you can buy the taste of the Vidalia onion all year long. She's been selling Vidalia onion products since 1980, when she began cooking in her kitchen, labeling jars on the pool table in the playroom, and hauling them to market in a borrowed carpet truck. But the bright, sharp, sweet, pungent taste of pickled Vidalias caught on immediately, and Beverly quickly went from one employee and one product to 12 products—not counting the fresh onions she sells during the June-July harvest time.

Her Vidalia onion pickles are wonderful and are sold as far away as Harrod's in London. Golden with turmeric, these pickles are great garnishing a smoked salmon at the buffet table. She also sells relish, onion salad, mustard, salad dressing, and good old Georgia pecans and candied pecans.

Mrs. Franklin Conner's Onion Pie Supreme

The Conners have been "in onions" for six generations. Here is Beverly's mother's prize-winning recipe from a statewide contest for the Vidalia Festival in 1979.

Serves 6 in 1½ hours

3	cups thinly sliced Vidalia onions
3	tablespoons butter
1	half-baked 9-inch pie shell
½	cup milk
1½	cups sour cream
3	tablespoons flour
1	teaspoon salt
2	eggs, beaten
2	crisply fried bacon slices

Cook onions in butter until golden. Spoon into pastry shell. Blend milk with 1¼ cups sour cream. Blend flour and salt with remaining ¼ cup sour cream. Combine both mixtures with beaten eggs, then pour over onions. Bake at 325° F. for 30 minutes, or until center is firm. Garnish with crumbled fried bacon.

West Indies Salad

When the Bland family ran a contest for recipes using their onions, this one from Mrs. George P. Dance, of Pensacola, Florida, was their grand prize winner.

Serves 4
15 minutes preparation,
4–6 hours to marinate

- 1 Vidalia onion, finely chopped
- 1 pound crabmeat Salt and pepper to taste
- ½ cup light oil
- ½ cup cider vinegar
- ½ cup ice water

Follow these steps explicitly: Finely chop onion and place half in a bowl. Carefully remove any shell from crabmeat. Add crabmeat to bowl. Season with salt and pepper. Add rest of onion. Pour oil over crabmeat and onion. Pour vinegar, then ice water, over ingredients. Toss slightly—do not stir. Cover and marinate in refrigerator 4–6 hours.

SWEET VIDALIA ONIONS

Bland Farms   phone orders: yes
PO Box 506-K   800-841-3981
Glennville, GA 30427   visa/mc

Raymond and Ruby Jean Bland started farming more than 40 years ago. They knew even then that the special qualities in the Georgia soil-water-sun combination produced an onion so sweet you could eat it like an apple—as their grandson, Landis, does. Now, with son Delbert and daughter-in-law Sandra to help with the mail orders, the Blands are busy growing not only Vidalia sweet onions but tobacco and corn as well.

Using Ruby Jean's prize recipe, they now sell delicious pickled onions and pickle relish. Crisp, vinegary, a light, delicious winter condiment from a Georgia farmwife's pantry. You can order these all year long. They're beautifully packaged with green and buff-colored bonnets tied with gold ribbon. They'd make a great-looking gift.

Garlic

Garlic is believed to have originated in Siberia and then been hand-carried to Egypt, then to India, by way of the spice trade. Until a hundred years ago, its primary use was medicinal, being prescribed for everything from headaches to infections to heart disease. Even King Tut was found with six cloves in his tomb. But today, even though in some circles it is still known as Russian penicillin, garlic is grown and used primarily for culinary purposes.

Several varieties of this member of the lily family, sometimes known as the stinking rose, are cultivated commercially. What you see in the grocery store is mostly Italian. But you can buy from growers other superior types: Silverskin, a pure white, strong variety with better keeping qualities than Italian; rocambole, a strong French variety; white garlic, very strong and a good keeper; and, of course, elephant garlic—which is not, as any garlic grower will tell you, a true garlic at all but is nearer to a leek. It has a seed and is considerably milder than any true garlic; the garlic that will kiss and not tell.

The growers we have chosen all offer garlic they grow themselves, and with some added feature: either their garlic is organic, or they also offer a garlic product we found particularly interesting.

STATE FAIR-WINNING GARLIC

Mountain Meadow Farm phone orders: yes
826 Ulrich Rd. 503-560-3350
Prospect, OR 97536

Suzanne Nurfe and Michael Laslovich grow organic garlic of several varieties: Italian blue, rocambole, silverskin, white, and elephant. Their elephant garlic placed first at the 1985 Oregon State Fair and also was named outstanding specimen. Suzanne and Michael have been growing garlic only four years and still treat every order as if it were a present they were sending to their best friend. In addition to garlic by the pound, they braid garlic, make garlic oil (good for high blood pressure), and grind their own garlic powder, which is a far cry from the commercial chemical-laden junk. Michael and Suzanne also grow and dry beautiful flowers. Ask about them when you call.

GARLIC BRAIDS AND WHOLE PEELED GARLIC

K.C. Farms phone orders: yes
PO Box 189 408-628-3596
Tres Piños, CA 95075 visa/mc

Kit Sherman not only grows and braids beautiful, enormous heads of pure white garlic in lengths ranging from about a foot up to you-name-it in custom garlic chains (keep those vampires at bay forever) . . . but he also makes garlic wreaths, chile wreaths and ristras, bay wreaths, and cinnamon stick wreaths, all of which are not only beautiful to look at but are useful besides. They sent me a pint

---

Suzanne Nurfe's Elephant Garlic Broth

For a fine clear soup, strain and serve with cooked noodles or rice. Or at the last minute add snow peas, sliced zucchini, dumplings. Good for recipes calling for consommé.

Makes 1 quart of broth in 2½ hours

	Peels from 6–8 potatoes
1	large onion, peeled
2	carrots
1	stalk celery
1½	quarts water
1½	tablespoons olive oil
½	bay leaf
6	cloves elephant garlic
¼	teaspoon dried thyme
	Pinch of sage

Combine ingredients and simmer uncovered 2½ hours. Possibilities are now endless. Add water to maintain volume.

plastic container filled with huge, pure white, peeled cloves of garlic. At first glance, I thought it was sheer frippery, but by the time I had used them all I was hopelessly spoiled and nearly cried the next time I had to peel my own.

THE GARLIC LADY

Costello Farms phone orders: yes
2201 Clement St., Ste. 452 415-521-3298
Alameda, CA 94501 visa/mc: no

Shirley Costello Hocking grew up with garlic, and she will provide you with not only first-quality garlic but also garlic braids and a product she's offering for sale from an old family recipe: marinated garlic, a blend of garlic, herbs, spices, vinegar, and chile pepper. This is a bright, splashy taste that does not rely on salt, sugar, or MSG for its lift. Shirley Hocking sells garlic with this motto on every order: "Remember garlic for love and life." When you order, ask for her recipes calling for marinated garlic. These are solid, authentic California-style Italian dishes.

THE GRANDADDY OF GARLIC

Gilroy Farms Garlic phone orders: yes
PO Box 436 800-3-GARLIC
King City, CA 93930 visa/mc

Gilroy is the California town where they hold a huge annual festival dedicated to garlic. It's also where you can drive down the freeway and see the road strewn with garlic spilled from trucks like some ceremony to keep Count Dracula out of the county. If you order direct from Gilroy, you can order not only garlic but garlic braids, presses, T-shirts, festival posters, pottery garlic cellars, elephant garlic cellars, and—best of all—Gilroy's own *The Garlic Lovers' Cookbook,* a must in the library of any garlic-loving cook. They don't call Gilroy the garlic capital of the world for nothing.

RICES

Not so long ago, about all we had to choose from in rice was Uncle Ben's and Rice-a-Roni, but with the introduction of ethnic specialties, we've learned that there's as much variety in rice as there is, say, in bread. We're growing more interesting rices in America today, and what we don't grow is readily available by import.

There are at least 7,000 known varieties of rice, which fall into three main groups: short, medium, and long grain. Long-grain rices cook up light and fluffy with grains that separate—ideal for salads, curries, stews, and casserole dishes. Medium- and short-grain rices cook up tender and moist with particles clinging together—suitable for Asian dishes, croquettes, puddings, or rice rings, which benefit from the molding properties of these rices.

Most rices on the market today are produced by cleaning the grains to remove chaff, dust, and seeds, then removing husks from the grains. When only the outer hull and a small amount of bran are removed, the product is called brown rice, more nutty and chewy when cooked, with all of the natural nutrition remaining. When additional layers of bran are removed, the rice turns white and loses some of its natural nutriment. Some companies add back certain vitamins, then call the rice "enriched." Parboiled rice, like Uncle Ben's, has been steamed, and this aids in the retention of natural vitamins and minerals. Precooked ("instant") rice requires a minimum of preparation time but has been overprocessed in terms of nutrition and is the least desirable rice to buy.

WILD RICE

Deer Creek Wild Rice phone orders: yes
680 Jones St. 916-673-8053
Yuba City, CA 95991 visa/mc

Deer Creek was the first company west of the Mississippi to figure out a way to tame the wild native American grass we call wild rice. Hybridizing to get a non-shattering head, they made it possible for the first time to grow this rice commercially. The Indian way was to pole through the Minnesota marshes in a dugout canoe, pull the tall spears of grass over the sides of the boat, and knock the grains into the boat. That's why it was always so expensive. But now this California hybrid is available at a more reasonable cost. It's still expensive, but it swells up to four times its dry size, and can be bought or mixed at home with brown rice to good advantage. Deer Creek not only sells wild rice by the pound, but also have good-looking gift packages. Call and ask for their brochure.

TEXMATI RICE

Farms of Texas Co.   phone orders: yes
PO Box 1305   713-331-6481
Alvin, TX 77512   visa/mc

A hybrid from long-grain rice of the type we associate with Uncle Ben's and an Indian rice called basmati, this long-grained nutty rice comes either brown (husk on) or polished white. It will soon be available in an "instant" rice. They also mix this rice with Minnesota wild rice in a blend they call Royal—16 percent wild, 27 percent Texmati brown, and 55 percent Texmati white. Delicious! I love this rice. It cooks up like good, long-grain, grain-apart style rice, but with an added nutty aroma and taste. I plan to order 25 pounds of Texmati brown for use as our everyday rice.

CALMATI RICE

Estus Gourmet   phone orders: yes
1499 67th St.   415-653-0496
Emeryville, CA 94608

A year ago, Estus Gourmet introduced Calmati, an aromatic brown rice grown in California but originally grown in India and known there as basmati. Now, they've blended this rice with California's non-shattering wild rice and they call it "Two Indian" rice. This makes a nice 50-50 blend that is chewy, aromatic, and great with poultry meals.

WILD PECAN RICE

Conrad Rice Mill   phone orders: yes
PO Box 296   318-364-7274
New Iberia, LA 70560   ae/visa/mc

This rice is, neither wild nor mixed with pecans but is, rather, plain long-grain rice that was planted in south Louisiana on an old pecan plantation. Much to everyone's delight, the rice has taken on the subtle flavor of pecans. Sold under the brand name Konriko. You can also buy from them plain long-grain rices. And do visit their mill if you're in south Louisiana. America's oldest rice mill, it's on the National Register of Historic Places. This rice is so tasty, all it needs is a pat of butter. Delicious.

BASMATI

See also: The Ethnic Pantry for sources for imported basmati, Thai sweet sticky rice, and Asian jasmine rice.

MEXICAN

See also: Maison E. H. Glass, Inc., for Mexican rice with peppers and extra-fancy wild rice.

ARBORIO

See also: G. B. Ratto, International Grocers, for Italian Arborio rice, basmati, and Wehahoni—a California hybrid from basmati, sold unhulled.

KOKUHO

See also: H. Roth & Son for Kokuho, a Japanese short-grain rice, and Texas Patna, an all-purpose long-grain white.

Popcorn Rice Picante

You can make this savory rice pudding using plain long-grain rice with good results, but using popcorn rice gives it an added nutty dimension.

Serves 4 in 2 hours

1	cup cooked rice
2	eggs, lightly beaten
2	tablespoons butter
1	cup grated white New York cheddar cheese
½	cup fresh cilantro leaves
1	fresh jalapeño, seeded and minced
1	small onion, peeled and minced
1	clove garlic, pressed
¾	cup half-and-half
	Salt and pepper

Place cooked rice in a buttered 2-quart soufflé dish. Combine remaining ingredients and mix with rice, seasoning to taste with salt and pepper. Bake uncovered in a hot-water bath at 350° F. until a knife stuck in the center comes out clean (about an hour).

(Hot-water bath: place an oven-proof pan on the oven shelf with an inch or so of warm water in it. Place soufflé dish in the water.)

POPCORN RICE

See also: Community Coffee for popcorn rice, a white rice that has a popcornlike aroma when cooking and a nutty flavor.

FRUITS AND NUTS, FRESH AND DRIED

America's orchard growers were among the first to offer their products directly to the consumer by mail order. Roadside stands from Florida through south Texas and on to California made tasteful arrangements of their dates, oranges, prunes, walnuts, whatever, tied them up with colored cellophane, stuck a bow on them, and shipped them off by special order. My mother remembers the box of oranges shipped up from south Texas on the freight car for Christmas when she was a kid on a wind-swept Texas panhandle ranch. The whole family would take the buckboard to town, stand on the brick siding at the train station, feel the ground beneath their feet rumble and shake as the steam engine wheezed into the station, and wait patiently for the freight to be handed down. By the time they had driven the 40 miles back to the ranch, the kids were full to overflowing with sweet south Texas oranges.

Today the only reason to order fruit and nuts through the mail is to get a better quality than you can buy at the grocery store. I have limited the choices here to orchards that hand-pick and sell these riper, bigger, and better fruits and nuts.

PEERLESS PEARS

Harry and David
Bear Creek Orchards
Medford, OR 97501

phone orders: yes
800-547-3033
visa/mc

Harry and David wrote the book on the shipping of perishable fruit. They developed a drop-ship system that means your order is filled from a regional warehouse and gets to you within a couple of days. The pear is one fruit that is never allowed to ripen on the tree, so it is ideal for shipping. Picking, packing, and shipping are an absolute science with these pear growers. Reliability is their middle name. From the beginning, in the heart of the Depression as a mail-order shipper of pears, Harry and David has grown to include other fruits, baked goods, candies, and even toys. Last year the family sold out to a big tobacco company, and the natives around here mourn the loss of the "localness" of this company. But the pears are still reliable.

HOMEGROWN PEARS AND APPLES

Pinnacle Orchards   phone orders: yes
PO Box 1068   800-547-0227
Medford, OR 97501   ae/visa/mc

This is the little guy all of us locals are rooting for. Pinnacle grows pears of three or four varieties as well as apples, and they offer for sale a number of Oregon regional food specialties as well: cheeses, nuts, sausages, salad dressings, preserves, even baked goods.

   This company is locally owned and operated and feels like a member of the community. They also use a drop-ship system to guarantee that perishable pears will arrive perfectly ripe.

GARGANTUAN KIWIS

The Kiwi Ranch   phone orders: yes
192 Hwy. 99E   916-695-1448
Gridley, CA 96948   visa/mc

Gary and Pamela Pigg grow kiwis and sell them from November to Easter—singly, by the pound, or by the bushel. If you want enormous, perfect ones, specify. If you want "canners," ones that may not look as pretty but will make splendid jam, specify. You can get your order as you wish it, and priced accordingly. Gary and Pamela also make a wonderful kiwi jam and kiwi chutney. They even sell "Kiwi Kid" dolls. The thing I like about kiwis is that they contain an enzyme that keeps gelatin from setting. Anything that strikes a blow against Jello, I'm all for.

Benedictine Compote with Crème Fraîche

For a dramatic end to dinner that requires no rehearsal at all, flambé stewed fruits and nuts. Allow about six pieces of dried fruit per diner, choosing from black mission figs, apricots, apples, pears, prunes, raisins, or any combination thereof. Place fruit in heavy-bottomed saucepan, barely cover with water, add a cinnamon stick, juice and zest of a lemon, and honey to taste. Gently boil until fruits are soft. Stir in a handful of nuts—walnuts, pecans, hazelnuts, or almonds. Remove to dessert dishes.

For a nice piece of theater, line up the dessert dishes on the dining table, with crème fraîche alongside. Say something to heighten the anticipation; then, leaping nimbly back to the stove and using a metal measure, over medium-high heat, bring ¼ cup 80-proof Benedictine or other brandy to just under the boil. Return to the diners—who, if you have done your warm-up properly, will be waiting with bated breath . . . or at least will still be waiting—light and pour flaming liquor over fruits and nuts. Spoon a teaspoon of crème fraîche atop each, and serve to dazzled diners.

DRIED FRUITS AND NUTS

Timbercrest Farms	phone orders: yes
4791 Dry Creek Rd.	707-433-8251
Healdsburg, CA 95448	visa/mc

Rancher Waltenspiel looks a good bit like the man in "American Gothic," and when you look into his tanned, creased face, you know he didn't get into farming as a tax dodge. He and his co-grower wife, Ruth, own an orchard just 75 miles north of San Francisco, where they grow and dry a variety of fruits and nuts. Waltenspiel products are grown organically and are free of added sugar, sulfur dioxide, and other preservatives. They ship the same day they receive orders and include recipes with every shipment. Their apricots, pears, and peaches are all allowed to ripen completely before they're picked and dried.

Just this year Ruth has begun to sell two great salad dressings she makes, one for fruit and one for green salads. The fruit dressing is a mayonnaise type with dates in it, good enough to eat out of the jar with a spoon. The dressing for greens is also a mayonnaise type but with sun-dried tomatoes in it, imparting a pale pink color and tart, pungent tomato taste. Both are delicious.

The Waltenspiels were among the first to offer California sun-dried tomatoes and marinated sun-dried tomatoes. Even Mr. Waltenspiel is shocked by the sales of those two items. He told me, scratching his head and looking apologetic, "Well, it's not like catsup, but people still like it." Indeed. Call for a catalog and see the full line, 20–30 varieties.

JUMBO HASS AVOCADOS

George Bliss Premium	phone orders: yes
Avocados	805-969-3676
PO Box 5749	visa/mc
Santa Barbara, CA 93108	

George Bliss's father was a soil inspector in Maryland in the 1920s when he got the bug to go to California and make his fortune. After a careful search he chose a southerly exposure tempered by the Pacific breezes just outside Santa Barbara as an ideal location for his farm. Later, George, Jr., went to agricultural school and decided avocados were the fruit of choice. Today, George Bliss, Jr., grows avocados you have to see to believe. A rich green-gold with a high oil count, so dense and heavy in your hand you feel like you're holding a baby bowling ball, these avocados weigh in over a pound apiece and are the best I've ever seen or tasted. You can only get these from April through November.

RUBY RED TEXAS GRAPEFRUIT

Pittman & Davis   phone orders: no
PO Box 2227   512-423-2154
Harlingen, TX 78551   ae/visa/mc

About the same time Harry and David were tromping through New York offices trying to drum up orders for pears—during the Depression when all orchards were suffering—Frank Davis, Sr., and Howard Pittman were trying to figure out how to stay alive in the valley. They'd been shipping vegetables by railway express but about the time of the Depression, roads got better and orders got worse, and they were really at their wit's end. Mrs. Davis, who worked in the company as a "proofreader," making sure orders were properly addressed, came up with the idea of concentrating on gift baskets and Christmas orders. Mrs. Davis was right. Soon they were out of the vegetable business altogether.

During the harvest, from November through March, Frank Davis ships grapefruit from south Texas and from Florida, depending on where he can get the best specimens. The south Texas ruby red is by far the best, but if they get killed off by frost, the Florida Indian River, which was hybridized from the Texas variety, runs a close second. Frank also ships pears, pistachios, cheeses, and meats. He has an impeccable reputation for quality and can be trusted to get the goods to the destination, ripe and on time.

One interesting aspect to Pittman & Davis is that they'll let you order Christmas fruit and pay later, billing you in January. It's just a little thing, but it makes them people I just plain like.

Ported Figs Stuffed with Whole Almonds

Serves 2 in 10 minutes

6 Timbercrest mission figs
¼ cup port (or sherry)
¼ cup ricotta cheese
6 whole toasted almonds

Soften figs by boiling in water to cover, up to 20 minutes. Drain, remove to bowl. Add port, cover, and refrigerate overnight. Next day, remove figs from port, slice partially through in an X pattern, and stuff with ricotta. Arrange on dessert dishes and top with almonds.

How to Ripen a Hass Avocado

Place avocado in fruit bowl at room temperature until it yields to gentle pressure when held in the palm of your hand. Skin color will change from green to black on a Hass as it ripens. For faster ripening, place the avocado in a plastic bag with a piece of banana peel. Gases released by the banana peel will hasten ripening. *Never* place an unripe avocado in the refrigerator. But, once you have brought the avocado to its proper ripeness, you may store the ripened, uncut fruit 3–4 days in the refrigerator. Serve at room temperature for best flavor.

To Market To Market Puckered Plum Cake

Kathy Parson of To Market To Market packs Sunray prunes in her gift baskets (see index) and tucks in this recipe, which produces a cake that is moist, succulent, and delicious. If I have them I like to use black walnuts in this recipe.

Serves 10 in 1½ hours

- 1½ cups Sunray colossal prunes
- 1 teaspoon grated lemon rind
- 2 cups sifted flour
- 1 teaspoon baking powder
- 1 teaspoon baking soda
- ½ teaspoon salt
- 1 cup soft butter
- 1 cup sugar
- 2 eggs
- 1 cup sour cream
- 1 teaspoon vanilla
- ½ cup brown sugar
- 1 tablespoon cinnamon
- ½ cup chopped walnuts

Pour boiling water over prunes and let stand 15 minutes. Drain, pit, and dice. Add lemon rind and set aside. Grease and flour a 9-inch tube pan. Sift together flour, baking powder, baking soda, and salt; remove ¼ cup and toss with prunes. Cream butter and sugar until fluffy. Beat in eggs one at a time. Slowly beat in flour mixture alternately with sour cream and vanilla, beginning and ending with flour. Fold in prunes. Combine brown sugar, cinnamon, and nuts. Turn

CONTINUED ON PAGE 77

PERFECT PRUNES

Sunray Orchards phone orders: yes
Rte. 1, Box 299 503-839-4116
Myrtle Creek, OR 97457

Oregon produces a good deal of the nation's prunes, the largest and most succulent variety being the Moyers. Sunray ships various sizes. "Colossal" size is no mere example of inflated language but is an accurate description of fruit—as big as a golf ball, truly aromatic with the pungent, tart pruney smell and taste. They're wonderful.

WASHINGTON APPLES

Serendipity Orchards phone orders: yes
PO Box 303 509-687-3941
Manson, WA 98831 ae/visa/mc

Washington is known for its apples, and Pat and Dick Bailey grow a variety known as Lake Chelan Red Delicious, a great apple to eat out-of-hand. Their orchard, located in Chelan Valley and watered by the glacial waters of Lake Chelan, is known worldwide for the quality of its apples. This apple bears little resemblance to that scrawny red delicious you buy at the grocery store for the kids' lunch sacks. This is a world-class eating apple.

DESIGNER APPLES

Apple Attractions phone orders: yes
PO Box 3202 509-826-1330
Omak, WA 98841

David Guthrie has figured out a way to put a message on a red delicious apple. You can say happy birthday; merry Christmas; go jump in the lake. Using a secret method—they will say only that it is free of chemicals, dyes, or preservatives—the Apple Attractions people produce custom gift fruit with a message and design like an edible greeting card, healthier than candy and longer-lasting than flowers. Call for a price quote.

VERMONT APPLES

See also: Hickins Mountain Mowings Farm.

AMERICAN NATIVE FOODS: FORAGING FOR FUN AND PROFIT

American Spoon Foods	phone orders: yes
411 E. Lake St.	616-347-9030
Petoskey, MI 49770	visa/mc

Justin Rashid and Kate Marshall are a pair who can be said to have been in the right place at the right time. Friends of Larry Forgione, chef of New York's An American Place, Justin and Kate began foraging for Michigan's wild morel mushrooms for Larry's restaurant. When they began, a couple of out-of-work actors from New York, kicking through the woods in their home state of Upper Michigan, they had no idea that they would be swept up in the tide and would soon be known as the country's fastest-growing entrepreneurs of wild native American foods. As Kate Marshall said, "We were going to be movie stars."

So much for Hollywood. In the quaint tourist town of Petoskey, where cherry orchards abound and wild berries grow in such abundance you couldn't pick them all if every citizen of the town were conscripted for a month of Sundays, the Marshall-Rashid family has made a name for itself. In groceries.

It's just that one thing led to another. From the mushrooms, they discovered the wild berries in northern Michigan. Larry developed some recipes for them, and they began putting up wild berry and fruit preserves whose most striking assets are that they are more fruit than sugar, have no artificial pectin, and speak with such authority that even the toast will pay attention.

In addition to the morels, boletus, and oyster mushrooms, their provisions include watercress, lamb's-quarter, cattail shoots, wild strawberries, blackberries, and elderberries. They've added smoked buffalo sausage; the rarest, palest raspberry honey; hazelnuts; black walnuts; and jams beyond description. They've dried Michigan's

CONTINUED FROM PAGE 76

one-third of batter into pan. Sprinkle with one-third brown sugar mixture; repeat layering twice. Bake at 350° F. 55 minutes or until done (springs back at a touch). Cool in pan on rack 10 minutes. Remove from pan.

Grilled Pork Tenderloin with Michigan Dried Tart Cherries

Serves 2 in 45 minutes

1 small pork tenderloin
    (9–11 ounces)
    Virgin olive oil
    Fresh cracked pepper
    Fennel seed
    Dried Red Tart Cherry
    Sauce(recipeonpage79)

Have pork at room temperature. Tuck thin end under and skewer. Brush with oil. Sprinkle with pepper and fennel seed. Grill over medium-hot charcoal to an internal temperature of 140° F., turning several times. Remove to heated platter, cover and let rest 8 minutes. Slice on diagonal. Fan out pieces on plate. Spoon on cherry sauce.

Black walnuts are splendid in pies. Just substitute them for pecans in pecan pie recipes. I also like to use them with pomegranates and orange juice in a duck sauce. Sauté shallots in butter, then mix in duck broth, orange juice, and black walnuts. Reduce, season with salt and pepper, then add pomegranate seeds. Pour over roast poultry—duck, pheasant, Cornish hen. Looks gorgeous. Tastes even better.

Peanuts originated in South America, where archaeologists have unearthed peanut-shaped jars made by the Incas. The peanut was taken to Africa and Asia by Spanish explorers, then back to Virginia on slave ships. During the Civil War, goober peas—as the Confederate soldiers called them—were prized for their quick energy. The peanut contains only polyunsaturated fats, and the food energy it provides compares thusly: 1 pound of peanuts = 2½ pounds of steak, or 4 quarts of milk, or 32 eggs. The peanut contains more protein than eggs, dairy products, and many cuts of meat.

cherries into a product like a raisin, only red and tart. New products every season—depending on the weather. Call or write for a catalog.

CRACKED EASTERN BLACK WALNUTS

Missouri Dandy Pantry   phone orders: yes
212 Hammons Dr. E   417-276-5121
Stockton, MO 65785   visa/mc

If you have ever been so ambitious as to attempt to remove the meat from a black walnut, you will see why this company provides a valuable service. They procure 100 percent Eastern black walnuts, then crack them for you and send them out, shelled, in 1-pound packages. The black walnut is one variety that's so pungent, it seems to lose nothing in the shelling—except the yellow stain on your fingers and the curses when you mash your thumb with the hammer.

BOILED-IN-OIL JUMBO PEANUTS

Hubbard Peanut Co.   phone orders: no
PO Box 94   804-562-4081
Sedley, VA 23878

In 1953, after having had three babies in 18 months—a daughter, then twins—Mrs. Hubbard knew she couldn't go back to teaching high school, so she began boiling peanuts using an old family recipe and selling them at the drugstore. Pretty soon, friends began asking her to ship them out for gifts, and her mail-order business was launched.

Today, the Hubbards prefer direct mail order because peanuts are perishable. What you get when you order is a 2-pound tin of giant-sized peanuts that have been water-blanched, then boiled in coconut oil. This labor-intensive method produces a peanut like you've never tasted before. They come salted or unsalted and are crisp, crunchy, and flavorful. Keep them in the icebox, Mrs. Hubbard says, or even the freezer.

The Hubbards are a good example of the individuality possible in a small company. Even though their peanuts have been served everywhere including the White House, they still refuse to carry Visa or MasterCard—that would raise their prices by 5 percent, they say, and they don't want to do that. They still prefer to sell directly to the customer. This way they can tell you how to take care of the goobers. And they will never allow their nuts to go into a grocery chain. Too common.

CRISP COATED NUTS

Kakawateez, Ltd.   phone orders: yes
130 Olive St.   419-422-5732
Findlay, OH 45840

Don Schieber was hatching baby chicks for a living when he went to Mexico in search of a new site. But he fell in love with these crisp, sweet-salty nuts and hunted down their maker, who was a Japanese fellow making them in his kitchen. He taught Don how to make 'em, and Don went back home to Ohio and said to his brother, "We're getting out of the chicken business."

Peanuts, filberts, Brazil nuts, pistachios, macadamias, almonds, cashews, and redskin peanuts are all subjected to the Totem process during which they're covered with alternate coats of flour and syrup, then dry-roasted and sprayed with soy sauce. Don named the company Kakawateez because that's the phonetic spelling of Cacahuates, which is "peanut" in Spanish. So what do you call the origin of this? Mexican, Spanish, Japanese, or Ohioan? I'd say a little bit of all of them, and Ahmurrican through and through.

HAZELNUTS

Dundee Orchards   phone orders: yes
PO Box 227   503-538-1063
Dundee, OR 97115

You can get first-quality giants here as well as ground and broken nuts for baking—fresh and good, not just the

---

American Spoon Dried Red Tart Cherry Sauce

½ cup dried red tart cherries
1 small head garlic, peeled
⅓ bottle Barolo wine
2 tablespoons butter

Combine cherries, peeled whole cloves of garlic, and Barolo in saucepan. Bring to boil. Lower to simmer and cook, uncovered, until reduced by half. Cut butter into pieces and swirl into sauce.

"If you mix American Spoon wild blueberry preserve with crème fraîche and eat it with French toast or blintzes, breakfast will never be the same again."

New York Magazine
February 8, 1982

American Spoon's dried red tart Montmorency cherries from Michigan are exquisite after dinner. Soak in brandy or vodka. Serve in a cone-shaped glass. Or, over the best scoop of ice cream you can lay your hands on, flambé them by warming the spirited cherries, then pour the flaming cherry liquor over the ices. Or dip in chocolate and serve with strong, black coffee. It's that little bite that finishes dinner with a bang.

Dundee Hazelnut Butter Sauce for Lamb and Pork

Makes 1 cup in 10 minutes

- ½ cup hazelnut butter
- 2 tablespoons lemon juice
- 2 tablespoons soy sauce
- 1½ teaspoons Worcestershire sauce
- 1 tablespoon orange juice
- ½ cup water
  Dash of Tabasco sauce

Combine all ingredients in saucepan over low heat. Cook and stir about 5 minutes, adding more water if necessary for saucy consistency.

Dundee Suggestions for Hazelnut Butter

Mix with equal parts of soft butter and serve over sautéed fish or steamed vegetables.

Substitute in equal measure in any recipe calling for peanut butter or other ground nut.

Mix in equal proportion with brie or cream cheese and spread on crackers.

sweepings from some giant operation. They also make pure hazelnut butter, both creamy and crunchy.

All the products offered are handmade by Mary Mills Weil and Marlyce Tolvstad, partners who have learned to prune and water with the best of them.

HAZELNUT SNACKS

Pacific Hazelnut Farms phone orders: yes
20495 Butteville Rd. NE 503-638-0582
Hubbard, OR 97032 visa/mc

Ersel and Joan Christopherson dry-roast a good bit of their crop and sell them just salted or lightly salted and flavored: sour cream and onion, garlic and onion, and barbecue. They also make double-chocolate-dipped hazelnuts, hazelnut toffee and nougat, and hazelnut milk chocolate cheesecake.

HAZELNUTS AND WALNUTS

A & B Nut Basket phone orders: yes
1685 N.E. Kennedy Lane 503-640-4887
Hillsboro, OR 97124

Bill McCann was a mess sergeant in the Air Force before he retired and went into the nut business. He's created a mist of sugar and salt that he uses to coat jumbo hazelnuts. He also combines jumbos with Chambers Nine walnuts. The Chambers Nine is a special variety developed at Oregon State—as Bill McCann says, "a nice, big nut." He also makes hazelnut butter. As he says of his new career, "all in all, it's kind of a fun thing."

BULK HAZELNUTS

Westnut phone orders: yes
PO Box 125 503-538-2161
Dundee, OR 97115 visa

The Baker's Pack containing sliced, diced, and whole hazelnuts is a good choice here, as is the 5-pound box of fresh, shelled whole hazelnuts. Be sure to ask them to send you their Oregon Hazelnut Primer, a 32-page recipe book. Also available is a chocolate and hazelnut torte.

CALIFORNIA WALNUTS AND ALMONDS

T.J. Farms   phone orders: yes
3600 Chico Ave.   916-343-2294
Chico, CA 95828

Mary and Dave Moss farm 150 acres of walnuts, almonds, kiwis, and vegetables. You can buy from them first-quality nuts, kiwi jams, vinegar, and trail mix. One thing about buying directly from the farm: you can get very fresh nuts at a price considerably lower than you'd pay in the local store.

NONPARIEL BLANCHED ALMONDS

Nunes Farms Almonds   phone orders: yes
PO Box 146   415-459-7201
San Anselmo, CA 94960

Maureen Nunes not only sells her family's almonds in the shell, but also offers them blanched, roasted, chopped roasted, and salted, or in an almond toffee crunch. For heavy-duty bakers, this would be a good source for nonpareil supreme blanched almonds that still taste like something when you use them in baked goods.

BEYOND GARLIC: PISTACHIOS, CASHEWS, MACADAMIAS

Golden Valley Nut   phone orders: yes
170 Rucker Ave.   408-842-4893
Gilroy, CA 95020

There's more to Gilroy than garlic, as the pistachio nut growers will tell you. You can buy, direct from the orchard, giant, first-quality pistachios salted or unsalted, without that awful red dye or any other artificial preserva-

The first hazelnut tree planted in Oregon, according to Joan Christopherson of Pacific Hazelnut Farms, was in Scottsburg about 1857. The Northwest climate is as ideal for growing hazelnuts (filberts) as their native France, and now 97 percent of our nation's crop comes from the Willamette Valley in western Oregon. Today, we even export hazelnuts back to Europe, where their popularity has remained firm. There are many hazelnut growers in Oregon. I'm giving you just a few who offer superior nuts and special treatments that I found interesting.

To toast almonds: Spread in a single layer in shallow pan. Bake at 300° F. for 15 minutes, or until they just begin to turn color. Remove from oven. Their residual heat will finish the process.

To roast almonds: Spread ½ teaspoon of butter or oil over surface of a shallow pan. Add almonds in a single layer. Roast, stirring often, at 300° F. for 15 minutes, or until they just begin to turn brown. Remove from oven at once.

Moroccan Chicken Tadjeen with Almond Rice

Sweet fruit and honey, tart lemon, and crunchy almonds complement chicken in this piquant Northern African dish.

Serves 4 in 1 hour
(marinates overnight)

1	3-pound cut-up fryer
¼	cup soy sauce
¼	cup dry sherry
2	tablespoons honey
¼	cup lemon juice + ½ teaspoon peel
1	clove garlic, pressed
1	teaspoon curry powder (or to taste)
¼	teaspoon *each:* ginger, oregano, black pepper, and thyme
2	tablespoons butter
1	large onion, thinly sliced
2	tablespoons olive oil
8	pitted prunes, chopped

CONTINUED ON PAGE 83

tive. Golden Valley also sells almonds, cashews, macadamias, walnuts, and pecans, grown close by and guaranteed fresh. This is the place to buy nuts in bulk, not in some cute gift pack where you pay for the package as well as the product.

PISTACHIO HEAVEN

CIF Nut Ranch   phone orders: yes
825 Hinckley Rd.   415-692-8000
Burlingame, CA 94010

Under the brand name Sunranch, CIF sells giant, first-quality pistachios vacuum-packed in jars and cans. If you like pistachios, you should buy from these people at least once, to get their pistachio cookbook. Such recipes! Quenelles stuffed with veal and pistachios; croissants with a ham-pistachio filling; a terrine with pistachios and foie gras and truffles; pistachio-filled sole rolls; chicken breast or breast of veal stuffed with pistachio filling; lamb risotto and pistachios; venison and pistachios; empress pistachio gelee; pistachio crème; pistachio truffles; pistachio eggnog and ice cream. Can you stand it?

TEXAS NATIVE PECANS

Pecan Producers   phone orders: yes
  International   1-800-22PECAN (national)
Drawer 147, Dept. A   214-872-1337 (TX)
Corsicana, TX 75110   ae/visa/mc

Anybody who's ever spent any time at all in Texas knows the native pecans that grow along the broad creeks and sluggish green rivers are the best in the world. They are also the second hardest nut to crack—the black walnut being the first. Now, at last—salvation! Hayden Crawford has bought up all the premium-quality native pecans he can find and is cracking them for you. You can buy freshly shelled native halves, pieces, or (if you must) Stuarts and Desirable halves—those are the large papershell hybrids derived from the native, easier to crack but a drier, less flavorful nut. These are *the* nut dealers in Texas, and if you want anything from almonds to walnuts, call up Hayden and he's probably got it.

GEORGIA PECANS

Sunnyland Farms, Inc. phone orders: yes
21 Willson Rd., Box 549 912-883-3085
Albany, GA 31703 visa/mc

Jane and Harry Willson have groves of Stuart and Schley pecans, which they offer by the 5-pound box at a very reasonable price. They also sell mammoth halves, toasted and salted nuts, and broken pecan meats. All their prices are postpaid. Not only do you get first-quality Georgia pecans this way but, I swear, they're cheaper than they are in my grocery store—where they're old, unreliable, and hardly worth the sack I bring them home in.

GIANT BRAZILIAN CASHEWS

The Squire's Choice phone orders: yes
35 S. Main St., Box G-2 800-523-6163
Yardley, PA 19067 ae/visa/mc

On plantations in the Brazilian back country, the world's largest cashews are grown. Brought to the United States and roasted in 4-pound batches in peanut oil, these make an impressive gift. Expensive, yes. Better than $13 a pound, but such luxury. All done up in a 2-pound red box. Merry Christmas.

GEORGIA PEACHES AND PECANS

Callaway Gardens phone orders: yes
  Country Store 800-282-8181
Pine Mountain, GA 31822 ae/visa

Callaway Gardens is to Georgia what Harry and David is to Oregon. The big, regional country store that started out as a roadside stand selling peaches and pecans has

CONTINUED FROM PAGE 82

8 dried apricots, chopped
2 cups hot, cooked rice
½ cup toasted almonds
½ red bell pepper, sliced thinly

Marinate chicken in the next seven ingredients, covered, in the refrigerator at least 2 hours or as long as overnight, turning occasionally. In 10-inch skillet, melt butter and sauté onion until golden. Remove from skillet. Drain chicken, reserving marinade. Add oil to skillet; increase heat to moderately high and brown chicken pieces. Pour off excess fat. Place onion on chicken; add fruit and pour marinade over all. Reduce heat to low, cover skillet, and simmer 30 minutes. Remove lid and finish cooking another 15 minutes. Meanwhile, cook rice and toss with almonds and red pepper. To serve, place chicken pieces around edges of large platter. Mound rice in center, cover with cooked fruit and pan juices.

Real Texas Pecan Pie

This may look like your regula-tion pie recipe, but it's a case of technique making the differ-ence. Just a little thing really, but what a superior result: dissolve the sugar. You'll see the differ-ence. A good step to add to any pies of this nature: Osgood, nut pies, fruit and nut pies.

  1   unbaked 9-inch pie shell
  1   cup sugar
  ½ teaspoon salt
  1   cup dark corn syrup
  3   eggs, beaten
  ½ cup butter
1½ teaspoons vanilla
  2   cups chopped pecans

Preheat oven to 375° F. In a small saucepan, combine sugar, salt, and corn syrup. Heat until sugar dissolves. Meanwhile, beat eggs until foamy. When syrup is hot, add butter; stir to melt. Now add vanilla, pecans, and eggs. Pour into prepared pie shell. Bake for about 40 min-utes, or until knife inserted in fill-ing comes out clean. Cool on a rack. Can be served with or with-out whipped cream.

grown to be a big tourist stop and mail-order business. You can still get good Georgia pecans they procure from the Malatchie Farms, and you can still get peach pre-serves. You can also get grits, bacon, ham, muscadine jelly (made from their local wild muscadine grapes and mysterious beyond reason), chowchow, and watermelon pickle. All of it is good, real Southern cooking. Call for a catalog. They even have an all-peach cookbook called *The Peach Sampler,* a real treasure for cookbook collec-tors and peach lovers.

CHAPTER 3

THE PROTEIN PURVEYORS

I. Pâtés and sausages
II. Game and game birds
III. Red meat: Prime lamb, veal, pork, and beef
IV. Fish and shellfish
V. Caviars
VI. Escargots

Why in the world would we devote a whole chapter to the mail order of lamb chops, steaks, lobsters, sausages, and ducks, when everybody knows you can run down to the neighborhood supermarket and get everything from Chateaubriand to a live lobster who spends his last days crawling sluggishly about the floor of a greenish grocery store aquarium?

This gets to the heart of the notion of *Satisfaction Guaranteed.* Protein purveyors who pay their rent from the proceeds of mail order know they must offer something beyond what the grocery stores do. Without exception, the meat and fish vendors I have included offer products that are superior in taste, of a higher grade (based on USDA meat grading standards), and fresher. In many cases, the vendors have monitored the product from the ground up, meaning they know what the animal was fed, whether it had chemicals introduced into its diet, how old it was, and so on. Vegetarians, please turn the page before you feel weak, but some of these people stand in their kitchen taking your order as they look out the window at the animal still on the hoof. In other words, you are buying from a farm and the animal is custom-butchered for you.

There really are differences in taste between grocery store chickens and free-range birds. Prime beef is superior to the usual "choice" that's available at the supermarkets. And to receive a lobster within 36 hours of its being scooped from the cold North Atlantic, as opposed to its having been trapped in a local aquarium for God knows how long, makes a not-so-subtle difference in taste. We're all so benumbed by the usual provender, we've forgotten what truly fresh meat and fish taste like. Begin ordering from these folks, and, trust me, you'll be spoiled forever. Never again will you be able to face Safeway bacon or a Winn-Dixie ham. Even though these products do cost more than you'll pay in any grocery store, you'll be getting premium meat and fish. The absolute luxury of this is beyond explanation.

PÂTÉS AND SAUSAGES

Pâtés and sausages were developed in the Middle Ages to make use of and preserve scraps of meat. Every French village, in addition to its bakery, dairy shop, and greengrocer, had a *charcuterie*. The word developed from *chair* (meat) and *cuit* (cooked) and referred both to the shop and the product. The parsimonious French made use of every bit of the animal—carefully grinding, then blending the meat with spices.

Refrigeration didn't come about until late in the 19th century, and the art of meat preservation was a highly developed craft. Today, a few people, who either apprenticed in France or had a gifted French mother, are still able to produce these colorful, richly flavored blends of meats, vegetables, and seafood.

The pâtés are perhaps the most versatile member of the charcuterie repertoire. Traditional pâtés use mainly pork, but also livers, poultry, and game, blended with wines, spices, and liqueurs or brandies. The interior may be studded with nuts, truffles, or whole nuggets of tongue, veal, or other choice unground meats. Nouvelle Cuisine has created an interest in fish pâtés and vegetable pâtés, which are highly flavored but lighter than the traditional pork and game pâtés.

Pâtés served in their cooking dishes, usually a deep earthenware crock, are known as terrines. If cooked in a pastry, they're called *en croute*. A mousse is a smoother, creamier version of pâté that is usually more spreadable and frequently more delicately seasoned.

Foie gras, a fatted goose or duck liver, traditionally is made by French farmers who force-feed their geese or ducks with corn, stroking it into the bird's throat through a tube. This produces a large, engorged liver. It's against the law in the United States to force-feed birds, and a lot of French foie gras (188,000 pounds in 1981) is flown to this country. I have found a source for American foie gras made in New York state (see index for D'Artagnan). Imported foie gras is cooked to death. Better you should buy the domestic variety, which can be cooked only until rare, as they do it in France. Pâté de foie gras means the foie gras has been blended with pork or pork liver.

Sausages, or *saucisson,* may be cured or smoked so that they are *sec* (dry and hard, like salami) and require no refrigeration, or they may be fresh, soft, and juicy, requiring both refrigeration and cooking. *Boudin noir* is a blood sausage that becomes positively black after cooking, and *boudin blanc* is a white sausage made with veal or poultry and usually bound with white bread. *Andouille* is a kind of tripe sausage.

Of course, the French aren't the only ones who know how to make sausages. Every culture has its means for preserving bits and pieces of foods. We have included the best we could find of American-made French, German, Portuguese, Cajun, and even one incredible "hobo's" sausage that's no baloney.

BIG APPLE PÂTÉS

**Les Trois Petits Cochons
(3 Little Pigs)**
453 Greenwich St.
New York, NY 10013

phone orders: yes, through
Marshall Field's/
Neiman-Marcus
800-M-FIELDS/
800-322-INFO
ae/visa/mc

Alain Sinturel and Jean Pierre Pradie, both coming from families of French chefs and charcutiers, first met in London, then later by chance in New York. Pooling their resources, they were able to acquire an 11-by-13-foot, two-story carriage house where, with secondhand equip-

How to Serve Pâté

For a classic first course in a French meal: a single slice of pâté on a bed of lettuce with French bread, cornichons, a dash of spicy mustard, and a glass of wine. For lunch or picnic: a pâté and croissant sandwich with spicy mustard, cornichons, lettuce, and a sprig of parsley. For the strictly vegetarian: serves two slices of vegetable pâté on a luncheon plate with watercress, tomato, parsley, sprouts, radishes, and cherry tomatoes. Or create a mixed plate combining pâtés, grapes, blood oranges, and brie, garnished with cornichons and curly leaf lettuce. Serve with French bread and mustard. Make a charcuterie sampler board, combining a selection of pâtés, sausages, and specialty meats, bounded by parsley, sauerkraut, cornichons, dark bread, mustard, and butter.

Pâtés, mousses, and sausages are served with wines. Mousses call for light-bodied reds or any white. The game pâtés go with light-bodied reds, dry and semidry whites. The bracing country pâtés, *Poivre Vert* and *Forestier*, demand a full-bodied red. According to the Messieurs Pradie and Sinturel, a good-quality Beaujolais is the best all-around choice; served cool, it goes well with all pâtés.

ment, a loan, and Gallic guts, they opened their own charcuterie in 1975. It wasn't long before Craig Claiborne, James Beard, and Mimi Sheraton found them, and once their reviews hit the papers, the two French chefs began to see black ink in their ledgers.

Both are idealists and refuse to use chemical additives in their fresh pâtés. Instead they use the traditional preservatives: red pepper and cloves, which have an antiseptic effect; sage, marjoram, and rosemary, which, combined with the meat's fat, slow oxidation and rancidity; and ground nutmeg, mustard seeds, angelica, ginger, and coriander, which retard discoloration. Because their pâtés contain no nitrites, they aren't bright pink but a more muted, dark, rosy tan color. These fresh, delicate pâtés, sold in pound loaves, require about 24 hours to prepare, three to four days to properly age, and are good for about 30 days, uncut. Once they're cut, they'll keep in the refrigerator, properly wrapped, no longer than 10 days. These are precious morsels.

You can choose from *Campagne*—coarsely ground pork with onion, garlic, and herbs; *Poivre Vert*—finely ground pork with green peppercorns and cognac; or *Forestier*—pork and chicken livers flavored with cèpes and Madeira.

There are three game pâtés, blending pork with rabbit, prunes, and Armagnac; duck with pistachios, Grand Marnier, and orange zest; and venison with juniper berries and cognac.

They offer three delicate mousses, made from duck livers, chicken livers, and truffles; and finally a silken goose liver and Sauterne mousse, which they call *Mousse Royale de Foie d'Oie au Sauterne*. They also offer a couple of vegetable pâtés, a salmon mousse, a French garlic sausage, and real imported cornichons, cèpes, and truffle breakings in juice.

These virtuoso pâtés cost about $10 a pound and will provide you with the makings of a nonpareil picnic. Call the 800 numbers and see just what combination of pâtés and mousses the two stores are offering. As we go to press, Neiman's offers 5 assorted pounds for around $70 postpaid, and Marshall Field's offers 3 pounds with a jar of cornichons for about $58. If you're in New York, stop by the charcuterie, where they also offer quiches, galantines, and salads so good they have rendered the New York food press nearly speechless with joy.

SAN FRANCISCO PÂTÉS AND SAUSAGES

Marcel et Henri   phone orders: yes
415 Browning Way   415-948-1883
S. San Francisco, CA   (The Works, Los Altos)
94080   visa/mc

Henri Lapuyade came to San Francisco from his native France in 1949. After serving a rigorous apprenticeship with Lucien Heyraud, the legendary chef at San Francisco's Palace Hotel, Henri began experimenting with pâtés. Remembering the recipes his mother used in her French restaurant, Henri began offering the pâtés from the charcuterie he established at the top of Russian Hill. He is largely responsible for the popularity of pâtés in this country.

You can still visit the original shop. Just try to decide among the 32 choices, including duck, pork, chicken liver, rabbit, pheasant, salmon, and then the blends. One of the best is the *Pâté Forestier au Genièvre,* a blend of pork, chicken livers, fresh mushrooms, brandy, and juniper berries. Henri's pâtés, galantines, and sausages are as good as they get. Try Henri's once and you will, as Henri encourages, *parlez-vous pâté.*

CALIFORNIA SAUSAGES AND PÂTÉS

Le Pique-Nique   phone orders: yes
  Charcuterie   415-532-0250
1924 E. 14th St.
Oakland, CA 94606

Who would think that an Irish guy from Oakland could make French sausages? But for seven years, Dennis Donnegan has been doing just that. Dennis operates a small, intimate charcuterie and produces some outstanding handmade pâtés. You will get personal service from him, just like the old days when the butcher would really help you out. Currently, Dennis makes and ships seven pâtés, including one splendid *Campagne* variety of coarsely ground pork and pork liver blended with whis-

All Usinger's employees are invited to eat breakfast and lunch, courtesy of the company, in company dining rooms—separated, I might add, into "boys" and "girls" rooms. This stems from an old German tradition of companies feeding the help. It also serves as an ongoing quality control so that the employees are the first to taste everything they make. Here's a recipe that was developed in their dining hall in the tradition of beer 'n' brat that made Milwaukee famous . . . ahem . . . as they say.

Bratwurst à la Vern

Serves 4 in 45 minutes

- 2 Bermuda onions, coarsely chopped
- 2 tablespoons butter
- 1 tablespoon Worcestershire sauce
- 2 tablespoons cider vinegar
  Salt to taste
- 2 tablespoons brown sugar
- ½ teaspoon paprika
- 1 12-ounce bottle of beer
- 8 bratwurst links (1½ pounds)

In a heavy saucepan, cook onions in butter until lightly browned. Add Worcestershire, vinegar, salt, brown sugar, paprika, and beer. Simmer 5 minutes. Add bratwurst and simmer uncovered for 25–30 minutes, or until done. Serve with brown bread and beer.

key, eggs, fresh garlic, and spices, then wrapped in caul. Dennis also makes a fabulous ground pork and chicken liver pâté with marinated whole chicken breast running through the center, seasoned with rosemary and whole pistachios. His pâtés are light, deftly seasoned, and all delicious. Dennis also makes a good garlic-fennel sausage and a good fine-herb sausage made with fresh spinach and parsley, then doused with plum wine. All pâtés and sausages are shipped second-day air.

GERMAN-STYLE SAUSAGES

Usinger's Famous Sausage   phone orders: yes
1030 N. Third St.   414-276-9100
Milwaukee, WI 53203

With more than 80 sausages on their list, all made using German and Eastern European traditional recipes, most without chemical additives and packed in natural casings, the Usingers have a place in Milwaukee's heart—Milwaukee being a town where five kinds of sausages are sold at the local ball games and where hostesses have wine-and-sausage-tasting parties routinely. Usinger's has been making sausage here since the 1880s: blood sausages, liver sausages, sausages to be cooked, summer sausages, and lunch meats, everything from Milwaukee's favorite bratwurst to a renowned landjaeger heavy with garlic.

We found the Braunschweiger to be as pale and delicate as any pâté. Lean, it has a slight aroma of suet. The little Hildescheimer, on the other hand, was softer, rosier in color, and had a mild, gentle flavor. What they call goose liver is studded with pistachios (still hand-peeled in Usinger's plant by a woman who's worked there for years) and beef tongue. The Hessische Landleberwurst is smoked and aromatic with onions. Fresh liver sausage is the only one that's not smoked, and it's a light tan color. Mash it with cream and cognac and people will say *mais oui*. We even liked the wieners they sent, packed in natural casings and good enough to make you whistle "take me out to the ball game."

A most staggering aspect of these sausages is their price: ranging from $2.79 to $3.29 a pound. Just take a gander at the supermarket prices, think about chemicals, and make your decision. With a 5-pound minimum, they'll charge you 90 cents to pack, the price of the dry ice, and the actual shipping charges. But still . . . such a deal. Quality.

BEST SUMMER SAUSAGE

Sheboygan Sausage Co.   phone orders: yes
PO Box 1123   414-458-2143
Sheboygan, WI 53082   minimum order: $20

In the heart of the Depression, a German sausagemaker joined the many other Germans in Sheboygan, Wisconsin, and began plying his trade. It wasn't long before Sheboygan was known as the bratwurst capital of the world. Not only is the company famous for this Wisconsin favorite but they have gained a national reputation for summer sausage, a dry, dark sausage that requires no refrigeration and is always favored in the winter . . . despite its name. In a taste test we conducted here, comparing Sheboygan to three others, we found Sheboygan to be a tangy, salty, smoky, vinegary version of summer sausage that seemed the best of the ones we tried. Sold in 12-ounce, 18-ounce, 2-pound, and 4-pound sizes, it sells for an astounding $2.20 per pound, plus shipping. Sheboygan also makes coarse-ground bologna and a fine Polish sausage. They do have a $20 minimum order and use nitrites.

THIS IS NO BALONEY

The Daniel Weaver Co.   phone orders: yes
PO Box 525   800-WEAVERS (U.S.)
Lebanon, PA 17042   717-274-6100 (PA)
                        ae/visa/mc

If you thought that pale, smooth stuff they sell in the deli case—almost quivering with pigs' snouts and lips and ears and white bread pudding—was baloney, I have good news. Real baloney—or, as adults are supposed to say, bologna—is made from 100 percent beef, 90 per-

---

Polish Sausage Cooked in Molasses

1½ pounds Polish sausage
⅓   cup dark molasses
1   teaspoon German
    mustard
6   cups cold water

Prick casings of sausage with a fork to prevent bursting. Combine molasses, mustard, and water in large saucepan. Bring to a boil, then add sausage. Cover and simmer 25 minutes. Remove from liquid and cut into serving pieces. Serve with hot sauerkraut or just-steamed red cabbage and black bread.

cent lean, and is about the color and texture of a real good San Francisco salami. Around Lebanon, Pennsylvania, famous for this German-style sausage, the best source for real Lebanon bologna is Weaver's. Daniel Weaver first tried his luck in Mexico after emigrating from Germany, but his smokehouse was burned down by Pancho Villa, so he retreated to German relatives around Lebanon and started over. Now, almost a hundred years later, his company still makes this sweet-sour, smoky bologna the same way. I guess you can thank Pancho Villa for this one.

Back in those days, every farm made sausages to preserve its meat supply for the winter, refrigeration being measured by the length of the winter only. The story may be apocryphal, but Weaver's Hugh Miller says that one particular hobo was in great demand in the county around hog-killing time because he had a way with sausage. According to Hugh's story, the hobo revealed his recipe for baloney and thereafter mysteriously disappeared. Someone was heard to say, "I would kill to know how to make that baloney." Who knows? Talk's cheap. Maybe the story's baloney. Ask Hugh.

One of the interesting aspects of this kind of sausage is that it requires no refrigeration. The natural fermentation that takes place during its long, cool smoking preserves the sausage.

In addition to the Lebanon bologna, the Weavers also make Baum's Sweet Bologna, a sweeter/tangier version of the same sausage. Call for their catalog. They also sell first-rate ham, bacon, Canadian bacon, and even the famous Strode's Scrapple, which comes in a can and originated in Philadelphia.

PORTUGUESE SAUSAGES

Gaspar's Sausage Co., Inc. phone orders: yes
PO Box 436   800-542-2038 (U.S.)
N. Dartmouth, MA 02747   617-998-2012 (MA)
                               visa/mc

Rosy, ham-laden linguica and its hotter cousin chourico have been made since 1927 by Manuel Gaspar and sons. Manuel came from Lisbon to New Bedford, Massachusetts, in 1927 and made sausage in his garage for years, using more ham than other pork to achieve a traditional Portuguese style. He moved to the North Dartmouth plant in 1954 but still makes the sausage the traditional Portuguese way. The ham-heavy pork is first ground, then mixed with spices that include garlic, black pepper, vinegar, and enough paprika to make the sausage blush permanently. It is allowed to marinate until it "smells right," they say. Then it's fed into natural hog or beef casings and hand-twisted at random intervals. Now the sausage is wheeled into a smokehouse where it remains at 140° F. about three hours. Then the sausage gets a cold shower and is blast-chilled. When you get it, remember to cook it, for this sausage is smoked but uncooked. The Portuguese community around New Bedford is most fond of the sausage grilled and served on a roll, but we adored the soup recipe they included and highly recommend it.

SOUTH LOUISIANA ANDOUILLE AND TASSO

Oak Grove Smokehouse, Inc.
17648 Old Jefferson Hwy.
Prairieville, LA 70769

phone orders: yes
504-673-6857

Robert Schexnailder, being a good Cajun, began smoking meats as a hobby in his backyard. He used a tried and true Cajun-type smoker—an old refrigerator. A Ph.D. agricultural researcher at Louisiana State University, he just made the regional sausages for fun. *Andouille,* a Cajun smoked pure pork sausage, and *tasso,* a very highly seasoned Cajun smoked ham, are essential ingredients in many Cajun specialties, from seafood gumbo to chicken jambalaya. But one thing led to another. Today he and his wife, Babette, and their grown kids Yvette and Robert, Jr., now smoke thousands of pounds of meat daily: turkey, chicken, bacon, ham, and sausage, in addition to the *tasso* and *andouille.*

They've also developed Cajun mixes they send out along with their smoked meats so that people won't waste the scraps. Now you can have gumbo for one person, and

---

Portuguese Kale Soup

Serves 8 in 3 hours

- 1½ pounds linguica or chourico
- 1 pound shank meat or chuck roast
- 2 teaspoons crushed red pepper
- 1 onion, peeled and quartered
- 2 bunches fresh kale (or 4 10-ounce boxes frozen kale)
- 1 small head cabbage, shredded
- 4 cups cooked dried beans (or 2 20-ounce cans kidney beans)
- 6 small potatoes, peeled and diced
  Salt and pepper to taste

Combine meats, red pepper, onion, and salt in large saucepot. Cover with water and bring to a boil. Simmer until meat is almost done (about 2 hours). Add kale, cabbage, and beans to broth. When kale is about half cooked, add potatoes and simmer an additional 30 minutes. Adjust seasonings with salt and pepper. Serve with dark bread and a robust red wine.

Tasso Seafood Gumbo

Serves 8 in 3 hours

1	pound okra, sliced (2 10-ounce boxes frozen)
¼	cup light oil
½	pound *tasso*, sliced in strips
2	medium onions, chopped
2	tablespoons flour
1	large bell pepper, chopped
2	stalks celery, chopped
	Handful fresh parsley, cut fine
2	bay leaves
4	cloves garlic, pressed
2	teaspoons fresh thyme
8	ounces tomato sauce
2	quarts water
1	16-ounce can tomatoes, with juice
1	pound lump crabmeat
2	whole boiled blue crabs
1	pound peeled shrimp
	Salt, black and red pepper to taste
1	pint oysters and liquor
	Gumbo filé

In a large saucepot, smother okra in oil over low heat, covered, for 25 minutes. Add *tasso* and onions and cook 10 more minutes, covered. Sprinkle in flour; stir and brown the mixture. Add just enough water to keep it from sticking, then add pepper, celery, parsley, bay leaves, garlic, and thyme, stirring constantly. Add tomato sauce and simmer 5 minutes. Add water and tomatoes. Simmer uncovered about 2 hours. During last 20 minutes add crabmeat, blue crabs, shrimp, and salt and peppers to taste. Five minutes be-

CONTINUED ON PAGE 95

jambalaya for an intimate dinner for two—and all in 30 minutes. The thing that really surprises the Schexnailders is that right in their own neighborhood, where everybody knows how to make gumbo from scratch, the mixes sell real well. For 25 cents they'll send along a recipe booklet called *A Taste of South Louisiana,* with authentic Cajun recipes.

GAME, GAME BIRDS, AND A CHICKEN IN EVERY POT BESIDES

When Lawrence Forgione began American Spoon Foods in Michigan to assure himself a steady supply of fresh buffalo meat for his New York restaurant, An American Place, it was considered revolutionary. But before long, other restaurants were following suit; not only buffalo, but venison, quail, wild boar, and other such meats began springing up on restaurant menus. The enthusiastic restaurant goers, who kept badgering waiters for the source of these foods, soon created a consumer demand that had to be met.

Before that, the only home cooks who had access to game and game birds were those who happened to have a hunter for a friend. But with fast shipping, some changes in the law, and a growing interest in American native foods and exotic meats, now you can pick up the phone and order wild boar ribs, backstrap of venison, buffalo steak, and all manner of birds: quail, chukar, duck, goose, partridge, pheasant, squab, and wild turkey. Not only do these succulent meats enlarge the repertoire of the gourmand but also offer good alternatives to people who like the taste of red meat but want or need to cut down on fats. These wild fellows, who had to chase down their own dinner, are generally as lean and lithe as a long-distance runner. Many doctors recommend venison, for example, to people with cholesterol problems. Buffalo is sometimes the only meat that can be eaten by highly allergic people who cannot tolerate meat from animals that have been raised on so-called improved scientific diets in domestic feedlots. The people who grow game birds usually handle chickens and turkeys as well, so I have lumped these birds into this category, too, simply because it's convenient. I suppose it would be fair to say that a free-range chicken is about half wild anyway, and all the chickens here fall into that category.

One caveat about this section: The supplies for these are uneven. Some items are seasonal, and all depend on a favorable growing season. Call for price and availability on all items.

NEW ZEALAND VENISON

Wilderness Gourmet	phone orders: yes
Enzed Traders, Inc.	313-663-6987
PO Box 3257	ae/visa/mc/dc/cb
Ann Arbor, MI 48106	

Boneless backstrap of venison is the first item on the list from Enzed. This venison is grown in New Zealand, raised as we might raise cattle, flash-frozen, and shipped to customers by air. The venison backstrap looks much like filet mignon and is the mildest meat from the deer. Venison rib chop steak, sausage, and whole venison hinds are also available. We smoked a venison hind—they're about as big as a ham—and sliced it paper-thin for a big party. Delicious. The Nodine Sausagemakers in Goshen, Connecticut, make venison sausage for Enzed. It is smoked, lean and highly flavorful, soft, dark in color, and moist. Packed in natural beef casings, with 25 percent beef added to improve the texture. I recommend it.

In addition to the venison, the Enzed traders offer buffalo strip loins, franks, and burgers. Wild boar hams, pheasant, goose, turkey, goose sausage, and rendered goose fat—so necessary for authentic cooking of foods from southwest France.

See also: American Spoon Foods for fresh buffalo and buffalo sausages.

BOARING FOOD

Gordon-Thompson, Ltd.	phone orders: yes
410 W. Coast Hwy.	714-645-5180
Newport Beach, CA 92663	visa/mc

If you don't think it takes nerves of steel to stay in this business, consider the case of the wild boar, which is nothing but a domestic pig that went native several generations back. The survival of the fittest demands that only the meanest, most ridge-backed, curved-tusk, ugly, scary

---

CONTINUED FROM PAGE 94

fore serving, add oysters and liquor. Stir well, taste, and adjust seasonings. Add filé gradually until gumbo loses its sweetness —begin with a tablespoon. Fish out bay leaves and discard. Serve over rice.

Enzed Traders' Marinade for Venison or Elk

Because venison is so lean, the Enzed Traders recommend marinades to guarantee tenderness. Here's their favorite.

Makes 2¾ cups in 10 minutes

2	cups fresh orange juice
¼	cup dark soy sauce
¼	cup Worcestershire sauce
2	large cloves garlic, pressed
2	teaspoons cracked peppercorns
¼	cup port wine

Combine all ingredients in a nonaluminum container and place six venison steaks or one venison ham in the liquid. Cover and marinate in the refrigerator overnight.

For a good serving sauce, sauté 2 sliced onions in 2 tablespoons of butter, then add to marinade. Reduce by ¾ by boiling, stirring. Serve with sautéed medallions of venison.

Cumberland Sauce

For one of the best sauces for venison or elk, use Lieutenant Maury red currant jelly (see Maury Island Farming Co. under jams in index) for the perfect blend of sweet and tangy game sauce.

Makes 1 cup in 10 minutes

- 4   tablespoons red currant jelly (Lt. Maury)
- 4   tablespoons brown sugar
-     Grated rind of 1 orange
- 1   tablespoon orange juice
- 1   tablespoon lemon juice
- 4   tablespoons port wine
- 2   teaspoons Dijon mustard

Combine ingredients in small saucepan and raise to a boil. Serve with any dark red meat: venison, elk, boar, bear, or beef.

ones make it, and there are a good many of them holed up in Arkansas. That's where the Gordon-Thompsons go to get them. And they tell me—I swear I am not making this up—that the only way to get one is to let him tree you, then shoot him. I always thought the object of a hunt was to trap the animal, not to let the animal trap you—but they say that's not the way it's done in Arkansas. Anyway, the ribs are so good, they're like the best pork spareribs you ever had, with just a hint of wild, smoky, dangerous flavor to them. Ask for their special barbecue sauce, too. They tell me that the boars are in short supply in the winter because when the snow gets deep, a fellow tends to slip and can't climb trees fast enough. Ooooh-K. Whatever you say.

The Gordon-Thompsons also contract to buy Malaysian black tiger prawns, which come four to the pound and are shipped live, from far East Asia. Their latest shipment—about a thousand pounds—was held up in customs until the poor prawns expired. Why they didn't have a heart attack over that, I couldn't tell you—just tough, I guess. But they're sticklers for quality and only ship the freshest products. If you want something really exotic, like the black tiger prawns, let them hold your order until the lively things come swimming into their warehouse. You'll have them the next day. Also available are boneless quail and buffalo steaks. Call for their catalog and ask what's in today. The offerings change with the season.

FLYING BIRDS, FISHES, AND FRESH EXOTIC VEGETABLES

Flying Foods
  International, Inc.

1225 Broadway	phone orders: yes
Santa Monica, CA 90404;	213-395-1783
43-43 9th St.	718-706-0820
Long Island City, NY 11101	visa/mc

Four years ago, Paul Moriates, who was food and beverage controller at the Waldorf Astoria Hotel in New York, and his partner Walter Martin, who was assistant to the manager of the hotel, decided to ship foods that were plentiful in one area to another wherever there was a demand. They found that they could tap worldwide markets and supply New York area restaurants with once-unavailable exotic cuisine.

They began by emptying Walter's bedroom, flinging open the windows—it was the dead of winter—and running back and forth to the airport. After months of staggering up three flights of stairs with crates of perishable foods and storing them in their *au naturel* walk-in refrigerator and seeing the Dover sole encroach on Walter's ever-diminishing space, they could see that either the business would have to move or Walter would. So they opened a warehouse near Kennedy Airport.

Their business rose like a fine batch of bread. They added the Los Angeles area warehouse to take advantage of Pacific Rim products. Eventually they opened their warehouses to retail customers after restaurateurs like Piero Selvaggio of Valentino's and other chefs started recommending their Santa Monica warehouse to customers who wanted to cook their fine foods at home.

Their list of what's available changes seasonally and even daily, depending on all the finicky aspects of this crazy business, but the day I visited they had a good supply of game birds—partridge, pheasant, squab, and quail. Fresh free-range baby chickens. Smoked ducks, chickens, and turkeys. Goose liver from Israel. Mussels from Maine and Dover sole from France. Here's where you can get vials of cuttlefish ink to add color to pasta, red mullet from Brittany, langoustines from France, John Dory from the Sea of Galilee, turbot from the Netherlands, cheeks of monkfish from the Mediterranean.

Not only do they offer these perishable protein products, sent out within 12 hours of hitting their warehouse, but they also offer fresh garden produce in season. For example: mâche; hearts of palm; passion fruit; white asparagus from Argentina; radicchio; red, yellow, and purple peppers from Holland; trivissao; Maui onions; dried and fresh morels; chanterelles; cèpes; oyster mushrooms; fresh wood ears, and others. Call and see what's in today. They encourage visits to the warehouses on both coasts and remind you that when you shop with them, the retail fine-food buyer is paying wholesale prices.

TSAR NICOULAI

See also: California Sunshine Fine Foods. Up in Northern California, California Sunshine is a purveyor of exotica as well as fine fresh vegetables. Here you can find game birds including chukar, Culver ducks and duck breast, goose and goose breast, guineas, mallards, Muscovys, pheasants, poussin, quail, squab, and quail eggs. They have smoked capon, Long Island duck and goose, fresh rabbit, suckling pig, wild boar, caribou, antelope, venison, Sonoma lamb, and kid.

They are well known for their assortment of American caviars, golden, gold pearl, and sturgeon. They also sell Caspian, Beluga, Sevruga, and Osetra. They offer American foie gras, live crayfish from the Mediterranean, green-lipped mussels from New Zealand, and an array of smoked fishes.

They are primarily a wholesaler and impose a handling charge of $10 on all orders under $100.

AMERICAN FOIE GRAS

D'Artagnan phone orders: yes
399-419 St. Paul Ave. 201-792-0748
Jersey City, NJ 07306 ae/visa/mc

As Suzanne Hamlin of the *New York Daily News* says about foie gras, "Maybe you'll be lucky and hate it, thereby being able to set aside the foie gras money for potential college educations." Now that Ariane Daguin, the daughter of an internationally acclaimed French chef, and former apprentice at 3 Little Pigs Charcuterie in New York (see index), has started not only cooking and selling this velvety-smooth, unforgettable duck liver but also giving all sorts of advice on its use, we're all doomed.

It used to be you could get real foie gras only in France, because the American Department of Agriculture required that the tons of it shipped here be sterilized out of its very tasteful existence. And the American duck lovers have never been able to agree with the Frenchwomen who care for and feed special Moulard ducks—forcing them to swallow corn through a tube—that to be a future

How to Eat Foie Gras

The traditional French manner is to serve it as a first course. It is very rich; a pound easily serves 10 people. Serve a little colder than room temperature, in a pottery terrine, along with crusty French bread. The French provide a glass of hot water and a spoon alongside. Each guest dips the spoon in hot water, then scoops out the foie gras, spreading it thickly on the bread. The wine for this is a sweet Sauterne, which seems to cut through the richness and leave a clean, bright taste in the mouth.

If you buy raw foie gras, remember to cook it rare. You can sauté it carefully (it will fall apart if handled roughly) and serve it hot. Before you try this—it's something like gambling with your grandmother's social security check—better ask Ariane exactly how to cook it. You'd hate to ruin it. Too precious.

foie gras is a special destiny. Therefore it's still against the law to force-feed birds in the United States.

But science and technology will out. Two Israelis and an American in the Mongap Valley of New York have crossbred the Pekin and Muscovy and gotten what they called a "mullard" duck, which produces a rosy, velvety-rich liver without being force-fed. They also get magret, a "fat duck breast," from the same animal. Both the magrets and foie gras weigh about 2 pounds each. That's more than twice as large as what you'd find on a plain old Long Island or Pekin duck.

Ariane will send you a whole, cooked foie gras, about 2 pounds, personally prepared to its rare perfection by Ariane, then sealed in an airtight Cryovac pouch. Unopened and refrigerated, it will keep about 30 days. Opened, it stays fresh about a week provided you double-wrap it in foil and refrigerate.

Now for the shock. It's presently $65 a pound, plus shipping. In addition to the whole cooked foie gras, D'Artagnan also sells the rest of the duck: breast, magrets, legs, wings, hearts, and gizzards, and rendered duck fat, as well as whole ducks.

Drawing on her valuable apprenticeship at 3 Little Pigs, Ariane also cooks and sells *Pâté de Foie Gras au Sauterne; Galantine de Foie Gras au Confit de Canard,* wherein the legs are boned and stuffed with foie gras; *Confit de Canard; Magret Fume,* a hardwood-smoked breast; *Jambon de Canard,* in which the breast is formed into the shape of a miniature (½ to ¾ pound) ham, coated with pepper, and hung to cure until the richly flavored duck meat acquires a subtle taste and a silken texture; and *Gesiers Confits,* gizzards preserved in duck fat. When you call, ask for the recipe booklet that Ariane has written. It comes with the order.

Other game birds carefully selected and offered are California poussin, New York free-range chicken, Georgia quail, California squab and pigeon, New Jersey pheasant, California Pekin duck, New Jersey Muscovy and mallard ducks, Pennsylvania wild turkey, New Jersey guinea hen, geese, and partridges from three states.

They also have available on request: red tail venison from New Zealand, wild boar from Texas, Arkansas rabbit, antelope, axis venison, bison, elk, wild sheep, reindeer, wild hare, suckling pigs, and Corsican sheep.

Grilled Rabbit

Marinate the quartered rabbit overnight, then grill quickly over a fire that's had grapevines or apple cuttings added to the charcoal. Serve with a fine blueberry chutney and Texmati rice (see index) for a simple, delicious dinner. Gewürztraminer to drink, a salad of Belgian endive and goat cheese with a light vinaigrette dressing, your favorite chocoholic dessert. Who needs a rabbit's foot?

Serves 2 in 30 minutes; marinates overnight

- 1 cup light oil
- 4 cloves garlic, pressed
- 4 shallots, finely chopped
  Juice of half a lemon
- 2 sprigs fresh sage, or
  1 teaspoon dried
- 2 sprigs fresh thyme, or
  1 teaspoon dried
- 2 sprigs fresh rosemary,
  or 1 teaspoon dried
- 1 bay leaf
- ½ cup dry Vermouth
  Salt and red and black
  peppers to taste
- 1 rabbit, quartered

Combine all ingredients in non-aluminum bowl and submerge rabbit in marinade. Cover and marinate overnight in the refrigerator, turning occasionally. Grill rabbit, covered, until the juices run clear, turning with tongs and basting with the marinade often so that the skin will be an even golden color. Don't char it. Takes about 20 minutes total. Watch it every minute.

RABBIT AND RABBIT SAUSAGES

Triple R Ranch phone orders: yes
Rte. 2, Box 393N 503-359-9103
Cornelius, OR 97113

Shari Thomas raises and sells rabbits, whole or made into sausages and salami, to customers all over the Northwest. Among her customers are medical patients who require a high-protein, low-cholesterol protein source. The sausages and salami she makes from rabbit have no additives or preservatives. She calls them "lean links," and they're a good choice for a breakfast meat for those who need to avoid fats.

And, as you might have guessed, you can even buy rabbit pelts if you wish to make something to wrap the baby bunting in. And I tell you what: make Shari throw in a rabbit's foot with your order, just for good luck. 'Course, you'll have to come up with your own brass chain and holder. But think of the luck. I just can't bring myself to write down the recipe she made up for "Floppy Joes." If you want it, ask her.

GRAIN-FED PRIME POULTRY

Cavanaugh Lakeview phone orders: yes
  Farms, Ltd. 800-243-4438
PO Box 430 ae/visa/mc
Chelsea, MI 48118

Cynthia Feller carefully feeds her free-range birds grain and produces a fine chicken. She also offers capon, duckling, turkey, goose, pheasant, and quail. No chemicals or hormones are accidentally introduced to these birds, and she butchers and flash-freezes them right there on the farm before sending them out, on the theory that you're getting a fresher bird than if you went to a store and bought a so-called "fresh" bird that had been languishing under Saran Wrap a week.

She has perfected a honey glaze that she sprays on before smoking these birds. She sells them along with smoked spiral-cut hams. The smokehouse is right on the farm and uses choice hardwoods and carefully controlled time and temperature to get a succulent, smoky-sweet product. Call for a catalog that will tell you in detail what Cynthia is growing this year.

SUCCULENT GAME BIRDS

Wellington Farms
RD 2, Box 58 South Rd.
Millbrook, NY 12545

phone orders: yes
1-800-348-3412 (national)
1-800-336-3637 (NY)
visa/mc

George Oppenheimer lives in upstate New York in a country of undulating green hills, peaceful farms, and pleasant valleys. He got into the business of raising game birds by going to pheasant farms to purchase his own Thanksgiving and Christmas birds. Every time he set foot on one of those farms, he says, "I was attracted to the business end of it by seeing how the owners of these farms lived and how orderly they seemed to be able to manage their farms. It just appealed to me." So George began by talking with a few of them, writing to state universities and cooperative extension courses. He finally made the decision, and he says the real story of his beginnings in the bird business would be fodder for a novel. If you're ever up his way, stop by his little country store on the place and he'll tell you a bit of it.

Meanwhile, you can order these birds, which are truly free-range, being fed only organically grown feeds. Choose from pheasant, duck, wild turkey, guinea, geese, quail, and chukar—all ready to cook. George also smokes pheasant, goose, and capon at a reasonable price.

BONELESS POULTRY AND OTHER EXCEPTIONAL FOODS

Confidence Co.
#2 E St. Ste. 655
Santa Rosa, CA 95404

phone orders: yes
707-829-5201

In this mostly wholesale business, Sophie Sanders just sells what she happens to like: fresh poussin, pheasant, quail, Pekin duck, and grain-fed chicken. All grown right

Smoked Capon Salad

You can substitute other perfectly ripe fruits here as you find them in prime condition in the market. The ugli fruit has a wonderful sweet peachy plus grapefruit taste that's made for poultry. Substitute a Texas red grapefruit or pomelo. Any smoked poultry is equally delicious—turkey, duck, or quail.

Serves 4

- 1 head butter lettuce
- 1 bunch cilantro
- 1 ripe Hass avocado
- 1 ripe papaya
- 1 ripe mango
- 1 ugli fruit
  Juice of 1 lime
- ½ cup olive oil
- 1 smoked capon, deboned
  Red pepper flakes to taste

Arrange washed and dried lettuce on a flat serving plate. Strip out leaves of cilantro. Discard stems. Peel and slice fruits, holding them over a bowl to catch juices. Discard seeds and membranes. Whisk together lime juice with other juices and oil. Coat each fruit in turn in the dressing. Then artfully group fruit slices and capon atop lettuce. Sprinkle with cilantro leaves and red pepper flakes and dress with lime/oil dressing.

Sautéed Duck Breast in Peppercorns

Serve duck breast the way the French farmers do when they have them for supper: quickly sautéed in clarified butter, cut into paper-thin slices, and fanned onto a plate with a sprinkling of cracked peppercorns. Bulgur cooked in broth, baby zucchini sautéed with the meat, a Bibb/chicory salad with lemon-Chardonnay dressing.

In major markets you may find boneless duck breast for sale. Or you can lift duck breast from a whole duck, then use the rest of the duck to make stock and create a dynamite clear sauce using dried morels or other forest mushrooms. This is a two-day operation. One day for stock, and 15 minutes for final preparation at serving time.

Serves 2 in 15 minutes

- 2   tablespoons clarified butter or light oil
- 1   whole duck breast, boned, skinned, and patted dry
     Cracked peppercorns

Over medium-high heat, preheat dry skillet. Add clarified butter or oil, heat, then add whole duck breast. Cook, turning frequently, until breast seems firm when pressed with forefinger. This will produce meat that is red-brown glazed on the outside and cooked just to pink on the inside. Cut into paper-thin slices and fan onto dinner plate. Grind fresh peppercorns atop and serve.

there in her home county of Sonoma. You can get them with or without bones. Sonoma spring lamb, suckling pig, and goat are also available here. And, during their brief spring season, so are the biggest fresh morels I ever laid eyes on. Sophie also has frozen Périgord truffles, and smoked salmon not only from the Pacific but also from Norway and Scotland. On request, she will smoke any fish you ask for: monkfish, ono, Chili bass. You name it. Sophie is here to please.

GRASS-FED BUFFALO

The Great Western Buffalo Trading Co.
Star Rte.
Twin Bridges, MT 69754

phone orders: yes
406-684-5498
visa/mc

Visitors are always welcome at the century-old ranch located at the 18-mile marker on Route 41, between Dillon and Twin Bridges, Montana. This rolling green ranch was a Lewis and Clark campsite and now is dotted with peacefully grazing buffalo. The Western Pride buffalo raised here are fed only natural prairie grass, no artificial food or chemicals. They're only 3 percent fat, making buffalo meat a good choice for medically restricted diets. You can buy grassland buffalo meat, tinned barbecue, and ranch stew from these people . . . as well as skulls, mounted heads, or buffalo robes, should you be awaiting a casting call for a Western movie and need a costume.

RED MEAT: PRIME LAMB, VEAL, PORK, AND BEEF

The red meats presented here are prime, of a quality very hard to come by in a normal supermarket. The feed, handling, aging—everything—is controlled from the ground up. These meats, with the exception of the smoked products, are flash-frozen and sent to you in gel ice. You can have them on hand in your home freezer until the moment you wish to serve them. I would note that portions suggested by the purveyors seemed to me overly generous; for example, a half pound of meat not infrequently was said to constitute one serving. In cooking these meats at home, we invariably found we could feed twice as many people as suggested.

When I asked one seller of prime beef what she'd recommend I suggest about cooking it, she answered quickly, "as little as possible." And so it is with meat that's tender, flavorful, and perfectly aged. It requires no disguise, no tenderizing, no long, complicated procedure. The only thing that might make you nervous is the possibility of ruining a good piece of meat. For that reason, I gave these meats close attention when cooking them. And in trying recipes for this section, I have attempted to devise methods that are as foolproof as possible and sauces that enhance the basic good taste of prime meat rather than masking it. We have had memorable meals from these products. I had forgotten just how good a steak can be.

SPRING LAMB AND AGNEAU DE LAIT

Jamison Farms
RD 2, Box 402
Latrobe, PA 15650

phone orders: yes
412-834-7424

Sukey and John Jamison are urban people who had a dream. They wanted to provide a peaceful, slower-paced environment for their three young children. So 10 years ago, they traded in the Volvo for a pickup truck, gave up their apartment lease, and bought 108 acres on the outskirts of Crabtree, Westmoreland County, Pennsylvania. For a while they worked on the 100-year-old farmhouse and fences, while John kept his job as a high-powered coal salesman. But they soon stocked the place with sheep and now make their entire living raising lambs and sheep. They do everything with great care, from choosing breeding stock, to feeding and finishing the animals. What you get from the Jamisons is prime, pampered lamb.

You can buy young milk-fed lamb *(agneau de lait)* by special order, otherwise known as suckling lamb and very hard to find; or you can buy a regular spring lamb, about 40–50 pounds hanging weight, and cut to order: two legs, two shoulders, two racks, two loins, four shanks, and ground lamb. You can also order any of the particular cuts

Sukey Jamison's Lamb Shank Stew

Sukey makes broth from lamb bones, water, salt, pepper, garlic, and parsley. She simmers this about an hour, cools it, removes any fat from the top, and strains it. She then has it ready for use in soups and stews. You can substitute chicken broth or veal broth for this homemade stock if you wish. See Mail-Order Menus for full menu.

Serves 6 in 2 hours; freezes well

6	lamb shanks
	Flour
	Salt and pepper
2	tablespoons light oil
1	1-pound can tomatoes and juice
2	cloves garlic, pressed
1	medium onion, coarsely chopped
½	teaspoon dried rosemary
2	quarts stock (veal, lamb, or chicken)
6	medium carrots, cut in coins
4	small stalks celery, sliced
4	medium potatoes, chopped
¼	medium head cabbage, finely shredded
½	cup chopped parsley

Flour shanks, season with salt and pepper, and brown in oil in bottom of soup pot. Add tomatoes and juice, garlic,

CONTINUED ON PAGE 104

CONTINUED FROM PAGE 103

onion, and rosemary and sauté until onion turns clear. Add broth; cover and simmer about an hour.

Remove lid and add carrots, celery, and potatoes. Cook until tender, about 20 minutes. Add cabbage and parsley and cook until tender, about 15 minutes. Bones may be removed, or shanks may be served in soup bowls with the stew.

Rachel Nicoll's Quenelles de Veau

Rachel sends out a booklet with 25 of her favorite, well-tested veal recipes with every order. Here's one we really liked. See Mail-Order Menus for full menu.

Serves 4 in 45 minutes

1	pound ground veal
2	tablespoons butter
4	tablespoons flour
3	tablespoons *glace de viande*
¼	cup water
2	eggs
	Salt and pepper to taste
1	tablespoon heavy cream

Remove veal from refrigerator 15 minutes before preparation. In a small saucepan, melt butter. Add flour; cook and stir to make a light golden roux, about 10 minutes. Add *glace* and water. Cook and stir until mixture becomes very smooth and thick. Allow to cool. Blend with veal in

CONTINUED ON PAGE 105

you like. Sukey is even offering her ready-made lamb stew. I've included her recipe, which is so good we've made it a dozen times already. Sukey and I agree the shank is the ideal choice for lamb stew.

THE FATTED CALF: ROSY MILK-FED VEAL

Summerfield Farm	phone orders: yes
Rte. 1, Box 43	703-837-1718
Boyce, VA 22620	visa/mc

Jamie and Rachel Nicoll raise veal calves the old-fashioned European way: using real milk and fresh eggs. Nicoll veal looks different from "fancy grade" veal because it isn't dead white; it's rosy pink, aromatic, more tender and flavorful. So-called white veal gets its pale color and mushy taste because the animals are anemic. Commercially raised veal is fed a tetracycline-laced dry milk product and kept in such close quarters it can never move. As a result, the so-called standard of pale flesh is really a result of poor condition. But the Nicolls raise calves in hay-filled stalls. They're healthy. It costs them more to raise veal this way; they butcher when the animal is less than half the weight of a commercially raised calf, right at 200 pounds, but they're beginning to get results in terms of sales.

Jamie and Rachel began in the winter of 1983 with one cow, one calf, and two sacks of grain. Rachel was raised by an accomplished European cook and knew about sauces and special roasts and cuts. Jamie had enough courage to sell veal literally door-to-door from the back of his pickup truck—looking funny for a farmer, in his penny loafers and khaki pants. But within a year the two of them had received favorable attention from the people who count: Craig Claiborne thanked them for the veal they sent; Julia Child was so enchanted she made plans for a visit to their farm.

You can get any combination—from a whole calf, butchered carefully by Dutch butchers who use a knife instead of a saw, to various packages that might include scallopini, a 3-pound rolled roast, loin chops, and one thing Rachel provides with every order: a jar of homemade *glace de viande,* her own reduced veal glaze. It will turn the most novice cook into a chef with the opening of a jar. Shanks, liver, sweetbreads, and kidneys are also available. They also are beginning to raise baby spring lambs for sale. Ask when you call. Jamie and Rachel Nicoll want to be your *boucherie de la maison.*

ROAST SUCKLING PIG

Campbell's Farm phone orders: yes
PO Box 74 802-333-4072
Port Mills, VT 95058 visa/mc

Ron and Mary Campbell raise and sell a limited number of roast suckling pigs, weighing between 15 and 20 pounds each. They carefully raise these animals on a hand-mixed feed that guarantees the meat will be moist, tender, and tasty. You can get the pig either uncooked or smoked. If you'd like to reserve one for Christmas or Thanksgiving, when they're in very short supply, give the Campbell's notice by sending $25 to reserve one for you; they'll send it on the date you specify. A suckling pig feeds from 10 to 15 people and makes an impressive centerpiece for a big party. They'll send several recipes for you to choose from. The Campbells know their pigs— and their pig roasts—and they'll show you how.

AMERICAN PROSCIUTTO

S. Wallace Edwards & phone orders: yes
  Sons, Inc. 800-222-4267
PO Box 25 ae/visa/mc
Surry, VA 23883

When we received a red leather box with gold engraving on it, my husband, Joe, thought it was presentation pistols. It had that look and feel to it. But no, it was another Southern specialty, Virginia ham, sliced paper-thin, a deep brick-red, and lean as a *Vogue* model. This is the special gift box you can buy from Wallace Edwards, who dry cures hams after the fashion of the East Coast Indians who taught the first Virginia settlers how to do it. He calls his

CONTINUED FROM PAGE 104

a processor or blender. With machine running, add eggs one at a time. Season to taste with salt and pepper and stir in cream.

Using two teaspoons face to face, shape quenelles into small egg shapes. (It helps to dip spoons frequently in hot water.) Place the quenelles in lightly greased pan. Pour enough boiling water to cover them, taking care not to pour water directly onto quenelles or they will dissolve. Cover with a sheet of waxed paper and poach gently —never allowing water to exceed 180° F.—until quenelles are firm and float to the top, about 15–20 minutes. Remove carefully with a slotted spoon; drain. Coat with thin glaze of melted red currant jelly (see The Maury Island Farming Co.).

Or, instead of poaching, coat just-formed, uncooked quenelles with beaten egg and cloak with bread crumbs mixed with Parmesan cheese. Sauté in butter and oil until golden.

How to Cook a Virginia Ham

A 12-pound ham will provide the following servings: 500 1-inch diameter party biscuits, or 300 2-inch diameter biscuits, or 30 ample servings for dinner.

When you receive a whole uncooked Virginia ham, it requires no refrigeration. It simply should be hung in its burlap bag until you're ready to prepare it. These hickory-smoked hams frequently develop a mold on them, much like an aging fine cheese. Simply scrub the ham with a stiff brush under hot water before cooking. The mold is harmless and normal. For a juicier ham, you can soak the scrubbed ham submerged in water overnight.

Traditional cooking method: Place ham skin down in a large soup pot and cover with cold water. Raise to a simmer and simmer 20–25 minutes per pound. Add hot water as necessary to keep ham covered. When done, remove ham from pot and skin while still warm. You can then glaze it with brown sugar and cloves, scoring it into diamond shapes, and bake uncovered in a 300° F. oven for 30 minutes.

specialty the Wigwam, and it is smoked and cured for a full year, creating a highly flavorful ham that has gained a national reputation.

Italian prosciutto, a salt-cured ham of intense red color and rich taste, has been altered slightly by Americans. Our native product is sweeter and more tender than the Italian variety, but equally complex and arresting to the taste buds.

Edwards also sells a country-style hickory-smoked ham, cured six months, and delicious Virginia link sausages for breakfast, as well as thick-sliced lean bacon, featured in the Williams-Sonoma catalog.

SMITHFIELD HAMS

Gwaltney of Smithfield, Ltd.
Smithfield, VA 23430

phone orders: yes
804-357-3131
ae/visa/mc

The Smithfield ham—as distinctive, deep brick-red, salty, and full-flavored as it is—is the basis for real Southern cooking. Folded into a small hot biscuit, the Smithfield has served many a garden party. Actually it is simply a Virginia ham that is prepared in the town of Smithfield. These particular hams have been world-famous since Queen Victoria insisted they be shipped to her on a regular basis.

A Smithfield ham begins with a hog that is fed either oil-rich peanuts or acorns in addition to corn. Once chosen and specially fed, the hog is butchered and the ham salted for 35 days. Then it's washed and rubbed with black pepper and spends 21 days "equalizing" as salt penetrates the surface and equalizes throughout the flesh. Then the ham is smoked with red oak or hickory for 5 days and hung to be air-cured a minimum of 6 months. Eighteen months is considered ideal.

Temperature is of no importance in the aging of a ham. The 100° F. Virginia summer days have no effect on hanging hams. If you order one and unwrap it to discover it's covered with mold, think nothing of it. It's normal.

VERMONT COB-SMOKED HAM

Harrington's
Main St.
Richmond, VT 05477

phone orders: yes
802-434-4444
ae/visa/mc/dc

The wet-cure hams are quite different from their Southern cousins, being moist, pale pink, and milder in flavor. For better than a hundred years, the Harringtons have been using this old-fashioned Vermont smoking method, over corncobs and maplewood. In a taste test, the editors of *Cuisine* magazine found this to be the best ham in the country. It is, to our taste, delicious and well worth the money. It comes cooked or uncooked, bone in or out; you can even get it spiral-cut, which makes it a snap to serve at parties. The Harringtons also smoke to good advantage bacon, Canadian bacon, sausage, turkey, and pheasant. They've developed a catalog of other food products to go with the smoked meats.

MAHOGANY-SMOKED MEATS

Meadow Farms Country
  Smokehouse
PO Box 1387
Bishop, CA 93514

phone orders: yes
619-873-5311
visa/mc

Roi Ballard drives high into the Southern California desert mountains for aged mahogany with which to smoke his meats. This dense, exotic wood creates a smoky aroma so intense it permeates the box in which he sends you the ham. The ham is pale, moist, flavorful, and quite distinct in its mahogany smoke flavor. According to *Cuisine's* taste test, Roi Ballard's ham was the only wet-cure ham to buy west of the Mississippi. It is absolutely wonderful. We loved it. His bacon is equally delicious, and the jerky dried over that same intense mahogany smoke is outstanding. Ballard also smokes poultry. If you'll just give him a call, he will send you a virtual snowstorm of information about his products. His first occupation was marketing, and he knows how to get you to buy a pig in a poke. The flavor will bring you back.

How to Carve a Smithfield Ham

These hams are traditionally served cold and sliced paper-thin. Here's the best way to bring out the delicate flavor.

1. Place ham on platter, the flattest side down. Use a long, sharp, thin-bladed knife and make a cut straight down, through to the bone, about an inch away from the joint.

2. Slant the knife slightly for each succeeding cut and slice very thin diagonal slices into your original vertical cut.

3. As the slices become larger, decrease the slant. Eventually, the bone formation will cause you to cut smaller slices at different angles. The main idea is to keep the slices paper-thin, regardless of the shape or size of slice.

APPLEWOOD-SMOKED HAMS, BACON, AND SAUSAGES

Nueske's Hillcrest Farm	phone orders: yes
Meats	1 800-37-BACON (WI)
Rural Rte. #2	1-800-38-BACON (national)
Wittenberg, WI 54499	ae/visa/mc

Jim Nueske is this kind of a guy: When he went to San Francisco on business, he looked in the phone book for other Nueskes and called up the only one he found. Turned out it was his cousin, who remembered swimming in the river back in Wisconsin when he was a kid. So the two Nueskes are reunited and Jim's got his cousin selling hams in San Francisco as a sideline to his first job—selling orthopedic chairs.

The Nueskes are that kind of family. Jim and his brother Robert operate their father's smoking business using the time-honored European method of 24 hours of slow smoking that brings out the best in the fine pork they begin with. Applewood is the origin of the fine, sweet, mysterious flavor you'll find in Nueske hams, bacon, and sausages.

Along with California's mahogany-smoked and one Vermont cob-smoked, these hams were found to be the best in the country in a survey done by *Cuisine*. Moist, lean, sweet, and a deep red color, these pork products are first rate. Never any added fillers, binders, or extenders. The Nueske ham has no water added. Their sausages are just lean, tender meat and natural spices. You can also get a gift pack with good Wisconsin brie and French cherry preserves. Thank goodness these boys stayed in northwoods Wisconsin and didn't run off to the city for some damnfool reason.

CUSTOM PROCESSED MEATS

Roland and Son	phone orders: yes
Box 278	802-476-6066
South Barre, VT 05670	visa/mc

Until recently the Lefebvre family has been making fine cured and smoked meats using old family recipes and traditions, but just for custom orders. Almost by demand —people moved away and wrote back, begging, or out-of-town relatives tried the meats and couldn't get them out of their memory—the Lefebvres have decided to ''go public'' and sell through the mails. The ham we tried was sweet, delicate, aromatic, and had a fine texture with very little fat. It was too good for a ham sandwich and demanded a place of honor on the plate, with maybe just some dark bread and good mustard beside it. They cure their hams with maple syrup before cob-smoking them, but they also use chemical preservatives. Their summer sausage is vinegary sweet and dark as liver. They also smoke cheddar, which goes nicely with the ham. Quite naturally, they will still do custom meat orders. Call and tell them what you want. This is still a very small family operation.

PRIZE-WINNING COUNTRY HAMS

Roy L. Hoffman & Sons   phone orders: yes
RFD 6, Box 5   301-739-2332
Hagerstown, MD 21740   visa/mc

When third-generation butcher Donald Hoffman began entering national competitions for cured hams in 1976, he thought that he ''had the best product in the world.'' But he didn't win. Taking the experts' criticisms seriously, Don began tinkering with the aging, the cure, and the amount of smoke. Now, you can hardly beat him. In contest after contest, he takes the prizes. His ham is sugar-cured and hickory-smoked and melts in your mouth.

He got started in the mail-order business as a result of one of those contests. Merle Ellis had judged the contest and praised Hoffman's hams in his syndicated column ''The Butcher.''

Hoffman began getting letters requesting his catalog. At that time, it didn't even exist. But not being one to miss an opportunity, Hoffman developed one. In addition to his prize-winning country hams, he's developed a sugar-cured, hickory-smoked turkey that is as moist, flavorful, and delicious as any ham—with predictably fewer calories. The turkey breast is white and tender, and if you served it to a blindfolded panel of five, I'll bet a nickel three of them would say it was a ham due to the cure and

Pear Glaze for a Pink Ham

Glaze for a whole ham in 1 hour

3	pounds Seckel pears (field pears)
½	cup water
⅓	cup pear vinegar (or white-wine vinegar)
⅔	cup brown sugar
⅓	cup pear brandy

Peel and core pears and place in medium saucepan with water and vinegar. Cook until soft. Puree mixture, then return to pan and mix with brown sugar. Simmer until reduced and as thick as applesauce. Remove from heat and stir in brandy. Brush mixture generously over a fully cooked ham. Place ham in oven at 350° F., uncovered, and cook and baste until ham acquires a caramel-colored glaze, about 40 minutes.

Erskine Early's Redeye Gravy

Remove just-fried slices of country ham from skillet and pour off about half the grease into a small dish, leaving a couple of tablespoons in the pan. Heat until grease is almost smoking, then add about ¼ cup tap water. (Some people use a little coffee here instead of water.) It will boil and steam furiously while you stir it up with a pan scraper. When this has cooked a minute

CONTINUED ON PAGE 110

CONTINUED FROM PAGE 109

or two, pour it into the grease you previously saved, and presto! Redeye gravy. The gravy is fine "sop" by itself for biscuits, or pour it over the ham.

Omaha Steaks Korean Barbecued Beef

Delicious with a side dish of stir-fried snow pea pods and cashews. Try it with Texmati rice (see index). See Mail-Order Menus for full menu.

Serves 4
20 minutes preparation; 2–3 hours to marinate

- ¼ cup soy sauce
- 3 tablespoons brown sugar
- 2 tablespoons sesame oil
- ¼ teaspoon fresh ground black pepper
- 3 green onions and tops, thinly sliced diagonally
- 3 cloves garlic, pressed
- 1 tablespoon sesame seeds
- 1 pound tenderloin tips, thawed
- 2 tablespoons peanut oil

Mix first seven ingredients, then pour into a shallow dish. Place tenderloin tips in marinade, cover, and let stand 2–3 hours, turning occasionally.

Remove tenderloin tips from marinade and stir-fry quickly in 2 tablespoons hot peanut oil in a wok. Serve on a bed of rice.

the method. It's that good. Hoffman also smokes bacon and pork chops and makes a good summer sausage. His prices are very reasonable for the quality you're getting.

ATTIC HAMS

Burgers' Ozark Country-Cured Hams
Hwy. 87S
California, MO 65018

phone orders: yes
314-796-3134
ae/visa/mc

The Burgers began curing hams for sale during the Depression to augment their farm's earnings. They hung them in the attic, where the combination of cold winter and hot summer heightened the natural aging process and produced the best-quality country-style ham. Now their company cures hundreds of thousands of hams per year, but they still pick out the best 2,000 and attic-hang them. For this connoisseur and devotee of country cured ham, this is nonpareil. Call early and ask them to reserve you one. You'll get the most pronounced aged, country-cured flavor of any country ham on the market. They also sell memorable country-cured bacon at a price that equals the grocery store and tastes so purely pork that you'll never be able to eat grocery store bacon again without tasting the chemicals in it. They also cure and smoke poultry, beef, and sausages. We liked everything they sent us.

TENNESSEE COUNTRY HAM

Early's Honey Stand
Rural Rte. 2
Spring Hill, TN 37174

phone orders: yes
615-486-2230
ae/visa/mc/dc

Despite the name of this business—they sell what they refer to as pure "bee" honey—the long-standing reputation of this company comes from traditional Southern-style smoked hams, bacon, and a pure pork sausage so good it'll make you hit your uncle.

Using their catalog, you can find a lot of down-home products, including sorghum, watermelon pickles, and chowchow. In addition to their hams—which are, I warn you, shot through with salt—they sell some of the best sausage I ever tasted. Packed in an old-fashioned cloth "poke," it's smoked over hickory and is 100 percent pure pork, seasoned with homegrown red pepper, hand-rubbed sage, and natural spices.

MIDWESTERN CORN-FED BEEFSTEAK

Omaha Steaks International   phone orders: yes
PO Box 3300   800-228-2778
Omaha, NE 68103   ae/visa/mc/dc

Anybody who reads food magazines has seen Omaha Steak ads with James Beard's smiling face prominently displayed. When I ordered these steaks, I was mildly skeptical. I seriously doubted the meat could be that good. Guess what? It's that good. These carefully trimmed steaks, top choice and prime grade, are fully flavored, unsullied by any stray flavors to impair your enjoyment. The filets are melt-in-your-mouth good.

And they have other offerings in their catalog that provide not only good taste but in some cases even seem a bargain. Watch for their sales. Just like Harrod's, they sometimes offer filets at half off. Then's when you should go for it. Turning the pages of their catalog is like walking down the aisle in the best butcher shop you can imagine. They offer everything from trays of hors d'oeuvres through beefsteaks and roasts, other red meats, poultry, and fish. They even have cakes.

One of their best values is what they call tenderloin tips. These are 1-pound packages of flavorful beef tenders for use in shish kebabs or stir-fries and are great for Japanese preparations.

CHICAGO STOCKYARDS BEEFSTEAKS

Pfaelzer Brothers   phone orders: yes
16W347 83rd St.   800-621-0226
Burr Ridge, IL 60521   ae/visa/mc/dc

The Pfaelzer brothers began selling meat from the back of a wagon in the 1920s. Then they got their first mail order—a Texas oilman wrote them a letter saying "Send

---

Bourbon Pepper Filet Flambé

The Pfaelzer mini-cookbook they send with every order is so filled with delicious recipes, I wanted to cook every one.

Here's a choice when you are in the mood for a dramatic presentation. Just try not to set the curtains on fire. Or your eyelashes, either. See Mail-Order Menus for full menu.

Serves 2 in 30 minutes

 2   teaspoons whole black peppercorns
 2   6-ounce beef filets
 1   tablespoon sweet butter
 1   tablespoon light oil
      Salt to taste
 ¼   cup bourbon (or brandy)
 ¼   cup beef stock

Coarsely crack peppercorns in mortar and pestle. Press into both sides of filets and set aside for 30 minutes, covered.

In a 12-inch skillet or blazer pan of a chafing dish (this is a super tableside preparation), heat butter and oil. Cook steaks over medium-high heat to desired doneness, turning once with tongs (takes about 12 minutes for medium-rare). Now sprinkle lightly with salt. Pour bourbon over steaks. *Carefully* ignite. Allow flames to subside. Remove steaks to hot platter; keep warm. Add beef stock to skillet. Boil and reduce by half. Pour over steaks and serve.

Roast Chateaubriand with Oregon Blue Cheese, California Almonds, and Green Olives

This is the simplest way I know to cook meat, and in a way that is guaranteed to come out perfect, cooked to order. Certified Prime says a 2-pound Chateaubriand will serve four, but it will also provide a good lunch for two the next day with the leftovers, or a meal for six to begin with. Don't cut it in half, though. Cook it all of a piece. See Mail-Order Menus for full menu.

Serves 4 in 1 hour

1	2-pound Chateaubriand (beef filet)
1	tablespoon olive oil
	Freshly milled black pepper
1	tablespoon sweet butter
½	cup whole California almonds
¼	cup chopped shallots
¼	cup dry sherry
¼	cup crumbled blue cheese
¼	cup pimiento-stuffed green olives
¼	cup heavy cream

Rub filet with oil, then pepper generously. Place in a rack inside a roasting pan. Cover and set aside for 30 minutes. Preheat oven to 500° F. Place pan in oven. Bake 5 minutes at 500° F.

CONTINUED ON PAGE 113

T-bones"—and it occurred to them that people outside the cobbled streets of Chicago might like a decent steak now and then.

Even though the company is now owned by Armour, they still do business as if they were just a little butcher shop. You get good service and a dazzling array of products, from steaks to roasts, pork, veal, and poultry, both cooked and uncooked. They offer such a complete selection that you could assemble an entire dinner from their catalog, from hors d'oeuvre to dessert. The only place their size really shows is in their choice of desserts. Some are made by huge commercial bakers and are little better than what you'd find at the grocery store. Maybe they figure once you've eaten a good steak and lobster dinner, you won't care. Trust me on this, Pfaelzer: We care.

CERTIFIED PRIME BEEF AND LAMB

Certified Prime	phone orders: yes
4538 S. Marshfield Ave.	800-257-2977
Chicago, IL 60609	312-376-7445 (IL)
	ae/visa/mc

Four years ago when Martin Bergerson asked himself how he could compete with the big boys, he came up with one idea: meat that he would certify was *prime*. Other mail-order butchers buy and sell *top choice* as well as *prime*, and the customer can never be sure what he's getting. But Martin Bergerson has the USDA certify every box he sells. You have the federal government stamp on every order. Prime is not just some word tossed loosely about. It is the top grading for meats, as determined by federal inspectors, and only applies to beef and lamb.

That is why this company restricts its products to these two items. No big, complete catalog here. Just meat as good as it gets, sent out to you by one of the four or five employees of this little maverick in with the big bulls. Filets, strips, rib eyes, top sirloin, Chateaubriand, Frenched lamb chops, and loin lamb chops. That's all. But, I will say, all perfect. The Chateaubriand is trimmed of fat so that you get a perfect, lean piece of dark red meat, tender and tasty as it can get.

ANTIBIOTIC-FREE LEAN BEEF

Curling Iron Beef Co. phone orders: yes
PO Box 40416   303-242-1206
Grand Junction, CO 81504 visa/mc

The beefsteak you choose from the neighborhood super-market comes from an animal that was fed in a feedlot for about 150 days. The feeds may contain steroids for mus-cle growth, antibiotics for animal health, and hormones to speed weight gain. This animal is then rushed to the slaughterhouse, where it is hit in the head, cut up, and rushed to the supermarket within three days. That is mod-ern, commercial-type meat packing: efficient, economical, and iffy.

Old-fashioned beef was handled differently. It was raised on grass. After butchering, it was hung at least two weeks to age, and it came out a dark red, lean product. Much of its reputation for toughness came not from the meat itself, but from the cooking practices of the day.

The Curling Iron Beef Co. is now bringing beef to the consumer that's the best combination of the two systems. Hand-picking animals, they feed them from 90 to 100 days in a feedlot, carefully choosing feeds to eliminate the steroids, hormones, and tetracyclines so commonly used in commercial operations. They age the beef at least 14 days before cutting it. What you get is lean, tender beef that's USDA *good* classification and good for you. With-out the middleman, buying from Roger Heintz at Curling Iron is like having a rancher friend you can call up and order from. Roger raises the cattle, feeds them, oversees their aging and cutting. This is the meat purveyor of choice for those who wish to avoid the "improvements" of the modern age in meat packing. The only modern thing here is the styrene cooler and dry ice that surrounds your frozen beef. The contents are old-fashioned cowboy beefsteaks.

FISH AND SHELLFISH

There is nothing to match the excitement of awaiting that Federal Express guaranteed before-noon delivery of live shellfish. Now it is possible to enjoy not only shellfish

CONTINUED FROM PAGE 112

Reduce temperature to 450° and continue to roast until cooked to suit. You can place a meat ther-mometer in the meat and check it until it reads 125° F. for medi-um-rare. Or, after 15 minutes, you can check the meat every 5 minutes by cutting into it. This will take in the neighborhood of half an hour total cooking time. Remove roast from oven and let stand 10 minutes before cutting it into thick slices. Fan slices onto a serving plate, pour sauce down the middle, and serve at once.

While meat is roasting, make sauce in a 6-inch skillet. Heat butter and brown the almonds. Then add shallots and cook until clear. Add sherry and boil down to 2 tablespoons. Add blue cheese. Cook a minute as cheese melts. Add drained ol-ives and cut with cream. Taste and adjust seasonings. It will taste extremely salty. Don't worry. When you combine the sauce with the utter sweet good-ness of Chateaubriand, the fla-vor marriage is such that people around the table may seem, for the moment, to lose their ability to carry on a sensible conversa-tion.

but also every single regional seafood specialty—regardless of where you live—thanks to the fast shippers. In many cases, by ordering direct you are getting fish fresher than you could buy even from a retail fish market in your neighborhood, because you have cut out the middleman and are buying directly off the docks. Lobsters, clams, crabs, mussels, prawns, crawfish, scallops—all can be shipped to you live from their home waters . . . even if the waters are as distant as Malaysia. Isn't the world shrinking?

I have grouped these listings thusly: First are the specialty shellfish shippers who bring you their own regional specialties, such as New England lobsters and steamer clams, Florida stone crab claws, live Texas crawfish, Malaysian tiger prawns, New Zealand green-lipped mussels. Next come the caviars: American, Russian, and Iranian. Then I've listed three reliable general fish markets representing the Atlantic, Pacific, and Gulf of Mexico. The final listings are several good fish smokers.

CLAMBAKE IN YOUR KITCHEN

The Clambake Co.   phone orders: yes
PO Box 1677   617-255-3289
Orleans, MA 02653   visa/mc

If you were to hold a clambake on the beach at Cape Cod, you'd get up real early, head for the sand, dig a pit, line it with stones, build a furious fire that you'd feed and tend for three or four hours until it burned down to glowing coals, then you'd line the hot rocks with a specially gathered seaweed known as rockweed. Now you'd begin putting in the food. For each person: a live 1¼-pound chicken lobster; 10 small live steamer clams; 3 or 4 live blue mussels; a 3-ounce portion of codfish seasoned with dill and wrapped in poaching paper; an ear of corn; a piece of sweet Italian sausage; a quarter of a large Spanish onion; 2 to 3 red Bliss potatoes. Over all this you'd pour a couple of cups of beer or white wine, cover, and let it steam. The only other things you'd need to complete this meal are good bread and butter, plenty of beer and white wine to drink, and watermelon for dessert.

Can't wait for your next trip to New England? You can order exactly what I told you. It comes in a can and is shipped to you overnight air so that once you get it, the lobster, clams, and mussels are still alive and kicking. Remove the top, pour in your choice of liquid, cover it, put it on your stove, and in 25–35 minutes you've got your own clambake.

The Clambake Company began three years ago to serve the summer tourists on Cape Cod who wanted to try a clambake but didn't quite know how to get it all together. After people in New York began calling and asking them to put the cans on the bus (they just couldn't get the whole dazzling experience out of their heads), the mail-order business began. The cans come in four sizes: single serving, 2–3 people, 4–5 people, and 6–10 people. Call them up, tell them how many you want to feed, and they'll send it out. As we go to press it costs an astonishing $16 per person plus shipping, which becomes proportionately smaller the more you order.

LIVE LOBSTER AT YOUR DOORSTEP

Marblehead Lobster Co.	phone orders: yes
Beacon and Orne Sts.	617-631-0787
Marblehead, MA 01945	visa/mc

The day we had the lobster dinner, the anticipation was greater than Christmas for a kid. I had invited people over, I had set the table, now all I had to do was pray the lobsters got here, live and on time. With just 10 minutes to spare—11:50 A.M., to be exact—the UPS man knocked on the door and there they were, resting in their styrofoam, sleepy from the dry ice, but alive and kicking: four Maine lobsters, 4 pounds of live, fresh steamer clams. I soaked the clams in cold saltwater for the day to encourage them to spit out that Atlantic beach sand. I dropped the lobsters in boiling water. Melted some butter and squeezed a lemon. Made a salad, bought a loaf of bread and a good dessert. It was one of the easiest dinner parties I ever had in my whole life, and at about half the cost of taking the same number of people to a good restaurant for the same menu. We all agreed. It was the best lobster we ever ate.

Hugh Bishop and Brenda Booma, who own this young company, handle a complete line of lobsters and fresh seafood native to New England and will deliver anything you want from the North Atlantic: crab, sea scallops, swordfish in season, cherrystones, steamers, oysters, and mussels. Call them up and see what's in. Tell them what you want and on what day. Then call up the guests. This is more fun than anything.

ATLANTIC OYSTERS

The Cotuit Oyster Co.　　　phone orders: yes
PO Box 563　　　　　　　617-428-6747
Cotuit, MA 02635

For big, briny live oysters, call Cape Cod's premier small oyster farm, Cotuit. Fall and winter are the best times of the year to get these; they're dredged from the carefully tended beds and sent in the shell via UPS, usually 60 at a time, in an insulated gift box. All you need once you get them is a tool with which to open them. If you don't have an oyster knife, try a pocket knife. Hold the oyster in the flat of your hand in a towel, and run the knife up against the inside shell. It will soon turn loose. (If you're lucky.) Remember to sip the nectar that remains after you've eaten this fresh, delicious morsel. Old oystermen will tell you that's the best part.

FRESH SMOKED OYSTERS

Ekone Oyster Co.　　　　phone orders: no
Box 465　　　　　　　　206-875-5494
South Bend, WA 98586

Nick Jambor grows, fresh-smokes, and ships these Pacific oysters all over the nation from his 20-acre oyster farm. Along with his wife, Joanne Salley, he raises the shellfish in Willapa Bay, now believed to be one of the cleanest in the country. He first grows the oyster larvae to the swimming stage, then puts them into a tank with recycled oyster shells, to which the larvae attach themselves. Nick and Joanne then thread the shells about 6 inches apart onto long strings, which they transport by boat to the tideflats. There the strings are suspended while the oysters grow in their borrowed shells to delectable maturity.

Joanne and Nick sell some of their oysters raw, but they save the best for smoking. These are steamed, shucked, and put first into a salt brine, then brown sugar and spices. They're alder-smoked about five hours. The Jambors also smoke other Pacific fishes. Call them and see what's in the smoker today.

TEXAS FARM CRAWFISH

Texas Crawfish Farms   phone orders: yes
PO Box 2735   409-883-8244 or
Orange, TX 77631   409-768-1654

minimum order: 50 pounds

With the growing national appeal of Cajun food, it stands to reason that the good old boys would soon start farming for crawfish. Dan Harris and Joe Heinen are doing just that right outside of Orange, Texas, and they'll send you live crawfish in a chilly bath, anytime during the season from November to June. These little freshwater lobsters have a considerably lighter tab than their seafaring cousins. The day I called, the price was $1.20 a pound f.o.b. Houston. Dan says that with the usual overnight airfreight shipping, the total bill usually is in the neighborhood of $2 a pound, delivered to your door.

These crawfish farmers primarily service restaurants, as far away as Manhattan and Los Angeles, but they'll gladly ship to an individual. Only hitch is they have a 50-pound minimum. Since, as Dan says, crawfish are just for fun, the thing to do is arrange to have a crawfish boil in your backyard. Invite up to 30 or 40 people, get a keg of beer, make some potato salad and baked beans, spread the picnic tables with layers of newspaper. Boil the crawfish and show people how to suck out that succulent bite of freshwater lobster. Then let the good times roll. What a party. (See Mail-Order Menus for complete menu.)

Floridians have long considered stone crab claws to be the pride of Florida cuisine and too good to be shared with outsiders.

The shells are heavy. Ten pounds will only serve 10 people as an hors d'oeuvre or six for an entrée.

Chef Allen's Original Mustard Sauce

Makes 2½ cups, enough sauce for 10 pounds crabmeat

2 tablespoons Dijon mustard
½ teaspoon dry English mustard
1 pint good mayonnaise
2 tablespoons Worcestershire sauce
   Juice of half a lemon
2 tablespoons heavy cream
   Salt and freshly milled black pepper to taste

Whisk together mustards, mayonnaise, and Worcestershire sauce. Add lemon juice and blend until smooth. Slowly add cream. Whisk and adjust seasonings with salt and pepper. Refrigerate covered until ready to use. Keeps one week, refrigerated.

Shrimp Stuffed with Stone Crabmeat

Season cooked stone crabmeat with salt and black pepper and add just enough mayonnaise or

CONTINUED ON PAGE 119

FRESH STONE CRAB CLAWS FROM FLORIDA

Chef Allen, Inc.	phone orders: yes
20145-12 N.E. 3rd Court	1-800-327-8456 (USA)
Miami, FL 33179	1-800-432-2382 (FL)
	visa/mc
	season: Oct. 15–May 15

Through this embarrassment of riches, receiving foods from the UPS man on a daily basis, I am able to maintain my composure—mostly. Except when it comes to shellfish. Especially stone crab claws: heavy, perfumed, fully cooked, cold, glistening shrimp-pink with freckles, and black claws that look like a toucan in repose when you hold them up. And to top it off, fresh, fresh, fresh. Better than anything in the store. I get them sooner than the fanciest fishmonger on the West Coast.

You can't even imagine how good this crabmeat is. In the first place, the claws are a good 6 to 8 inches long, bigger than any I ever saw, and the meat is rich, sweet, and firm in texture. Chef Allen sends you a mallet to crack their thick porcelain shells, as well as yellow muslin scalloped doilies and green satin ribbon so that you can tie each claw up into a posy-from-the-sea before you serve it. Recipes are included. I'm telling you: if you want to just knock somebody out, send them these crab claws.

GOLDEN GULF CRAB

Golden Gulf	phone orders: yes
120 Virginia St.	205-433-3223
Mobile, AL 36601	

From very deep warm waters in the Gulf of Mexico comes this new kind of crab, the *Geryon Fenneri*—known to cooks as the Golden Gulf crab because it keeps its golden color when cooked.

The crab comes dressed, in lumps in 8- and 16-ounce plastic containers at about $10 a pound. They're also selling claws, Great Pearls (jumbo lump meat) and Golden Nuggets (leg meat) as well as the glorious whole crabs. This sweet, succulent crab comes fully cooked and requires nothing more than a little high-quality mayonnaise to make it complete.

GREEN-LIPPED MUSSELS

Fisher Brothers Fishery phone orders: yes
PO Box 965 414-435-4633
Green Bay, WI 54305 visa/mc

No, they don't grow green-lipped mussels in Green Bay. But this enormous general fish company, which normally ships everything from Alaskan snow crab to small pike and lake trout, is now sending New Zealand's own fancy mussels to customers. Four to five inches plump, the mussels are pink or cream-colored, and they do have vivid lime green lips on a black and orange shell. The pink-fleshed ones are female, the cream ones are male. They are grown on a string, much like Jambor's oysters, and as a result are free of sand and grit. These are mild-flavored, soft-textured mussels that lend themselves well to sauced preparations. Jane Hibler, Portland cookbook author and expert fish cook, recommends spooning sauces of cream, butter, and Parmesan over the just-opened mussels, then broiling them just until the cheese melts. Delicious. These are so good, the simpler the presentation, the better.

They come live in a 22-pound box, chilled and iced down. Don't let them freeze—it kills them—and don't let them get too warm. They'll keep in this chilled state about 10 days from harvest. If you see one open, run fresh warm water over it and see if it doesn't slam shut. If it remains gaping, it's dead. Throw it out. If you don't live near a decent fishmonger, be sure to ask Fisher Brothers to send you their price list. They sell absolutely everything frozen in the general fish line. They can be your mail-order fishmonger.

CONTINUED FROM PAGE 118

mustard sauce to hold crabmeat together. Use extra-large uncooked shrimp. Peel shrimp, leaving last section of outer coating and tail intact. Wash thoroughly. Starting at back, cut almost through shrimp lengthwise. Pack crabmeat mixture into shrimp, fold over, and wrap with ½ strip bacon. Secure with toothpicks. Broil until bacon is golden brown on all sides.

Shirley Barr's Golden Crabmeat Quiche

I never knew a real man who didn't ask for seconds on this one.

Serves 6 in 1½ hours

3 eggs, slightly beaten
1 cup sour cream
½ teaspoon Worcestershire sauce
1 medium onion, sliced paper-thin
3 tablespoons butter
1 cup (¼ pound) shredded Swiss cheese
½ pound fresh lump crabmeat
1 9-inch half-baked pastry shell
Salt and pepper
Italian parsley leaves

Preheat oven to 300° F. Combine eggs, sour cream, and Worcestershire sauce and set aside. Sauté onion in butter. Stir in cheese, crabmeat, and egg

CONTINUED ON PAGE 120

CONTINUED FROM PAGE 119

mixture. Pour into baked pastry shell. Lightly salt and pepper. Bake 55–60 minutes or until custard is set and a silver knife inserted in the center comes out clean. Serve hot. Can also be made into party-sized tarts. Garnish with sprigs of fresh Italian parsley. Good hot or room temperature.

WEST AUSTRALIAN LOBSTER TAILS

Australian Seafood Producers
11777 San Vicente Blvd., Ste. 500
Los Angeles, CA 90049

phone orders: yes
213-820-8150
visa/mc

As long as we're down under, we may as well include the large, succulent, firm, sweet lobster tails that are scooped from the cold waters south of Australia. These are harvested from the sea, then flash-frozen right on the boat. Each weighs from 8 to 10 ounces and is a feast. They'll also throw in a dozen jumbo shrimp, and lobster recipes besides. As we go to press they're working on a lobster/scallop/shrimp Australian Seafood Mix sauced with velouté that comes in a boil-in-a-bag, which you can simply snip open and pour over fresh pasta. Not even priced yet, but playing to good reviews. Ask about it.

MALAYSIAN TIGER PRAWNS

See also: Gordon-Thompson, Ltd.

These giant shrimp, which come four to the pound, are popular in Los Angeles and are moving East, enchanting all who try them. Gordon-Thompson is the man who brings them in through the Los Angeles Port still alive and ships them to customers within 12 hours of clearing customs.

When you get them, the tail tells the tale about freshness. It should be a steel blue or gray. If it has turned black, the prawn is too old. Send it back. Once you cook them, you'll be delighted to see the shell turn a gorgeous sienna orange color. These are so dramatic, I'd suggest presenting one of these quarter-pound dazzlers still in the shell, on a serving of fresh pasta with a light cream sauce, accompanied by nothing more than hearts of romaine with a vinaigrette and a crisp white wine to drink. The inherent dramatic look of this creature demands a spotlight presentation.

FRESH-TO-YOUR-DOOR FLORIDA SEAFOOD

Triple M Seafood/Filet Express
2821 E. Atlantic Blvd.
Pompano Beach, FL 33062

phone orders: yes
800-722-0073 (national)
800-323-0073 (FL)
ae/visa/mc

Here is a perfect example of how the home cook is benefiting from the demands of fine restaurants. When Triple M landed a contract to provide the Steak and Ale chain with fresh seafood, to be shipped out daily in small lots to each of their locations, they also landed for themselves a very favorable contract with Federal Express, so that air-shipping from their door to yours is ridiculously reasonable.

This means that on any day before 2 P.M. you can call them on their 800 number; they'll tell you what they hauled in with their own fleet of fishing boats; and before noon the next day you'll have fresh fish, custom-packed for you: portions, loins, filets, or whole fish. They'll send any amount you want. They'll send anything they've got. The Florida choices are delectable. And what is especially rare in this exotic food trade: They try really hard to keep their prices competitive with local markets.

The array includes stone crabs, swordfish, redfish, tuna (they're the largest purveyor of fresh tuna in America), snapper, grouper, pompano, salmon, clams, and oysters. They also have more exotic species like conch as well as a good selection of frozen fish. They will answer any questions you have about preparation and have a file full of recipes they'll send out with your order, on request. If you want sushi, this is a good source of impeccably fresh, just-caught fish for that.

NORTH ATLANTIC SEAFOODS

Legal Seafoods Market
237 Hampshire St.
Cambridge, MA 02139

phone orders: yes
800-343-5804 (national)
617-864-3400 (MA)
ae/visa/mc/dc

Keys Conch Chowder

The conch is the East Coast cousin to abalone, a tropical marine gastropod. You may have seen its brightly colored pink spiral shell for sale in tourist shops. This is also a popular shell for use in cameo carving. The meat of the conch is sweet and delicate, although, like the abalone, it requires pounding to make it tender. The bird pepper is a tiny, hot-as-the-devil pepper found in Florida. If you ever got one of those Christmas pepper plants for decoration, that's a bird pepper. You can substitute a small amount of other hot red peppers.

Serves 6 in 1½ hours

1	pound conch meat
2	large onions, chopped
3	garlic cloves, mashed
1	green pepper, seeded and chopped
8	ounces tomato sauce
6	ounces tomato paste
3	medium potatoes, diced
1	tablespoon dried oregano
½	tablespoon salt
⅛	teaspoon pepper

CONTINUED ON PAGE 122

CONTINUED FROM PAGE 121

1 bird pepper, minced
Sherry

Put conch through a food grinder, using coarse blade, or pound with mallet and cut into very small pieces. Cover with water and simmer 30 minutes. Add onions, garlic, green pepper, tomato sauce and paste, potatoes, and 3 more cups water. Add oregano, salt, pepper, and bird pepper. Simmer until potatoes are tender, about 30 minutes. Add a dash of sherry to each serving.

Here's the market made famous by Julia Child, who not only shops here with regularity but says so. An enormously busy mail-order firm, they've been sending out the provender of the cold North Atlantic for years. Prime soft-shell crabs, scrod, Cape Cod scallops, clams, blue mussels, monkfish, swordfish, their list is long. Call and ask for what you want. Not only do they have local seafood but they also try to carry fish from all over the world. They have a motto about their freshness: "If it ain't fresh, it ain't Legal."

PACIFIC FISHES

Pure Food Fish Market   phone orders: yes
1511 Pike Place Market   206-622-5765
Seattle, WA 98101   visa/mc

Jeff Amon's motto is, "Let us do the fishing for you." And his market in the famed Pike Place backs right up to the water. Here's where you can get that whole salmon, or a live geoduck clam, Willapa Bay oysters, Dungeness crabs, and various other West Coast fishes—some from as far away as Alaska.

Pike Place has catered to tourists a long time and began shipping fresh fish back home for them. It is sometimes a good idea to bark a little to get Jeff Amon's attention. He'll want to know you're not just some tourist he'll never hear from again. Let him know you want him to pick the best thing in the case for you. With a little prodding, he'll really go all-out.

CUSTOM CANNED SEAFOOD

Hegg & Hegg   phone orders: yes
801 Marine Dr.   206-457-3344
Port Angeles, WA 98362   ae/visa/mc/cb

Fred Hegg smokes salmon, tuna, sturgeon, shad, oysters, crab, clams, and shrimp. His smoking method derives from the Northwest Indian formula using alder and creates a dry and flavorful product. He's been mail-ordering these fish for 26 years to customers who just keep coming back. His reputation is sterling.

GIFT-PACKED SMOKED SALMON

Specialty Seafoods
1719 13th St.
Anacortes, WA 98221

phone orders: yes
206-293-0611
ae/visa/mc/dc

If you want to give smoked salmon or smoked oysters for a present, call up these people. We have found their products to be tasty, and they're foil vacuum-packed in a good-looking brown box with great-looking calligraphy. They have a good catalog of Northwest specialties, too. Write for it.

FRESH PICKLED AND SMOKED PACIFIC FISHES

Josephson's Smokehouse
    and Dock
PO Box 412
Astoria, OR 97103

phone orders: yes
800-772-3474 (national)
800-828-3474 (OR)
    visa/mc

Michael and Linda Josephson are third-generation owners of a dockside fish company that offers not only smoked fish but fresh Pacific fish as well. They made their national reputation, however, with their Grandfather Anton's recipe for traditional smoked salmon, which is firm, with a deep brown-orange skin and pale shell-pink meat inside. This is a rich, complex, irresistible flavor that comes either vacuum-packed from 1- to 10-pound pieces in plastic, or in a can. They also cold-smoke lox, and this produces a soft rosy-colored but saltier product, sort of like a ham. Salmon jerky, sometimes known as squaw candy, is hard stuff to chew but has a kind of smoky-sweet flavor and is popular with kids.

The Josephsons will ship fresh West Coast specialties: whole coho or Chinook salmon, salmon steaks, halibut, sturgeon, lingcod, Pacific snapper, albacore tuna, petrale, English sole, and mouth-watering razor clams in season.

These people are reliable. Call them. You can trust them.

TENNESSEE OAK-SMOKED SALMON

Captain's Pride
PO Box 231
Bellingham, WA 98227

phone orders: yes
206-676-0930
ae/visa/mc/dc

Jerry Davis looks like a cowboy, is a licensed fisherman, and likes to talk about the necessity for sharp knives in his business. The day I spoke with him, at a food show, he'd had such a crush of tasters, he'd gotten excited and shaved off the top of his knuckle. But never mind. Every business has its perils. Jerry Davis has perfected a smoking technique that is unusual in the Pacific Northwest. He ships Tennessee oak clear to Washington State to smoke his salmon because oak doesn't have the creosote smoke that is typical of Northwest hardwoods. The result is a fine, delicate, moist salmon taste. Jerry also has a good salmon pâté, a smoked cheese, and cooked crabs that he'll airfreight to you. He has pretty well mastered the fast shipping problems and can send good fresh fish products anywhere you want them quickly.

MEDITERRANEAN-STYLE SMOKED SALMON

Circle K Enterprises
4396 Enterprise Pl., Ste. D
Fremont, CA 94539

phone orders: yes
415-794-7453
ae/visa/mc/dc

This brand-new business uses an ancient technique for smoking salmon that combines fruitwoods mixed with hickory. The result is a moist, slightly sweet, smoky salmon flavor that is vastly superior to the sometimes dry Indian-style smoked salmon that's so popular on the West Coast. Mark and Jeanne Kostic say salmon is their only product and one they produce by hand, carefully, without chemicals or artificial preservatives. It keeps well and is nice to have on hand for impromptu parties.

SMOKED CATFISH

Pickwick Catfish Farm   phone orders: yes
Hwy. 57   901-689-3805
Counce, TN 38326

Betty and Quentin Knussmann raise catfish in a pond. When the fish get to be about a pound, the Knussmanns catch them and smoke them in a homemade smoker. Because they're thoroughly smoked, they don't really even need refrigeration. They're sent out through the regular mail; no shipments in the summer.

When we got ours—two fish wrapped in a plastic bag, pepper-hot, moist, and smoky with creamy chunks of mild, fine catfish—we intended to be circumspect about them and try one of Betty's recipes. But we were so taken with the taste we nearly ate the fish all in one sitting. I swear, I had to hide the second fish. The prices are more than reasonable, and this old Southern standby is a treat.

Betty Knussmann's Chopped Catfish

Serves 4 in 10 minutes

1   smoked catfish, deboned
1   medium red onion, finely chopped
    Best-quality mayonnaise
    Salt and pepper
    Squeeze of fresh lemon juice

Combine catfish and onion in bowl. Moisten with mayonnaise, season to taste with salt and pepper and a squeeze of fresh lemon juice. Chill. Serve on lettuce leaf with crackers.

THE QUEEN OF SMOKE

Kohn's Smokehouse   phone orders: yes
Rte. 131, Box 160   207-372-8412
Thomaston, ME 04861   visa/mc

Living on the central coast of Maine, where real estate prices still languish at 1950s rates and life in the slow lane implies more pressure than there is, Ute and Dietrich Kohn operate a smokehouse based on the principles they learned in their native Germany. They offer completely naturally smoked products at prices that will remind you of nickel ice cream cones. They will ship, postpaid in pine boxes, a chicken hand-rubbed with herbs and spices, then smoked until moist and tender. That's $13.50. A 5-pound salami of pork and beef, smoked three weeks to hold its flavor for months, is only $31. Call for quotes on smoked eel, salmon, herring, Gouda, bacon, ham, or beef. But for a real surprise, order a rosy red-brown Maine lobster, smoked in the shell. As Ute says, an utterly delicious gift. The price: $18.50. How's that for a Christmas gift?

The roes most commonly eaten are lumpfish, salmon, sturgeon, gray mullet, and cod. The most precious caviar comes from the giant Beluga sturgeon, which may be 14 feet long and weigh a ton. Beluga roe is the largest of the sturgeon family and is slate gray to black in color. The caviar berry should be firm, not sticky, and fresh-tasting. American caviar roe is mostly Sevruga grade and is smaller than the Beluga berry. Keta salmon caviar is made from Alaskan chum salmon and is a medium to large orange egg of superior taste. Golden whitefish caviar comes from the whitefish of the Great Lakes of North America. Black lumpfish caviar comes from the cold, clear North Atlantic waters surrounding Iceland. This roe is dyed red or black to look like sturgeon or salmon roe and is the least expensive caviar on the market.

CAVIARS

Caviar isn't a food. Caviar is a dream. A dream of power, romance, and exotic locales. So it may come as news to you, as it did to me, to learn that at the turn of the century 150,000 pounds of United States caviar were produced annually, mostly for export to Europe. About that time, American caviar was so abundant it was served free with a 5-cent glass of beer. *Albany beef* is what they called it, and at one time they even passed a city ordinance that one was not to serve sturgeon or its eggs to one's servants more than three times a week.

I learned all this from Mr. H. Hansen-Sturm, fifth-generation American caviar purveyor. According to Hansen-Sturm, most American caviar came from the Hudson and Chesapeake estuaries, but around the turn of the century overfishing nearly ended the existence of East Coast Atlantic sturgeon and Pacific Coast White Beluga sturgeon.

His family then turned to buying Russian and Iranian caviar for import back to the United States, but when the political situation got really rocky, along about 1976, Hansen-Sturm and others began to rejuvenate the American caviar trade.

Now you can get Sevugra-grade American caviar at about half the cost of imported ones. In this brief decade the American caviar makers have upped the production, until 45 metric tons were produced in the United States in 1982. That's a lot of fish eggs.

SPECIALISTS FOR AMERICAN CAVIAR

Hansen Caviar Co.　　　　phone orders: yes
391-A Grand Ave.　　　　201-568-9653
Englewood, NJ 07631　　　visa/mc

Long a wholesaler in the caviar trade, Hansen-Sturm has just begun a mail-order service to consumers. Perhaps the best introduction to caviar comes from his gift taster, which provides 1-ounce jars of Caspian Beluga, American sturgeon, American keta salmon, and Canadian Golden whitefish, all prepared with pure salt. You can taste and see what you like, then call and order your favorite. Hansen also imports sides of Scotch smoked rainbow trout and salmon. The fish are smoked in Scotland and have never been frozen.

THE CAVIAR SUPERMARKET

Caviarteria, Inc.
29 E. 60th St.
New York, NY 10022

phone orders: yes
800-221-1020 (national)
212-759-7410 (NY)
ae/visa/mc/dc

Louis Sobol sells everything from domestic and imported caviars, to caviar cruises and even a vintage car or two from his New York emporium.

Here's where you can get fresh broken-grain Caspian caviar—mild, perishable, and a bargain because the berries aren't perfect. Also Swedish gravlax (dill-marinated salmon), smoked eel, and smoked salmon. All this in addition to caviars that begin with Russian Imperial at about $400 a pound, Beluga Prime at about $300, down to the bottom of the barrel where the weight of the caviar has broken the berries and you get them at a bargain rate—a mere $120 a pound. Remember, too, that caviar pounds are only 14 ounces. They also sell a full range of American caviars, all at less than $100 a pound, and fresh foie gras, both American and French. (Skip the French; it's been sterilized, pasteurized, and cooked way past its rare perfection.) They also sell fresh Italian truffles in season, both black and white, at about $250 a pound.

They have a caviar sampler for around $30 that includes 1-ounce jars of Caspian Kamchatka and American sturgeon, and 2-ounce jars of Alaskan salmon and American golden caviar made from freshwater whitefish. About those cars . . . Louis Sobol even wants to sell his old MGA and his Bentley. Good grief!

Roasted New Potatoes with Sour Cream and Caviar

Serves 6 in 1 hour

12 small new red potatoes
Rock salt
Salt and pepper
1 tablespoon minced fresh parsley
½ cup sour cream
Oil for deep frying
8 tablespoons American caviar

Preheat oven to 450° F. Arrange potatoes on a bed of rock salt in an ovenproof baking dish (the salt draws out moisture, making the potatoes flakier). Bake until tender, about 30–35 minutes. Remove from oven, cut potatoes in half, and scoop out flesh into a bowl. Reserve skins. Mash pulp, season to taste with salt and pepper, and mix in parsley and half the sour cream. Set aside.

Bring oil to 375° F. in deep-fat fryer or wok. Drop in potato skins and fry until golden and crisp (5 minutes). Drain. Fill skins with mashed potato mixture. Top each with a dollop of sour cream and a teaspoon or more of caviar. Serve on a bed of hot rock salt if desired.

CHINESE CAVIAR

See also: California Sunshine Fine Foods.

California Sunshine imports Keluga sturgeon caviar from Manchuria. The Keluga sturgeon (Huso Dauricus) is perhaps the largest, some weighing a ton and producing up to 500 pounds of roe each. The roe is processed immediately on floating factory ships, then is sent by riverboat, four-wheel-drive trucks, trains, and airplanes—under constant 26° F. refrigeration—to California, where it is sold fresh under the Tsar Nicoulai brand by California Sunshine.

ESCARGOTS

This is your exclusive source for fresh California escargot, canned in the United States.

SO MUCH FOR THE SNAIL'S PACE

Enfant Riant
PO Box 357
Petaluma, CA 94953

phone orders: yes
800-453-5500
Bon Vivant
visa/mc

When journalist Tracy Brash went out to do a story on a snail ranch in Santa Rosa, he found the rancher had moved to Texas. The only thing he left behind was a book on raising snails. Soon gourmand Tracy was raising snails at his Tiburon home. "It beats stamping on them," he says. And then his old buddy from grade school, Mike Beyries, came to visit from L.A. He'd been working the clubs as a stand-up comic. "Stay! Sit! Play dead!" he'd say to the snail on his finger. The two started fantasizing about snails. When the sun came up and they were still at it, they shifted gears and began serious research.

Now, some two years and tons of snails later, these two are up to their keisters in snails. They buy them by the ton from farmers who call the snails pests. They feed them a mixture of soymeal, bran flakes, and trace minerals. After purifying them, they pack the snails in pure water instead of brine or broth as the Europeans do. This means they're not preflavored. You'll also find them tender, because they're not frozen before canning, which is what gives the imported products their rubber-band texture. When you buy a 7½-ounce can of three dozen escargots, you'll get a mini-cookbook, too.

They'll also sell you live snails. I just hope you don't have the same experience my friend did. Her Italian mother-in-law, a real dragon, came over from the old country for a visit dressed all in black, with her hair oiled down flat and her sensible shoes. Flaring her nostrils and breathing heavily, she heaved great pots of tomato sauce onto the stove as she looked this bride in the eye and said she was afraid her son would starve. She was hauling out the Italian recipes, and grating cheese, and planting basil in every pot she could find. Lord, she only had two weeks! On the last day, she bullied this poor girl into purchasing a large number of live snails from the bin at Antone's in Houston. She gave the quivering Southern belle a recipe for escargots, then hurled herself up the steps for the plane back to Rome. After a nice long nap, my friend arose, went to the icebox for a beer, opened the door, peered in, and guess what? The little gray ghosts had slithered out of the sack and had crawled up the walls. All over. Silently, silently. I think that girl ran straight for the string of divorce lawyers who used to hang out down by the courthouse. She knew she was licked.

Escargots Mendocino

For a splendid first course, try these small California snails (that's what Petit Gris means) just simmered in a good wine sauce.

Serves 6 in 30 minutes

3	large shallots
1	cup California Pinot Noir
1	cup beef stock
1	tablespoon flour
1	tablespoon butter
	Salt and pepper
36	Petit Gris escargots

Dice shallots and simmer in wine until reduced by half. Add stock and simmer 5 minutes. Combine flour and butter, then add to sauce to thicken. Stir until smooth. Adjust with salt and pepper. Rinse and drain escargots and add them to the sauce. Simmer 10 minutes. Serve at once with remaining Pinot and a loaf of hot sourdough French bread.

CHAPTER 4

CONDIMENTS

One secret of good cooking resides in the mysterious blending of spices and herbs that sauce the food. Culinary academies teach budding chefs how to season, how to sauce. Lucky daughters learn from old-country mothers the curious combinations of certain ethnic cuisines. These subtle tricks mean that particular foods sometimes seem unreproducible to the unenlightened cook. But in searching out the condiments for this chapter, I found some of the most innovative preparations imaginable available to the home cook.

I have divided the chapter into four sections. The first, Main-course Sauces, covers pasta, barbecue, and butter sauces to make main-course preparation a snap. Second are the Ethnic supplies for the preparation of specialty foods: Chinese, Japanese, Indonesian, Mexican, Cajun, and even sources for some of the real exotics, including East African. Following this is a section with a few wonderful chutneys and fruit sauces that work well with the ethnic preparations, as well as relishes and pickled vegetables, from fiddleheads to pickled okra. Last are the Salad makings: vinegars and oils, mayonnaise, mustards, and salad dressings—some really good ones.

Scallops Los Gatos

For Judyth's Mountain by Cynthia Kaiser, Chef, Hilarie's Restaurant

Serves 2 in 15 minutes

 8 ounces fresh scallops
 1 cup fish stock (or clam juice)
 ¼ cup dry vermouth
 ½ teaspoon minced shallots
 2 teaspoons ginger jelly
 ⅓ cup crème fraîche (or sour cream)
     Salt and white pepper to taste
 1 teaspoon minced chives

In a medium saucepan over low heat, poach scallops in stock, vermouth, and shallots until scallops are an opaque white—about 5 minutes. Remove scallops to a heated bowl and reserve. Raise heat and reduce sauce to half the volume, then add ginger jelly, crème fraîche, and salt and white pepper to taste. Reduce the sauce to a creamy consistency, return scallops to pan and heat for a moment. Serve over fresh pasta with minced chives.

MAIN-COURSE SAUCES

Here are sauces—for pasta, for shellfish, for meats—that took somebody a long time to prepare, naturally. But not you. They make your dinner preparation look like you apprenticed under a fine chef. These sauces enhance rather than mask, and none of them—let me repeat, none of them—has MSG or other abominations to give you a headache or worse.

THE BEST OF THE BEST: PASTA SAUCES

See also: Judyth's Mountain, Inc. The real inspiration for this book came when Mona Onstead sent me a boxload of sauces so delicious, I realized I could give up cooking and never care. Mona puts up her own original recipes for pasta sauces using fresh herbs and the best ingredients she can find, in 1-pound jars that are ready to spoon out for one, two, or six servings. This is the answer to what to serve after a hard day at work. The choices include: Herb Tomato with Bacon, carefully blended with basil, garlic, oregano, and thyme. Country Garden, fresh, fresh, made with tomatoes, zucchini, onions, carrots, olive oil, wine vinegar, lemon juice, garlic, and spices. Pepper Olive with Walnuts, a deep, delicious red made with red bell peppers, black olives, walnuts, a good fruity olive oil, garlic, and parsley. Cream Garlic—this is Alfredo in a jar; the first ingredient is sweet butter. California Almond with Leeks and Capers—my all-time favorite—made with fresh onions, capers, oil, almonds, lemon juice, garlic, leeks, basil, and Tabasco.

Ask for Mona's special cookbook, which tells how to use her various products. Her first product, pepper jelly, sets the standard for all others, being made with fresh, not canned, peppers. Mona Onstead is one of those rare treasures: an original cook. Anything she cooks, I'll recommend.

CALIFORNIA PASTA SAUCES

Golden Whisk phone orders: yes
1255 Post St., Ste. 625 415-528-3010
San Francisco, CA 94105 visa/mc

Making sauces she calls "Pasta Partners," Elinor Hill-Courtney makes one really outstanding sauce called Al-bear, a glorious blend of golden apricots, green peppercorns, black mustard seed, shallots, and garlic. Her Basically Basil is a brilliant green, aromatic blend of basil, garlic, Italian olive oil, and fresh herbs. There are a dozen others, ending with a Raspberry Razzle that cries out to be slathered over a rack of lamb; it combines raspberries, kirschwasser, and spices. All her sauces are intensely seasoned and can be extended with what Elinor calls luxury liquids: wines, cognac, veloutés, and cream.

HOMESTYLE SPAGHETTI SAUCES

Schiavone's Food, Inc. phone orders: yes
1907 Tytus Ave. 513-422-8650
Middletown, OH 45042 ae/visa/mc
  Minimum order: 1 case

Paul Newman can take his sauce home, because taste-tested against the Schiavone brothers' sauce, it just doesn't measure up. The Schiavones operate a restaurant in the heart of America: Middletown, Ohio, where they grew up. They call their place Casa Mia, and to eat there is to be in the bosom of a large, loving Italian family. They began canning Mama's sauce at the request (read pleading) of customers who wanted to take some home. This canned sauce looks no different than what you'd see at the grocery store, but crank it open and the aroma of garlic and Italian warmth and care rushes up to greet you even before you've heated it. The Schiavones sell the sauce by the case only, but the cost is so reasonable—as we went to press it was $12 plus shipping—you'll never have any reason to be without it. Around here, with a

Athena's Caviar

Serves 8 in 2 hours

2	large eggplants
1	cup best-quality mayonnaise
2	cloves
2	garlic cloves, pressed
2	tablespoons Basically Basil sauce
1	generous pinch oregano leaf
3	lemons for juice/garnish
½	cup poppy seeds
2	hard-cooked eggs Toasted baguettes

Pierce eggplants with a fork and roast at 350° F. until soft, 45–60 minutes. Cut eggplants in half, scoop out flesh into food processor. Add mayonnaise, cloves, garlic, Basically Basil sauce, oregano, and ½ cup freshly squeezed lemon juice. Blend well. Place mixture in a serving bowl and blend in poppy seeds. Garnish with remaining lemon and hard-cooked egg wedges. Serve with toasted baguettes.

Meatballs Schiavone Style

Although you will enjoy the Scia-
vone sauces over pasta or pizza
as is, with maybe a little cheese,
do try making Mama's meatballs
for a real Southern Italian
homestyle supper. Hot, buttery
garlic bread, a green salad with
the simplest vinaigrette, fresh
fruit or ice cream for dessert.
Simple . . . simply wonderful.

Serves 4 in 30 minutes

1	pound lean ground beef
2	eggs
¼	cup bread crumbs
¼	cup chopped fresh parsley
¼	teaspoon salt
2	teaspoons black pepper
¼	cup grated cheese (Parmesan and/or Romano)
2	large cloves garlic
2	teaspoons olive oil

Combine above ingredients in a
large mixing bowl. Mix well and
shape into golf ball sized
rounds. Brown in skillet in a little
additional oil, over medium heat,
until golden on all sides. Don't
overcook. Add to Schiavone's
Spaghetti Sauce in a saucepan
and heat to boiling.

generous dollop of Parmesan, it has become the after-
school snack of choice, either with just-cooked pasta or
spread on an English muffin and toasted for an impromptu
pizza.

MEDITERRANEAN SPECIALTIES

See also: Corti Brothers. Darrell Corti is a grocer of impeccable taste. He imports specialty products from Italy that
offer quick, brightly flavored solutions to "What's for dinner?" Riviera Caviar, sometimes called Olivia, is an olive
paste made from tiny black Taggiasca olives that grow in
the area of Oneglia on Italy's Western Riviera. Combined
with the olives are thyme, bay leaf, and extra-virgin olive
oil. In France, they call this Tapenade. It is a full-bodied,
direct flavor that can be used right out of the jar or can
be softened with butter or oil. One thing you may have to
get used to—it turns foods an alarming purplish-black,
looking a bit like squid ink. Mouth-watering if you're into
Mediterranean food but startling if you're new to it. Corti
also imports the best Italian brands of sun-dried tomatoes,
marinated in olive oil: Pomolia and Eden.

Don't forget he also makes that incredible sour orange marmalade so invaluable as a glaze for game birds.

MISSOURI BARBECUE SAUCE

Wicker's Barbecue Sauce phone orders: yes
Box 126 800-847-0032
Hornersville, MO 63855 visa/mc

A fellow named Peck Wicker from this 200-resident ham-
let in the bootheel of Missouri invented this barbecue
sauce for daubing on the pork he sold from his natural pit.
Like others, he began bottling it and selling it by customer
demand. I was leery of the stuff when it came in, because
it looks like water with cayenne pepper floating in it. But
this vinegar-based sauce with Peck Wicker's own combination of spices has proved to be a valuable addition to
the larder. A chicken, marinated in this sauce for the day,
then simply baked in the oven, comes out golden, crisp,

and about as satisfactory as if I'd cranked up the bar-becue.

Besides the good tangy taste that Wicker's sauce gives to chicken, shrimp, pork, or beef, the good news is that the whole 28-ounce bottle only has 70 calories. Weight watchers can call this a Free one. In fact, this is sold as a diet condiment. It is all natural, has only pure ingredients and no chemical or other preservatives. Be-sides the original, Wicker's also makes mesquite-flavored sauce, and a low-sodium that has 75 percent less salt than the original. You get a six-pack, any mix you wish, for less than $10 plus shipping. You can even get a T-shirt or apron that says "I'm on the sauce."

GOOD TOMATO-BASED BARBECUE SAUCE

K.C. Masterpiece   phone orders: yes
4340 Mission Rd.   800-255-0513
Prairie Village, KS 66206   visa/mc

This slightly sweet, tomato-based barbecue sauce—cat-sup made good—is what the grocery store barbecue sauces aspire to but don't quite achieve. Used lightly on a barbecued salmon, it is wonderful. The 19-ounce jars come in three flavors: original, hickory, and mesquite. Thick and rich, this is what is known as a table sauce, meaning that it contains too much sugar to cook with; it would burn on the grill. Concocted by a Kansas City child psychiatrist who got so taken with the backyard barbecue that he gave up his practice and now just pushes barbe-cue sauce.

CALIFORNIA-STYLE BARBECUE SAUCE

Lawson Enterprises   phone orders: no
170 Crivello Ave.   707-643-9238
Pittsburg, CA 94565

Otis Lawson grew up in an East Bay family of 13 children. Everybody had chores, and he picked cooking because

Corti's Salsa al Pomodoro (Sun-dried Tomato Sauce with Cream)

The creamy texture and pink hue of this intense tomatoey sauce make this a perfect example of rich yet simple dressing for stuffed pastas. Quick as a wink to make and mysterious as the Mona Lisa.

Serves 6 in 30 minutes

     3 tablespoons extra-virgin olive oil
     1 tablespoon butter
     ½ medium onion, finely chopped
     1 clove garlic, finely minced
     ¾ cup marinated sun-dried tomatoes, drained and coarsely chopped
     1 teaspoon sugar
     4 tablespoons soft bread crumbs
     2 cups broth (vegetable or chicken)
     1 cup half-and-half
        Salt and pepper to taste

Heat oil and butter in saucepan until foaming. Add onion and garlic, and cook slowly until onion is translucent. Add chopped tomatoes, sugar, and bread crumbs. Stir and cook slowly about 10 minutes. Add broth, then half-and-half, and cook another 10 minutes until thick and smooth. Adjust sea-sonings. Suitable for all stuffed pastas, cheese ravioli, tortellini, and lasagne.

Darrell Corti's Grilled Chicken with Olivia

Here's a Mediterranean barbecue that drips with the flavor of olives. Good with just-steamed green beans and fresh pasta.

2 hours to marinate;
30 minutes preparation
Serves 1

	Boned chicken pieces (2 per person)
1	6-inch sprig fresh rosemary, chopped
1	clove garlic, pressed
½	cup olive oil
3–4	twists freshly ground pepper
¼	cup Riviera Caviar (Olivia)

Marinate chicken pieces (with skin on) in a mixture of rosemary, garlic, olive oil, and freshly milled black pepper for at least two hours.

Start a lively fire in the grill using any hardwood (mesquite preferred). When the fire is going, remove chicken from marinade and coat pieces evenly with a thin layer of Riviera Caviar.

Drain slightly. When fire has burned so that coals are covered with a uniform gray ash, place chicken pieces, skin side down, on grill. Grill on the skin until lightly browned, being careful to douse any flare-ups. Cook and turn, basting with marinade, until pieces are uniformly brown and cooked through, about 20 minutes.

he didn't like working in the yard. His mama taught him to bake, cook, and can fruits. When his chores were done, he'd gather up some kids and play restaurant; he was the cook. Later, in high school, he made and sold pastries for spending money. So it seems a natural progression for him to bottle and sell barbecue sauce. As Otis will tell you, his barbecue sauce has three effects; first a deep smoky flavor, then a sweet taste, and a sort of spicy taste at the end. Otis's sauce is a deep, thick, rich kind that will be very familiar to those who grew up on Southern-style barbecue. It's wonderful.

NEW YORK STATE FAIR-STYLE BARBECUE

The Rob Salamida Co. phone orders: yes
133 Washington Ave. 607-785-4391
Endicott, NY 13760 visa/mc

Rob Salamida began selling his barbecue outside of taverns in his hometown, Endicott, New York, when he was 15 years old. He decided right then and there that the vinegar and Italian spice marinade he used could be bottled and sold—despite the fact that it looked like "river water." When he got a little older, he went to the state fair with his product, and before long, he had an order from a woman in South Carolina and his business ceased to be purely local. Not yet 30 years old, Rob Salamida oversees a burgeoning barbecue business.

He calls his version of barbecue the Spiedie (spee-dee), and it's actually an Italian-style meat marinade that can be used to prepare steaks, pork chops, roasts, chicken, lamb, and even mushrooms. His own Spiedie sandwich begins with 1-inch cubes of meat marinated in the sauce for 24 hours, then skewered and cooked over charcoal. Slide the meat off into a single slice of Italian bread or fresh hard roll, and you have a genuine Spiedie sandwich.

He also markets a chicken barbecue sauce that is again vinegar-and-spice based but with egg added; it is essentially what is well known in that area as the "Cornell U. Barbecue Sauce" and is commonly used to baste chicken at big outdoor fund-raisers. Rob makes no claims for inventing this sauce, he just bottles and sells it.

Both Rob's sauces produce a bright, pungent barbecue taste as different from California or Kansas City as you could get and still be in the same category.

FRESH HERB COUNTRY CONDIMENTS

Muirhead	phone orders: yes
Box 189, RD 1	201-782-7803
Ringoes, NJ 08551	ae/visa/mc

Doris and Edward Simpson bought an 18th century house in Hunterdon County, New Jersey, about 15 years ago and turned a portion of it into a restaurant. Doris is an expert with sauces and condiments. In response to demand by her customers, she now sells (from the restaurant or by mail) the following: compound butters made with her own fresh garden-grown herbs; dill and horseradish salad dressings; horseradish mustard; "creative" cooking sauce; pesto; sherry pepper; cranberry conserve; sweet-and-sour honey glaze; four-seeded mustard; apricot-jalapeño jelly; apple catsup; and a sweet-and-sour dressing.

The "creative" cooking sauce is particularly entrancing, a deep red, sweet, onion- and herb-seasoned sauce. Doris recommends a teaspoon of this atop oysters or clams on the half shell, broiled. Let me tell you, this is unforgettable. She sends cooking suggestions with all her condiments. Every one is boldly seasoned with the fresh herbs she grows in the backyard. You will become devoted to Doris Simpson if you begin cooking with her sauces.

CALIFORNIA SWISS BUTTER SAUCES

St. Gallen Gourmet	phone orders: yes
Kitchen	707-575-3207
1275 Fourth St. #218	ae/visa/mc/dc
Santa Rosa, CA 95404	

Chef Josef Keller operates the kitchen in a French Continental restaurant known as La Province. In addition to cooking and teaching others to cook, he now sells three

---

Chef Josef's Chicken Indian

Try papaya, kiwi, pear, and apple in this dish. Delicious.

Serves 2 in 15 minutes

- 1 pound uncooked chicken pieces
  Salt and pepper to taste
  Flour
- 2 tablespoons light oil
- ¼ cup dry white wine
- 2 heaping tablespoons Mild Curry Sauce
- ¼ cup heavy cream
- ½ cup mixed fresh fruit, chopped

Remove skin and bones from chicken and cut into uniform pieces. Season chicken pieces to taste with salt and pepper and dust with flour. Sauté lightly in hot oil. Add wine, Chef Josef's Mild Curry Sauce, cream, and fruit. Simmer 5 minutes. Serve over rice.

butter-based sauces for home cooks: garlic herb, lemon dill, and a mild curry. These sauces combine traditional professional European cooking techniques with the need for American convenience. He sends every mail-order customer a mini-cooking lesson along with the sauces, and, by doing what the good chef tells you, you too can produce a finely sauced meal at home. He first offered these sauces only to other restaurants but eventually agreed to sell them in 6-ounce containers. Made with all-natural ingredients that always begin with pure butter, Chef Josef's herb butters are like having a chef in the pantry.

CALIFORNIA CURRIES

Ikonna Foods   phone orders: yes
PO Box 7688   415-526-8650
Berkeley, CA 94707

Ike and Donna Sofaer bring to us their family's curry sauces, which originated in the Middle East, then evolved and expanded in Bombay, and ultimately wound up in Berkeley. This long evolution embraces exotic flavors, enticing aromas, and wholesome ingredients. Made from tomato paste, red wine vinegar, secret spices, garlic, onion, and turmeric, the curry sauces come hot or mild. There are no fats, no sweeteners, no artificial preservatives, emulsifiers, or synthetic additives. We did find that the ingredients separated on standing, but better that than some chemical stuff to hold it in suspension. You can make curry by doing nothing more than arranging chicken pieces in a baking dish, pouring Ikonna Curry Sauce over it, and letting it bake for an hour. What could be simpler?

INDIAN SPICES OF VERMONT

Spices of Vermont   phone orders: yes
PO Box 18   802-425-2555
N. Ferrisburg, VT 05473   visa/mc

Dr. Shah came to America from India as a renowned oceanographer, but he had this compulsion to feed people. To that end, he opened The Spices, my favorite type of restaurant, the small, family-run ethnic kind. He and his wife and children live above the restaurant. During the dinner hour, Dr. Shah acts as host while his wife, Neeta, does the cooking. It is, according to the *Burlington Free Press,* "as close as most diners will come to a meal inside an Indian home." The Shahs' restaurant customers are positively devoted to them. One man has visited 191 times.

You can buy from Dr. Shah his wife's own, hand-blended cooking sauces, mellow or spicy hot. Free of salt, sugar, and preservatives, these sauces combine tomato paste, vegetable oil, vinegar, spices, onion, peanuts, co-conut, almonds, and turmeric in a perfectly balanced cooking sauce. All you do is blend the sauce with sour cream, sink meat or chicken breasts in it, and bake. Neeta also makes and sells an all-Vermont-apple chutney that tastes like a dark applesauce spiked with cumin and other spices. These sauce blends and chutneys come in 8-ounce jars. If you combine Dr. Shah with Rumi Corporation's products (see index), you're getting the best of Bombay cooking brought to America. I wish those two could meet.

OHIO SUN-DRIED TOMATOES

Genovesi Food Co.　　phone orders: yes
PO Box 5668　　　　　513-274-7455
Dayton, OH 45405　　　visa/mc

Nicole Genovesi describes her first taste of sun-dried tomatoes in Italy 15 years ago as love at first bite. She experimented for years in Ohio but could never quite get it right without that bright Italian sunshine to dry the tomatoes. But once dehydrators became available and she tried that, she knew she had it licked. She offers the tomatoes put up in California Sciabica olive oil or sun-flower oil. Both versions are carefully seasoned with garlic, oregano, and salt. Although this is saltier than Timbercrest's version (see index), the one Nicole puts up in olive oil tasted even better to us than an expensive imported one in a taste test we conducted. Expensive but well worth it.

Caraluzzi's Fettuccine with Mussels and Dried Tomatoes

Nicole got this recipe from Mark Caraluzzi, founder and chef at American Cafe Restaurant, Washington, D.C.

Serves 4 in 20 minutes

3	tablespoons olive oil
3	tablespoons butter
1	shallot, minced
3	cloves garlic, minced
3	tablespoons dry vermouth
	Pepper to taste
1/3	cup Genovesi tomatoes
1	14-ounce can plum tomatoes
2	pounds mussels, scrubbed
1/2	pound fresh fettuccine
2	tablespoons Italian parsley, chopped

CONTINUED ON PAGE 140

CONTINUED FROM PAGE 139

Bring a large pot of lightly salted water to a boil over high heat.

Meanwhile, in a large skillet with a lid, melt oil and butter. Add shallots and garlic. Sauté over low heat until soft, about 4 minutes. Add vermouth and pepper and simmer 4 minutes more. Stir in all tomatoes and simmer 6 minutes. Add mussels to skillet, cover, and simmer until all mussels have opened, discarding any that don't; about 2–3 minutes. Transfer mussels to warm plate.

Meanwhile, cook pasta al dente—2 minutes for fresh, 5–8 minutes for dried. Drain cooked pasta and arrange on a large warmed serving platter. Spoon sauce on top, then arrange mussels on sauce. Sprinkle with chopped parsley.

HAWAIIAN TERIYAKI SAUCES

Sagawa's Savory Sauces   phone orders: yes
PO Box 22-001   503-659-4422
Milwaukie, OR 97222   visa/mc

Portland dentist Jim Sagawa grew up in Hawaii, and once he was established in practice in Oregon, he began trying to buy the sauces he'd grown up with. Couldn't find them, so he made one himself. Blessedly free of MSG or preservatives, his thick, brown, sweet, smoky sauce is a blend of spices and herbs. Here's an authentic Hawaiian taste that you can pour out of a bottle onto marinating meats or fish. Makes dinner a luau. We really like this stuff.

FROM OREGON WITH LOVE: JAPANESE TERIYAKI

Ikeuchi Trading, Inc.   phone orders: yes
2795 Anderson Ave.,   503-884-0219
  Ste. 6
Klamath Falls, OR 97603

Samuel Ikeuchi, who underwent six years of chef training in his native Japan before coming to the United States, has been making this ancient recipe for his restaurant customers for 15 years. Made from soybeans, wheat, salt, sugar, cornstarch, garlic, ginger, and spices, Sam's sauce, which he calls Humick Sweet Steak Sauce, is the color and texture of rich molasses. It has a sweet, smoky, mysterious taste and is good for steaks, chicken, spareribs, shark, salmon—even corn on the cob, according to Sam. It really does make teriyaki a breeze. Only problem is, now that Sam's selling it outside the restaurant, he can barely keep up with the demand, because his sauce is aged six to eight months in a crock and he didn't anticipate that people would want so much. By the time you're reading this, he should have a new batch, long cooked, aged and bottled, just ready for you.

VERMONT VEGETABLES AND MIDDLE EASTERN SPICES

E. A. Khalaj, Inc.
#27E-397 Saint Paul St.
Burlington, VT 05401

phone orders: yes
802-658-5996

I just love to see what happens to these new Americans when they combine their old-world skills with our American gardens. Calling their product "Kalachi," the Khalaj family makes an all-natural condiment that looks like barbecue sauce but with an Eastern twist. Combining Vermont vegetables with Middle Eastern spices, they've created a thick, tomatoey, vinegary, smoky, spicy table sauce with no artificial enhancers—just tomatoes, celery, brown sugar, corn syrup, oil, vinegar, onions, garlic, spices, salt, and pepper. You can make a fabulous Persian entrée using this condiment and currants in a baked lamb dish.

ETHNIC SUPPLIES: SPICES, HERBS, ET AL.

In addition to the ready-made sauces we have presented, you can find dry spice blends, supplies, and directions for several interesting ethnic cuisines.

NORTHERN NEW MEXICO SPECIALTIES

Casados Farms
PO Box 1269
San Juan Pueblo, NM
  87566

phone orders: no
505-852-2692
visa/mc

New Mexico cuisine is one of a few notably distinct American cooking styles. It all started with the Aztecs—from whom we get the word chile—and continued with Spanish, then Anglo, influences. The Casados farm folks raise the all-natural products necessary to make New

Posole

The New Mexican Christmas Eve tradition calls for posole, and cinnamoned hot chocolate to drink. This recipe serves Christmas revelers or others just in from the cold.

Serves 8; cooks all day

¼	cup chile molido (dark brown powdered)
1	head garlic, peeled
1	large onion, chopped
1	medium chicken, cut up
1	pound pork loin, cut in 2-inch cubes
2	cups posole
	Water to cover
	Salt and pepper

Condiments:

1	bunch radishes, sliced
1	head lettuce, shredded
1	purple onion, sliced
2	limes, cut in wedges
	Pequín chiles, crumbled

In a large soup pot, combine first seven ingredients. Simmer gently until chicken is tender and corn kernels have burst. (It takes practically all day. Those posole kernels are hard.) Adjust seasonings with salt and pepper. Simmer uncovered an additional half hour, then serve in deep soup bowls, with plenty of broth. Pass condiments for people to add as they choose.

Park Kerr's Fabulous Fajitas

Serve folded into hot flour tortillas, with a side of fresh salsa, guacamole, all the accompaniments. Plenty of beer to drink. Praline for dessert.

Serves 12 in 1½ hours work (marinates overnight)

1	1-pound jar barbecue meat marinade
1	Coors light beer (Park says drink the rest of the six pack)
2	medium onions
2	fresh green chiles
2	jalapeños
2	bunches cilantro
2	cloves fresh garlic
1	tablespoon El Paso chili powder
1	inside skirt steak, about 2 pounds
24	fresh flour tortillas

Accompaniments:
>   Salsa Primera
>   Sour cream
>   Chopped green onion
>   Cilantro leaves
>   Guacamole

Mix marinade with beer. Coarsely chop onions, chiles, jalapeños, cilantro, and garlic. Stir in chili powder. Combine all ingredients in a glass dish and dredge steak in marinade; cover and refrigerate overnight. (Park says he always makes extra and freezes the raw meat in the marinade so he can be ready to fajita in a flash.)

About an hour before serving time, fire up the barbecue grill. Cook skirt steak until brown

CONTINUED ON PAGE 143

Mexican meals: corn, chiles, pine nuts, and spices. Here is your source for posole, the whole corn necessary for the stew of the same name. Get real New Mexico chile Caribe, coarsely ground and fresh as the devil; atole, the roasted blue cornmeal; panocha, a sprouted whole wheat flour.

In addition to the New Mexican staples, you can order ristras, strung dried red peppers, up to 60 inches long. One of the best combination items they have is a tin box about the size of your mother's jewelry box, decorated with birds and flowers, containing their own authentic New Mexico cookbook and a dozen New Mexico musts, including molido, posole, chicos, atole, and herbs. This is a fabulous introduction to New Mexico-style cuisine and highly recommended. They'll throw in this good little cookbook with the purchase of any five items. It's a gem.

AUTHENTIC TEX-MEX SUPPLIES

The El Paso Chile Co.　　phone orders: yes
100 Ruhlin Ct.　　　　　　915-544-3434
El Paso, TX 79922　　　　visa/mc

Park Kerr and his mama, Norma, started this company in 1981 from Mama's recipes for Salsa Primera (a fresh tomato sauce), barbecue meat marinade, and a chili powder. Chili powder is to the Texan what curry powder is to the Indian. And Norma Kerr's chili powder is a fine, authoritative blend of ground chile peppers, garlic, and the herbs it takes to get a true Texas chili powder. One of the reasons her chili powder exceeds others on the market is that Norma Kerr is a stickler for freshness. The flavors of chiles volatilize all too soon, and what you buy in the grocery store will often make a real Texan cry, tasting just kind of hot and metallic. But Norma Kerr's? That's chili! For chili con carne.

The Kerrs also sell a variety of ristras, wreaths, and decorative items, including a wheat straw star known as the kitchen wheat blessing, for good luck in the kitchen, Southwest style. Write for their catalog, which shows their own Mexican clay goat, Chivo, filled with their products, and also a charming Mexican twig basket brimming with other Southwestern cuisine favorites—recipes included.

Park's big contribution is the fajita marinade and recipe. This is the real McCoy.

INDONESIAN SPICES

Mrs. De Wildt	phone orders: yes
RD 3	215-588-1042
Bangor, PA 18013	minimum order: $10

Spices, in antiquity, were used as currency. JoAnne DeWildt Boots found spices to be as good as gold when World War II separated her from home and funds. Born and raised in the Netherlands East Indies, JoAnne was just graduating from high school in Australia when the Japanese invaded her home, imprisoning her father, mother, and sisters. JoAnne joined the Dutch forces and, in 1945, met and married fellow Dutchman John Boots.

After the war, the Bootses came to New York. The law prevented their withdrawing any money from their overseas accounts, so JoAnne's mother, still in the colony, took their money and purchased rare East Indies spices, which she shipped to them in New York. They began selling them to friends. By the time they had gotten all their money out of the East Indies, their newfound friends and customers had come to count on the spices. Their business was launched.

For 33 years the Boots family has operated this mail-order spice company. You can find the most exotic Indonesian specialties here: the fiery sambal, a chile paste, sweet soy sauce, krupuk, and various prepared foods. Cookbooks and Dutch specialties, including first-quality cheeses and chocolates, complete their offerings.

The Bootses also operate an inn and restaurant in the Poconos, about an hour out of New York City. At a very reasonable rate you can enjoy a rijsttafel (rice table) buffet that includes steaming white rice and a dozen side dishes. JoAnne does all the cooking, John Boots will make you his famous "Selectail," Java's answer to the daiquiri, and you will have the opportunity for a rare evening of Colonial splendor, Dutch East Indian style.

CONTINUED FROM PAGE 142

on the outside and still pink on the inside. Cut on the diagonal into thin fajita slices and serve in hot flour tortillas with the accompaniments.

Indonesian Rijsttafel (Rice Table)

From Mrs. DeWildt's Selecta Restaurant in the heart of the Poconos, Route 191, north of Bangor, Pennsylvania 18013. Telephone: 215-588-1042. By reservation only: Friday, Saturday, and Sunday evenings.

Salad: Gado Gado (assorted vegetables, spiced peanut dressing, and dry-fried onions)

Nasi: white rice and 12 side dishes

Telor Kerrie (eggs, green beans, peppers in curry sauce)

Babi Ketjap (pork in sweet soy sauce)

Sajur Lombok Kool (cabbage and peppers in spiced chicken broth)

Sambal Goreng Tempeh (spiced cultured soy cakes, fried with onions and peppers)

Ajam Pedis Djawa (Java spiced chicken)

Rendang Sumatra (spiced beef, eggplant, and zucchini, the only hot dish on the menu)

Serundeng (fried spiced coconut with peanuts)

Ikan Terie (fried dried anchovies)

CONTINUED ON PAGE 144

CONTINUED FROM PAGE 143

Pisang Goreng (fried bananas)

Krupuk Udang (fried tapioca-shrimp wafers, the Indonesian "bread")

Sate Babi (barbecued pork on skewers with spiced peanut dressing)

Sambal (hot chile paste) served on the side

Dessert: mixed tropical fruits on ice cream

Coffee or Tea

A WORLD OF TASTES

The Ethnic Pantry phone orders: yes
PO Box 798 312-223-6660
Grayslake, IL 60030 visa/mc

Here's the best idea since the Orient Express. Ken and Jan Anderson have put together a collection of ethnic dinners, including Indian, Thai, Indonesian, North African, East African, Mexican, Brazilian, and Middle Eastern. What you do is ask for their list—it is long and impressive. Then you pick out what kind of ethnic dinner you want to give, send in your order, and you'll get the exotic spices and herbs, recipes, directions, and a shopping list for the fresh items you'll need to complete a dinner for four people. From India, for example, they offer chicken in buttermilk sauce with spicy green beans and tomatoes, and basmati rice and pappadoms (lentil wafers). From Thailand comes hot-and-sour shrimp soup, chicken and spinach with peanut sauce and Thai rice, shrimp chips, and fish sauce.

I tell you, we have never quit talking about the chicken-cashew curry dinner we had from The Ethnic Pantry. Their spices and herbs are fresh. Their recipes are easy to follow. You can produce memorable meals from this. If you don't live in a cosmopolitan town full of fine ethnic restaurants, this is an excellent introduction to exotic cuisine. They have a whole catalog full of preplanned dinners, à la carte selections, general items from the countries of origin, spices, and herbs. What a super idea.

MAIL-ORDER CHINATOWN SUPPLIES

The Chinese Kitchen phone orders: yes
PO Box 218 201-665-2234
Stirling, NJ 07980 visa/mc

Since we moved away from San Francisco, I've had to send friends to Chinatown on errands of mercy for me. But no more. Now I have my own Chinese grocery store, all in a neat catalog that offers everything from lily buds to solid brass Mongolian hot pots—the condiments, the cookbooks and cookware, dried mushrooms, noodles, rice, grains, spices, vegetables, and teas. Even kits that offer everything a beginner needs.

They also have some of those hard-to-find tools you see in every Chinatown shop but nowhere else: bamboo-handled strainers, ladles and spatulas, bamboo steamers. All the good stuff.

THE REAL TEXAS CHILI KIT

Hachar Imports   phone orders: yes
PO Box 1579   512-723-9141
Laredo, TX 78042

Robert Hachar imports things from Mexico: spatterware in red, blue, and white, for example; gorgeous hand-blown clear Mexican glassware; tinware. But what he's done that's really fun, he's teamed up with The Real Texas Chili Company and will send you a chili kit that includes a big blue spatterware chili pot, four plates, four bowls, spoons, even a red-checkered hot pad, plus chili mix and instructions for making chili at home. Of course, you'll have to provide your own armadillo, buffalo, or Longhorn. Robert Hachar does not import road meat. Chili or no.

CREOLE TRIPLE TREAT

Bon Melange   phone orders: yes
115 Davis Ave.   601-452-3258, or -2140
Pass Christian, MS 39571   visa/mc

Malee Hearin grew up in New Orleans. In moving around, she discovered other people wanted to know how to prepare Creole foods. In addition to a French Market Bean Soup, she offers a Creole Triple Treat: Rockefeller Sauce, made with spinach and Creole spices; Bienville Sauce made with mushrooms, vegetables, and Creole seasoning; and a little thing she calls Cajun Beginnings, dry spices that can turn meat and seafood into *étouffée* and jambalaya. Malee sends instructions and recipes and will even tell you how to make Mississippi mud, a famous dessert of pecans, chocolate sauce, and vanilla ice cream.

PURE SPANISH SAFFRON THREADS, MEXICAN VANILLA, AND MUSHROOMS

Vanilla, Saffron Imports   phone orders: yes
70 Manchester St.   415-648-8990
San Francisco, CA 94110

I was sure glad to learn that Juan J. San Mames is importing these pure items: Spanish saffron threads, at $4 per gram; pure Mexican vanilla beans and extract; and those incredible gorgeous Mexican morels and cèpes, picked, then dried in the hot Mexican sun, and packed in FDA-approved bags for import. You can order the small size, which are the European chef's favorite; medium, which the Americans like; or large, which Mexican chefs stuff with meat or cheese. These fine, strong, nutty morels reconstitute quickly and are soft to the bite. They're clean and light-colored because they're grown in the forest mantle and not in a burned-over area. Best quality. His Mexican vanilla is also FDA-approved and that delicious, pungent kind so potent you can use half as much. This resource is a real find.

CHUTNEYS, FRUIT SAUCES, RELISHES, AND PICKLED VEGETABLES

In the days before refrigeration, fruits and vegetables were preserved in jars with vinegars, sweeteners, and spices. We have gathered some of these new/old favorites that go particularly well with the curries, barbecues, and Latin American combinations we've just been discussing.

BOMBAY CHUTNEYS VIA DENVER ATTORNEY ENGINEER

Rumi Corporation
1324-A E. 17th Ave.
Denver, CO 80218

phone orders: yes
Colorado Ambrosia
303-872-3875
visa/mc

When a guy named Rumi Engineer left his home in Bombay for the United States to study law, he brought along his family's recipes for chutneys. After 20 years or so, Rumi decided to take a leave of absence from the law and, on the suggestion of friends who had been the proud recipients of Rumi's gift chutneys, decided to plunge into the chutney-making business himself. He rented a Quonset hut with metal ribbed sides, a sign that still announced its former tenants—Mexican Food Sellers—a 40-gallon pot, and a stove. As Rumi himself says fondly about his first chutney kitchen, "It's hideous." On his first day in business, he began at 9 A.M., peeling, seeding, chopping, seasoning, and stewing the first batch of chutney. By 11 it was ready. Eleven P.M., that is. Later he would hand-pack and ship the entire order, alone.

Now two years, tons of chutney, and six flavors later, Rumi is supplying genuine Bombay-style chutneys to some of the toniest food establishments in the United States. He still makes the chutneys in small batches, balancing the flavors between sweet, sour, spicy, and subtle. He uses nothing artificial to preserve or stabilize. The spices and sugars do that.

The flavors Rumi makes currently are: fruit, a mild apple, peach, and pineapple chutney; mango, the traditional style similar to Major Grey's; tomato, one of my favorites—hot, thick, and smooth; Lemon-date, an extra-hot blend of spices coupled with the crisp, tangy lemons and mellow taste of dates; cranberry, available only from October to January, especially nice with holiday birds; carrot, perhaps the most interesting, with a nice crunch from finely grated carrots, made from a secret recipe used for Indian wedding ceremonial feasts.

Rumi has a new curry blend out that gets comments from "too mild" to "too hot," depending on the origin of the taster. To my taste, it is well balanced but could stand additional cayenne. Try it and see what you think.

Chutney originated in India but was made popular in the West by the British. Chutney derives from the Hindi word *chatni*, which literally means "lickable."

We all know that chutneys of many persuasions are delicious when drizzled over a brick of cream cheese and served with a decent water biscuit. Don't forget other possibilities: Peach halves filled with mango chutney. Tomato chutney as a marinade for scallops, shrimp, and firm whitefish; then skewer fish alternately between chunks of green pepper and onions; grill, serving additional chutney as a dip. Blend ¼ cup of chutney into mayonnaise for a new fruit dressing. A dollop of chutney atop a broiled chop makes it seem like you thought about dinner for more than a minute.

Apricot chutney with curry dabbed onto Cornish hens during last 10 minutes of a 50-minute roasting period at 400° F. gives the birds a golden glaze.

Rumi Engineer wants people to know that chutneys are not just for Indian dinners. He marinates poultry, ribs, chops, and steaks in chutney before grilling. He glazes that most American of birds, the turkey, with his cranberry chutney. As far as Rumi and I are concerned, Rudyard Kipling can take a flying leap. An American Thanksgiving turkey glazed with a Bombay-style chutney made in Denver by an Indian attorney named Engineer in an old Mexican restaurant just about covers the compass. East meets West, and South and North to boot. And it tastes good besides.

VERMONT MAPLE MUSTARD AND CHUTNEY

Sterling Mountain Maple phone orders: yes
PO Box 17   802-644-2487
Waterville, VT 05492   visa/mc

Calling their products Vermont Country Naturally, Susan Wylie and her husband make an English-style chutney sweetened with maple; Maple Apricot Mustard; Fire and Spice Mustard; Mint Chutney; Tutti-Frutti Sauce, which looks like what applesauce ought to be but isn't quite; Rum Raisin Apple Butter; and Maple Madness marinade and dressing. The mustard is particularly enchanting: made from apricots, maple, limes, citrus fruits, several imported mustards, just a touch of horseradish; on a duck it is just too much. A great product.

BOMBAY SAUCE, CHUTNEYS, AND CONSERVES

La Casa Rosa   phone orders: yes
107 Third St.   408-623-4563
San Juan Bautista, CA visa/mc
  95045

A Central California institution, La Casa Rosa is a restaurant in a classic California mission-style house that was originally built in 1858. Since 1935, La Casa Rosa has offered condiments for sale there and by mail order, made in the restaurant kitchen from the surrounding California provender plus herbs out of the restaurant's own garden. Their famous Bombay Sauce is bright yellow, sweet, and saucy, a perfect complement to curry. They also offer 20 or 30 chutneys, spiced watermelon rinds, preserves, and jellies including a spectacular pomegranate.

VERMONT SPIRITED CONSERVES

Pan Handler Products   phone orders: yes
4580 Maple St.   802-244-5597
Waterbury Center, VT   visa/mc
  05677

Patty Girouard makes three fruit and nut conserves that just beg to be on the table with roast meats. Blueberry Bourbon, made with what it's named for plus apples, raisins, walnuts, and lemon juice, is thick, rich, and complex. Apple Rum Walnut Conserve tastes like a Grade A apple pie filling with a punch. Strawberry Amaretto is a deep plum color and mostly sweet. These all go into Kerr jars with flats and lids and look like homemade.

NORTHWEST SPICY FRUIT RELISHES

Pristine Fruits   phone orders: yes
PO Box 2373   503-935-7510
Eugene, OR 97487

Laurie and Mark Whitham use the fine fruits and berries of the Northwest to create all-natural products: Apple Chutney, Cherry Chutney, and Marion Blackberry Gourmet Sauce. The chutneys are made particularly pungent by the use of cider vinegar and lemon juice. Both contain fresh ginger and have a generally fresh taste. Stir the blackberry sauce into yogurt for a real treat.

CRANBERRY CHUTNEY

Stowe Hollow Kitchens   phone orders: yes
Box 6830, RD 2   802-253-8248
Stowe, VT 05672   visa/mc

This excellent cranberry chutney is salt free and nicely balanced, being a deep cranberry red color and quite splendid with poultry.

DISTRICT OF COLUMBIA CONDIMENTS

Homespun, Inc.   phone orders: yes
3205-C Sutton Pl. NW   202-244-7712
Washington, DC 20016

Jane Becker's stores change from year to year, depending on the crop. Last year, the peach trees got hit by a late frost, so the chutney was snuffed out, but the tomatoes bore like crazy, so she put up a lot of dilly tomatoes. She's been praised for her cranberry catsup and chutney, as well as for preserves including gingered pear and tomato. We are particularly taken with lemon relish, a lemon, cucumber, onion, and pepper relish best served with smoked meat and Jarlsberg cheese.

TASTE OF TEXAS SAUCE

Dickie Davis   phone orders: yes
PO Box 668   915-396-2444 or -4421
Menard, TX 76859

Dickie Davis and her granddaughter Clara Treadwell were putting up salsa about six or seven years ago when they got to fiddling around with the ingredients. Tomatoes, peppers, onions, sugar, and spices. Pretty soon they had something new: hot, sweet, tomato red, and peppery. They call it simply Sweet & Hot, and they mostly sell it in pint jars through the country store in Menard.

When you go into this store, you feel like you're visiting kinfolks. You're invited to sit down and have a cup of coffee. People will press freshly baked goods on you and show you just how far they got with the quilting this week. Mrs. Davis keeps her relish in the store and only makes it in small batches on her stove at home. It will scorch if cooked too fast or too hot. But, she says, now she just keeps putting it on the bus, 'cause people do want it so. In fact, after her son did her taxes last year, he told her she should give up ranching (she owns two ranches outside Menard) and stick with Sweet & Hot.

HERBS, HERBS, HERBS

Hilltop Herb Farm　　　phone orders: yes
PO Box 1734　　　　　713-592-5859
Cleveland, TX 77327　　ae/visa/mc

Madalene and Jim Hill retired to the Sam Houston National Forest in 1957. All they planned to do was a little gardening. But Madalene's passion for herbs and for cooking soon proved unstoppable and now she has gardens, a dining room, a canning kitchen, and greenhouses. Her dinners are legend. And the provender of the kitchen spills over into the shop they call Gallimaufry. Ask for a catalog. They have herbal jellies, jams, marmalades, pickles, chutneys, relishes that taste just like you remember your grandmother making, herbal salts, and Hilltop seasonings.

　　Madalene Hill is an original. Where else could you purchase a custom-blended tea called Tranquilitea made from the Java dogwood tree, chamomile, peppermint, linden, yerba maté, spearmint, agrimony, hops, marigold, rosehips, borage, comfrey, elder, woodruff, rosemary, thyme, lemon balm, lemon verbena, and blackberry? Just reading the list aloud calms me down.

PLAIN GOOD COUNTRY LIVING

Clearview Farms Cannery　phone orders: yes
RD 1　　　　　　　　　802-933-2537
Enosburg Falls, VT 05450　visa/mc

Caroline Longe can't help it. She likes to feed people. Whenever her dairy farmer husband and his helpers

come inside the house, she's always asking them to taste something. She used to make quilts, and whenever one of her customers came to pick up an order, she'd insist they have a bite to eat. In fact, Caroline has decided that when she dies, she doesn't want a funeral, she wants a potluck. And a tape of her voice will be playing, saying, "Eat, eat. You'll feel better."

So, long on energy and nurture, Caroline began selling her canned goods. If you'd like good home cooking that would make a Vermont grandmother proud, call up Caroline and order: piccalilli, maple cranberry orange relish, honeyed carrot relish, zucchini relish, cranberry orange jam, maple carrot delight. How can I tell you which one was best? We just popped the flats off, got forks, and began tasting them one after another. Delicious.

ALL-AMERICAN ANTIPASTO

Lois Anna's Antipasto   phone orders: yes
20155 Independence Dr.   612-934-6754
Brookfield, WI 53005

When Gimbel's in Milwaukee, Wisconsin, put an ad in the paper inviting local people who had a food specialty to market it in the store's newly designed Market Place, Lois Anna Litzau took a jar of her old-favorite recipe for antipasto down to the store. She had an order immediately. She and her two daughters, Beth Lohman and Nancy Greenwood, began making and selling the antipasto from a rented church kitchen. The response was so good that they soon had orders from surrounding states.

Crisp, fresh vegetables in a light, piquant tomato sauce, packed in a 1-pound jar, make an instant salad that you can keep in the refrigerator and spoon out in portions. Cauliflower, green pepper, onions, mushrooms, olives, and peas, hand-cut and hand-cooked in the kitchen of the Brookfield United Methodist Church by a mother and two daughters. Having a jar of Lois Anna's antipasto on hand is like having a CARE package from home—mother's comfort in a jar.

EGGPLANT PÂTÉ

Cowboy Caviar   phone orders: yes
PO Box 1178   714-493-3318
San Juan Capistrano, CA
   92693

When Jerry Farrell was a kid, his mother used to make this eggplant spread from an old Russian recipe. Besides eggplant, this piquant spread also contains onion, green pepper, garlic, tomato paste, catsup, and a little salt and sugar. Jerry always liked it and along about 1981 decided to market it. He and his wife were trying to decide what to call this Russian version of caponata when, on their way to a football game, they hit on the name Cowboy Caviar. Do you suppose the Dallas Cowboys were playing? Anyway, this pâté tastes real good, although I don't know whether a cowboy would eat it or not. Besides downing it as an hors d'oeuvre, you can fold it into an omelet.

At the winter food show in Los Angeles, it won a prize because of its Mexican influence. Don't you love it? A Russian recipe, given a Cowboy label by an American on his way to a football game, and it reminds some expert of Mexican food. That's what happens to us here in the melting pot. We just absorb everything and bring out our own American version.

WHEN THE CHIPS ARE DOWN

Desert Rose Salsa   phone orders: yes
PO Box 5391   602-743-0450
Tucson, AZ 85703

When Patti Swidler and her slightly cosmic dentist husband Steve moved from Chicago to Tucson a dozen years ago, they'd never tasted Southwestern cuisine. Now, by native lights, they're experts. Vegetarian and sold on purity, they put up salsa with no sugar, no water, no artificial colors, flavors, or preservatives. You can identify everything you see in Patti's salsa: chunks of sweet tomato, jalapeño peppers, onions, carrots, herbs, and spices. Using a secret low-heat process, the Swidlers manage to seal in a jar the just-made fresh taste of tomato salsa you find in a good Mexican restaurant. You can get this in medium, hot, or Conmemorativa (our favorite, very hot and a little darker in color, a little smokier). She also offers Alberta's Peppers, cherry peppers preserved in olive oil, vinegar, garlic, herbs, and spices.

MARINATED CALIFORNIA VEGETABLES

Miss Scarlett/
 Div. of Rhett, Inc.
PO Box 1488
Burlingame, CA 94010

phone orders: yes
415-342-9234

A whale of an olive. Giant mushrooms. Stuffed eggplants. Miniature artichokes. Calamata olives. Spiced olives. Greek olives. Drunken onions and olives in vermouth. All in 12-ounce jars with no artificial preservatives. How Miss Scarlett survived the war and Reconstruction and found herself in the Bay Area is a story best left untold, but she sure wasn't kidding when she said, "I'll never be hungry again." Highly seasoned, a little salty, but a gorgeous addition to a table of crudités. Ask for a mixed case.

A PECK OF PICKLED PEPPERS

Mick's Peppouri
1707 S. 74th Ave.
Yakima, WA 98908

phone orders: yes
509-966-2328

Ginger Mick and her husband grow peppers in this sun-drenched valley of the Pacific Northwest. Combining two kinds and three colors of peppers—bells and jalapeños, red, yellow, and green—Ginger and Walt Mick put up about as pretty a pack of pickled peppers as I ever peeked at. Thick, meaty peppers with no salt or preservatives added. These are sweet, hot, and delicious. Plus they just look so good in the jar, you may not even want to open them.

THE REAL PICANTE

Van De Walle Farms   phone orders: yes
5310 Old Hwy. 90 W.   512-436-5551
San Antonio, TX 78227   visa/mc

Van De Walle's motto is, "We grow it. We know it." They used to supply a famous picante maker with peppers, but when that family concern was bought out by a large company that used its multinational buying powers to buy inferior imported peppers, the Van De Walles said: Well, shoot, we'll just make the picante ourselves. This is the real McCoy, the genuine article. The kind no self-respecting Tex-Mex lover would ever be without. Picante sauce that comes very mild, medium, and hot. (Forget the hot—only a stainless-steel throat could endure it.) They also pickle peppers and sell nacho jalapeños packed with hot carrots and onions; *pico de gallo;* a premium fajita marinade concentrate; a jalapeño relish that will make you wish for the Alamo. They're not kidding when they say farm-fresh flavors in a bottle. We have to keep ourselves supplied with this stuff by the case from now unto perpetuity.

PIMIENTO PRODUCTS

Pat's Pimientos   phone orders: yes
PO Box 5   408-385-5756
King City, CA 93930

Pat Gill, her husband, Allen, and Frances Williams farm 40 acres in sunny California and sell pimientos fresh, relished, and in jam. They let their peppers sun-ripen until they're bright red, sweet, and meaty, and use old family recipes to make this hot, peppery, sweet relish and its even richer cousin, pimiento jam.

CATSUP BEYOND BELIEF

Jasmine & Bread   phone orders: yes
RR 2, Box 256   802-763-7115
S. Royalton, VT 05068

Sherri Maurer can't stand waste. She used to make catsup from her leftover tomatoes. One year, she didn't have quite enough tomatoes but she did have some apples, so she put the two together, seasoned it, did some adjusting and changing, and pretty soon she had something so good her friends said it was Beyond Catsup. And the name stuck. Like many of her fellow Vermonters, she decided to go into business. With help from the Vermont Department of Agriculture, she decided she'd need two tons of tomatoes the first year. The farmers she called were flabbergasted. Yankee thrift made them more than a little wary. But that was three years ago. She made and sold 4 tons' worth herself the first year. And now the farmers call *her*. She expects she'll need eight tons this year.

Try this tangy mixture of tomato and apple as a glaze for meats and fish, a marinade, or salad dressing. It lives up to its name.

VEGETABLE AND FRUIT JELLIES

Sunny Meadow   phone orders: yes
PO Box 437   802-253-4641
Stowe, VT 05672   visa/mc

Peter Koeck makes a variety of fine products, from fresh pâtés to chutneys. But he's best known for his vegetable and fruit jellies. His tart-sweet lemon jelly is really nice. Apple chutney made from local Vermont apples is tart and mysterious-tasting. He's a good cook.

PURE AND FANCY FOODS FROM VERMONT

Blanchard and Blanchard   phone orders: yes
Upper Pasture Rd.   800-334-0268
Norwich, VT 05055

Probably the most staggering success story in Vermont is that of Melinda and Bob Blanchard. Bob comes from a long line of merchants. At the age of 12 he used to hang out in back of his grandfather's general store and build chicken coops. Melinda used to play hookey to help her mother make curries for dinner parties. So, putting their dreams together, they left New York and moved back to Norwich, where they opened a small cookware store and lived in a tent with their small son. Melinda's concoctions were so good her friends said she ought to sell them in the store. So in 1983 she did. Bob designed the good-looking blue and white logo, and the rest, as they say, is history. The canning kitchen has moved to larger and larger quarters. The Blanchards are out of the tent. Everything they make is pure and natural. Watch for their new line of baked goods.

Here's what you can get at the moment: seven mustards; a half-dozen salad dressings, including a Lemon-Pepper Vinaigrette to make you cheer; a half-dozen dessert sauces; five marinades; and now their latest and maybe the best of all—can you believe it?—catsup. New England chunky style that begins with fresh tomatoes, onions, celery, red and green bell peppers, cinnamon sticks, and other natural seasonings. This is pure, wholesome, honest catsup and is what Richard Nixon ought to order for those eggs he likes with catsup for breakfast. You are what you eat.

PICKLED OKRA

Talk o' Texas   phone orders: yes
435 S. Oaks   915-655-6077
San Angelo, TX 76905

For under $15 you can send a case of the best pickle the gods ever invented. I am talking, of course, about the

---

Lemon-Pepper Pasta

Serves 6 in 15 minutes

1	pound fresh linguine
¼	cup minced red onion
1	12-ounce bottle Lemon-Pepper Vinaigrette
1	cup tiny peas
1	cup green beans, sliced
1	cup mushrooms, sliced
2	tablespoons sweet butter
2	red sweet peppers, cut in thin strips
3	tomatoes, chopped
6	scallions, cut into ½-inch slivers
¼	cup fresh chives, minced
1	cup pitted black olives
¼	cup freshly grated Parmesan cheese Freshly milled black pepper

Cook pasta al dente in boiling water. Drain. In large bowl, toss pasta with onion and half the Lemon-Pepper Vinaigrette. Allow to cool to room temperature.

Cook peas, beans, and mushrooms quickly in butter. Don't overcook.

Add all ingredients except cheese, black pepper, and remaining dressing to pasta and toss. Toss with enough vinaigrette to coat. Top with grated cheese and freshly grated black pepper. Serve at room temperature.

venerated Talk o' Texas Pickled Okra. Just in case you never tried it, it's crisp, hot, sour, and spicy. Everything you want in a pickle and not a bit like slimy old boiled okra. Without spending a dime on advertising, or a red cent for added preservatives, the Talk o' Texas folks have made their pickles the talk of anybody who loves okra. You can get original or hot. Take your pick.

PICKLED GARLIC AND STEMS, GARLIC CANDY

Sorabol Restaurant   phone orders: yes
372 Grand Ave.   415-839-2288
Oakland, CA 94610   ae/visa/mc

At the San Francisco Gourmet Food and Wine Show, where the senses were assaulted by the sights and smells of more than 8,000 food and wine entrants, a few products stood out. Or perhaps even leaped out. Pickled garlic, garlic stems, and garlic candy were offered by only one person. And that person managed to draw a crowd with the seductive aroma of sautéing garlic. Young-Ran Hong stood, sautéing from daylight to dark, overwhelmed by the response to the product she has been offering to her restaurant customers for years. In the electric skillet, bubbling in hot butter, were pickled garlic stems and buds, looking like little green beans combined with some kind of pure white nut. The aroma was dizzying. The taste, a subtle garlic perfume without the bite of raw, fresh garlic, was enticing. Even the candied garlic was fun. It's the same idea as candied ginger, which Sorabol also makes and sells.

The manufacturer of these ancient Oriental delights, Young-Ran Hong, has operated a restaurant in Oakland and has made these products for her customers, along with garlic in soy sauce and kimchee, for several years. She was surprised by the response to her products. When I asked her for a business card, she stepped back. She couldn't get over it. She shook her head and sighed. "I never been famous before today. I never need name on card. Now. Television. Magazine. Book. One day. I never been famous before." Young-Ran Hong enjoyed her 15 minutes of fame. You will enjoy the pickled garlic. It comes in 4- and 6-ounce jars.

SALAD MAKINGS

Here are the best oils, vinegars, salad dressings, mayos, and mustards that I saw and tasted.

Oils

These oils are extra-virgin, meaning they are cold-pressed one time only and the first squeezings from the olive or nut is what you get. No chemical abominations. No heat. Nothing but the essence of the taste you want.

BEST CALIFORNIA OLIVE OILS

Santa Barbara Olive Co.   phone orders: yes
PO Box 3825   805-683-1932
Santa Barbara, CA 93105   visa/mc

For two generations, the Makela family has grown olives in this strip of land ideal for their production. Craig now produces what to my mind is the best extra-virgin olive oil money can buy. Cold-pressed, a lovely green-gold color, clear as crystal, the first pressing only. Fruity but not over-bearing. The chefs at Hugo's and Spago order it; so do Michael Hutchings and Julia Child. This is the best there is. And his olives! Enormous, perfectly graded for size and quality, and put up in a variety of ways, 13 in all, from wine-cured to jalapeño-stuffed. The perfect martini olive, soaked in vermouth, comes from the Makelas.

VARIETAL OLIVE OILS

Nick Sciabica & Sons   phone orders: yes
PO Box 1246   209-577-5067
Modesto, CA 95353

Dan Sciabica now heads a family venture that's been in place for four generations. Growing olives and producing oil using the time-honored methods practiced by his Sicilian grandfather, Dan makes a splendid extra-virgin olive oil from pesticide-free fruit carefully picked *from the tree,*

Jo's Christmas Eve Sicilian Sfinghi

Gemma Sciabica makes pastries with olive oil instead of butter or shortening. Because the taste is intense, she only uses half as much. I had always wondered why I couldn't reproduce the taste I found in North Beach bakeries. Here's the secret. These are the California Italian answer to New Orleans beignets, another form of the good old American doughnut—but with an olive oil difference. For other choices, ask for Gemma's cookbooklet. There's more.

Serves 10 in 30 minutes,
+ 2 hours rising time

    4   cups flour
    1   teaspoon salt
    1   tablespoon yeast,
        dissolved in ¼ cup
        warm water
    1½ cups warm milk
    4   tablespoons extra-virgin
        olive oil
    3   eggs
    ¼   cup sugar
    2   teaspoons vanilla
        Pure olive oil for
        cooking

Place flour in large mixing bowl. Make a well in center and add all ingredients except oil for cooking. Mix well, kneading at least 10 minutes, until dough is smooth and elastic. Cover and let rise until double in bulk, about an hour. Punch down and let rise again, about 20 minutes. Punch

CONTINUED ON PAGE 161

not off the ground. Dan's mother, Gemma, is in charge of quality control. Here's how that works.

In Gemma's kitchen, around the stove and spilling off the countertops are bottles and bottles of different pressings of olive oil, from dark green to light gold. When Gemma gets one to test, she opens it, rubs some on the back of her hand, sniffs it, and holds it up to the light. Then she tastes it. If the oil is cloudy, off-tasting, rough to the touch, or a dozen other subtle cues that only Gemma understands, it is rejected and won't get the Sciabica or Marsala label.

You can buy from the Sciabicas olive oil that comes from a particular variety of tree: Mission, Mission Organic Green, or Manzanillo Variety Organic Green. The Mission is the more common variety of tree for producing olives for oil, but the Manzanillo variety, rare and more expensive, is fruitier, light, and delicious. With this particular variety, I found I could use about half the usual amount.

IMPORTED FRUIT AND NUT OILS

See also: Soufflé de Paris.

Wendy Edgren not only brings us those airy soufflés, but she also imports first-quality walnut and hazelnut oils, as well as an extra-virgin olive oil from France, called Moulin Moderne from Christian Rossi, winner of gold medals for the past five years in French competitions. The oils come in bottles almost too pretty to believe, shaped like Greek urns and appropriately called Athena (16 ounces) and Athos (about 8 ounces). Wendy also brings in first-quality French imported green olives with lemon, Provence-style olives, green olives with fennel, as well as pickled shallots, garlic cloves, eggplant, and mushrooms. All of these products taste good. They are pricey, however. Luxe. Luxe.

See also: Corti Brothers for Italian extra-virgin olive oil, a greener, fruitier oil than any other. First quality.

Vinegars

Specialty vinegars are springing up everywhere. But be careful: Don't buy one that has a distilled white vinegar base. In taste-testing vinegars, if you stand them up side by side, from distilled white through cider, then wine and up through champagne vinegar, you'll see there are the same differences you'd find in wines—from rotgut to fino. Flavored vinegars vary from delicate raspberry up through the robust balsamic vinegar, a deep red-wine vinegar aged in vats of different woods. Every time the vinegar is transferred from one vat to the next, it becomes darker, richer, and more mellow. In Italy, where it is made, balsamic is as treasured as truffles and is used not only in salads and cooking but even as a nightcap.

Use potent vinegars (including balsamic) with hearty foods: cabbage, game, fennel, lamb. The more delicate fruit vinegars should be used in vinaigrettes, for chicken or fruit salads, or in a sauce for fish. You can even enjoy a tasty fruit vinegar, a tablespoon or so at a time, in a cold glass of club soda for a refreshing, cooling (read nonfattening) drink.

We have taste-tested white-wine vinegars flavored with garlic, basil, tarragon, mint, rosemary, blueberry, raspberry, and some fresh herb mixes. These vinegars are pure, good quality, and delicious.

CONTINUED FROM PAGE 160

down and pinch off pieces of dough that you can comfortably stretch to 2-by-4-inch pieces. Deep-fry in 2 inches pure olive oil until golden brown on each side. Drain. Sprinkle with cinnamon, sugar, honey, or syrup.

VARIETAL WINE VINEGARS

Kimberley Wine Vinegar Works
PO Box 40, Hunters Point
San Francisco, CA 94124

phone orders: yes
415-822-5850
visa/mc

The best American varietal wine vinegars in America are produced by Larry and Ruth Robinson, who began by making vinegar in their San Francisco Victorian. They've since moved out to the old Naval Shipyards, where they still use the traditional French Orléans method of converting wine to vinegar in oak barrels. This method, filtering

Ruth Robinson's Marinated Mushrooms

Serves 12–15 for party
10 minutes preparation;
2 days to marinate

- 1 pound fresh mushrooms
- ¾ cup virgin olive oil
- 2 large garlic cloves, crushed
- 1 teaspoon sugar
- 1 teaspoon salt
- ¾ cup Kimberley Cabernet vinegar
- ¼ cup minced parsley
- ¼ cup minced onion

Clean mushrooms. Combine remaining ingredients. Pour over mushrooms in nonaluminum container. Cover and refrigerate 2–3 days, stirring when you think about it. Drain before serving. Good with Valley lahvosh heart crackers.

out bacteria rather than chemically changing or pasteurizing the wine, takes six months. The delicate esters that flavor wines are carried over to the vinegars when they're prepared in this way without heat, without chemicals. Commercial chemical processes, in contrast, take only three days.

Ruth and Larry named their vinegars for their daughter, Kimberley, and make four kinds: Chardonnay, Cabernet, sherry, and a garlic-scented Cabernet. The Cabernet is aged in oak two years before beginning to turn to vinegar; the Chardonnay, six months. The sherry vinegar is one of the finest cooking wine vinegars I've ever used. The Cabernet tastes so good, it makes a fine salad dressing, with or without oil.

RASPBERRY VINEGAR NONPAREIL

Kendall-Brown Foods
PO Box 3365
San Rafael, CA 94912

phone orders: yes
415-499-1621

Barbara Kendall begins with fresh raspberries and the highest-quality California white-wine vinegar. Her raspberry vinegar stands up in taste tests with imported vinegars and is more fruity and fresh than any of the competitors. I guard my bottle of Barbara's vinegar jealously and won't let anybody else use it. It's so intensely raspberry that just a little used to deglaze the pan will create a perfect sauce over a just-sautéed fish filet. Barbara's vinegar is used in the best restaurant kitchens in San Francisco.

Barbara has also developed two splendid salad dressings: Raspberry-Walnut and Dill-Horseradish. Both work admirably as marinades as well.

NATURAL HERB VINEGARS

Peppicini Herb Farm
PO Box 1143
Santa Ynez, CA 93460

phone orders: yes
805-688-8217

Diane Wilder's interest in herbs began when she lived near Hearst Castle. She used to walk in the woods a lot and learned many edible plants and herbs. She loved showing young children these treasures of the forest, and now she's found a way to share her love for herbs with the world.

Calling her products Bella Vinegars, she begins with the best-quality white-wine vinegars, that she pours into ornate 8-ounce glass bottles made from an antique mold. She then feeds in fresh, organically grown herbs from her garden, caps the bottles, ties satin ribbons around the bottles' necks, and includes a cork so that once the cap is off, the cork can be used instead. The bottles themselves are such beauties, I'll bet this stuff walks off the shelves in gift stores, just from the look of it. And the taste—exquisite. Here are the choices: basil, cilantro, oregano, lemon thyme (made with champagne vinegar and smooth as silk), rosemary, and potpourri, made from tarragon, oregano, rosemary, red and black peppers, lemon thyme, and a blend of champagne and cider vinegars. Diane also flavors safflower oil with peppers and garlic. She even adds rosemary to local honey, and although she reports some buyer resistance, I found this was a fine glaze for a roast chicken.

Since she does not begin to bottle until her own garden herbs begin to reach their full flavor potential, she does not sell from December to April. Diane wraps her beautiful bottles in colored tissue paper. To open a package from her is a gift in itself. She grows herbs lovingly and prepares the herbal products the same way. The care shows.

FRESH FRUIT AND HERB VINEGARS

Herbs & Spice
PO Box 653
Astoria, OR 97103

phone orders: yes
503-325-1215
visa/mc

Betty Cier has translated a lifetime interest in gardening and cooking into fine herb products. She puts up fruit vinegars that make wonderful spritzers when mixed with club soda, and herb vinegars using herbs her daughters

---

Barbara Kendall's Fresh Salmon Salad

Serves 4 in 15 minutes

- 1 pound fresh salmon, poached in court bouillon, then broken into chunks
- ½ cup Raspberry-Walnut dressing
- ½ medium jícama, cut with melon baller
- ¼ pound Chinese snow pea pods, barely blanched
  Toasted whole walnuts

Combine all ingredients. Can be refrigerated or served immediately at room temperature.

Barbara Kendall's Warm Duck Salad

In a serving bowl, combine two or three kinds of deep-green lettuce leaves with coarsely chopped walnuts and sliced pear tomatoes. In sweet butter, sauté chunks of duck breast with shallots and button mushrooms. Remove meat and vegetables from skillet, place atop greens. Splash raspberry vinegar into skillet to deglaze, boil it up, and pour over the salad. That's California.

Betty Cier's Glazed Rock Cornish Hens

Serves 2 in 1½ hours

 2 Rock Cornish hens
   Salt and pepper to
   taste
 3 tablespoons strawberry
   vinegar
 ¼ cup strawberry jam
   Fresh strawberries
   Fresh Italian parsley

Preheat oven to 350° F. Rub hens inside and out with salt and pepper. Place on a rack in a shallow baking dish and roast uncovered 30 minutes. Meanwhile, combine strawberry vinegar and jam. After birds have cooked a half hour, coat them with strawberry glaze. Continue cooking until golden-glazed and done, about another 30 minutes. Garnish with fresh strawberries and Italian parsley.

grow organically for her. One of her newest and best flavors is cranberry. You could use the preceding Warm Duck Salad recipe with turkey breast and cranberry vinegar for a delicious luncheon salad. Here are the vinegars Betty is making at the moment: strawberry, raspberry, orange spice, blackberry, marion berry, and blueberry. Herbs include dill, garlic, purple basil, burnet, lemon, mint, garlic, and tarragon. Once Betty has dropped the fruits or herbs into the jars and poured in the white-wine vinegar, she caps the bottles, dips them in colored wax, and ties a ribbon around their necks. They're almost too pretty to open.

Betty also hand-blends her fresh herbs and makes a fine bread mix she'll send you. She calls it Herbal Beer Bread Mix; the beer acts as yeast, giving an almost cake-like texture to this well-balanced savory bread, which is on the table in less than an hour. Betty Cier is a good gardener and a good cook.

OREGON FRUIT VINEGARS

Oregon's Own Gourmet　　phone orders: yes
　Vinegars　　　　　　　503-282-6258
4307 N.E. Brazee
Portland, OR 97213

Marsha Johnson cold-processes her own vinegars, then adds Willamette Valley raspberries, blackberries, and blueberries right to the bottle. She ages the vinegars so you get a highly aromatic, clear vinegar with whole berries floating inside. Keeps best in the refrigerator. There's a three-bottle minimum order; try one of each.

See also: Corti Brothers for balsamic vinegar, imported and of the first quality.

Salad Dressings

If you have found homemade salad dressings beyond your ken, and if you abhor commercial dressings laced with chemicals, help is on the way.

BEST CALIFORNIA FRUIT AND WINE DRESSINGS

Cuisine Perel   phone orders: yes
PO Box 1064   415-435-1282
Tiburon, CA 94920

Leonardo and Silvia Perel are two of the most innovative cooks I know. Coming to Northern California from Argentina less than five years ago, they bring classic cooking techniques and Latin influences to the bounty of West Coast cuisine. Their salad dressings, free of artificial preservatives and made with the fresh fruits and wines they find locally, are just simply too good to be true. The lemon Chardonnay has won "best of show" in national contests where the competition is fierce. Their champagne mustard dressing is my personal favorite. Both dressings are smooth, creamy, pungent, and perfectly balanced and can lift salad greens to new heights.

The Perels are constantly coming up with new products. Lately they've added mustards, blended with fine California wines, Chardonnay, Sauterne, Chenin Blanc, and champagne. Their chutneys are original as well: grape apricot, grape peach, and a piquant grape. Their Zinfandel tomato sauce makes pasta a banquet. Call for a current list.

CALIFORNIA CLASSIC SALAD DRESSINGS

Cook's Classics, Ltd.   phone orders: yes
1111 Stanley Way   415-397-0202
Palo Alto, CA 94303   (Postmark S.F. shop)
                             ae/visa/mc
                             3-bottle minimum

Another of these incredible new businesses, Cook's Classics began in October 1983 at a Culinary Carnival. Offering her all-fresh salad dressings, sans sugar, MSG, or artificial preservatives, she had enough orders in one day to put her in business. Sheila makes five flavors using fresh garlic, fresh herbs, and premium spices. It is hard to

As a true salad lover, Sheila Cook has great ideas:

Lettuce, avocado, walnuts, and mandarin oranges make a great salad with Curry-Almond dressing.

Arrange on a platter barely cooked broccoli, cauliflower, baby carrots, and asparagus. Garnish with red flame grapes and splash Tarchon dressing over all.

Combine 3 cups cooked garbanzos and ¾ cup finely chopped purple onion with salt to taste. Dress with 6 tablespoons Apple-Honey-Mustard and ¾ teaspoon cumin. Fabulous.

Combine 4 cups spinach, 1 cup thinly sliced red onions, 1 diced apple, ½ cup bacon, ⅓ cup chopped pecans, and an optional ½ cup chicken or shrimp. Blend with Apple-Honey-Mustard.

Cook's Classic Potato Salad

Boil 8 small unpeeled diced red potatoes just until tender. Toss with ½ cup of any Cook's dressing. Add ½ cup diced celery, ½ cup thinly sliced red onions, 1 cup chopped Italian parsley, ½ teaspoon sweet fresh basil, salt and pepper to taste. Use additional dressing to taste.

say which tastes the best: Garlic; a tarragon dressing called Tarchon; a sweet-piquant Apple-Honey-Mustard; Caesar; or Curry-Almond.

The only thing better than the way they taste is the way they look, with an Art Nouveau label for each flavor. Sheila also includes a recipe brochure for stunning salads. Her brochure has that charming combination of food sophistication with a touch of "Hints from Heloise" thrown in just for your edification—such as suggesting that you wash a week's worth of lettuce at a time, then place it in your clothes washer on the spin-dry cycle to properly dry before preparing the salads. I love it. As Sheila herself says, "I use the same exact recipes in my own kitchen. So basically we have homemade dressings in a bottle." Sheila Cook's salad dressings are memorable. Even if you don't choose to dry your lettuce in the washing machine, you'll be glad you bought from Sheila.

GREAT COOKS FROM CHICAGO

Beautiful Food   phone orders: yes
546 Chestnut St.   312-446-4066
Winnetka, IL 60093   visa/mc

Charie McDonald started a take-out place in this Chicago suburb after years of experience as a cooking instructor, founder of the Chicago Culinary Guild, and student of Simca Beck. Following Simca's advice to use only the finest ingredients, Charie began getting requests in her shop for bottles of the perfectly balanced dressings she used on salads.

In the spring of 1982 she began bottling the dressings for her shop customers. But you can't keep a good thing local long, and now her light, low-sodium vinaigrettes are for sale nationwide. Choose from the original made with highest-quality olive oil, or the light one made with safflower oil, or the lemon vinaigrette made with olive oil and lemon juice. Beautiful Food also offers blue cheese and poppy-seed dressings and wonderful sweet mustard sauces.

Charie McDonald says, "I'll cook anything. Whatever they want. Chocolate chip cookies. I don't care. I just want to make my customers happy." The people who try her beautiful food are very happy.

FITNESS DRESSINGS

Victorian Pantry   phone orders: yes
PO Box 222   408-734-0907
Saratoga, CA 95071

With an eye to fitness as well as taste, the Victorian Pantry cooks make dressings from pale virgin olive oil and soy oil blended to lighten the calorie load. They use no salt but achieve intense flavors by carefully blending pungent herbs and spices. Try capers and cheese; red pepper basil; brandy honey; and olives and tarragon. These are all delicious.

NARSAI'S MUSTARDS AND DRESSINGS

Narsai's Restaurant Market   phone orders: yes
389 Colusa   415-527-7900
Berkeley, CA 94707

Narsai sells the dressings and mustards that make his Northern California restaurant famous. You can now take home Citronnade, a delicate, lemony dressing with Dijon mustard and coarse black pepper. In the restaurant they use it with salad greens, bunches of fresh herbs, cheese, and fruits on a plate. Narsai also makes mustards of pure stone-ground mustard and flavored with white wine: tarragon, green peppercorn, or sweet old-fashioned made with brown sugar, like a good German mustard. Besides the Citronnade, he also offers feta cheese dressing made with olive oil, lemon, mint, and garlic; and a basil dressing vinaigrette that brings alive just-blanched vegetables. If you call, don't forget Narsai made his reputation with dessert toppings he calls Decadence. With good reason.

BEST LITTLE DRESSING IN TEXAS

La Martinique Dressings   phone orders: yes
Pace Foods   512-224-2211
PO Box 12636   minimum order: 1 case
San Antonio, TX 78212

In the early part of the 20th century, when Frenchwoman Esther Allidi came to Austin, Texas, with her Escoffier cookbook in hand, she opened up broad vistas of taste thrills to the movers and shakers in the state capitol from her restaurant, which she called The Liberty Bell. Making salad dressings from her classic recipes, she began bottling and selling them to customers. Now, more than 50 years later, people who otherwise wouldn't miss Texas at all get positively misty-eyed over the unavailability of La Martinique dressings. There are three: Poppy-seed; a clear vinaigrette with Wisconsin blue cheese; and a French dressing that is the real Escoffier-style French, not one of those usual American abominations.

The family has now sold the salad dressing business to busy Pace, but the Pace people still do things by hand. Seven women peel and chop the onions and garlic for the French vinaigrettes. Until recently they were still putting labels on by hand, but Pace does have a machine for that. Time marches on. You have to buy this by the case. It comes in 8-ounce and 16-ounce bottles . . . the same plain-vanilla bottles Madame used. She put the money into the product, not into the package. It paid off.

Mayonnaises and Mustards

Lord, there are a lot of mustards. And a mayo or two worth talking about. I tried to hold this list down to just those that really stood out. I eliminated the clones (how many sweet hot mustards can one stand?) and offer to you the best I could find. The list is as abbreviated as I could make it.

CALIFORNIA GARLIC MAYONNAISE

See also: Norman-Bishop.

Carrol Norman not only knows her way around chocolate but also makes a garlic mayonnaise and a garlic mustard that will knock your socks off. Using the good Gilroy garlic from just down the road, she blends this with homemade first-quality white mayonnaise and a smooth light mustard to create two wonderful sandwich spreads. There is so much garlic in each of these spreads, the vampires will stay away indefinitely.

SAN FRANCISCO WHOLE-SEED MUSTARD

San Francisco Mustard Co.   phone orders: yes
PO Box 883962   415-435-5211
San Francisco, CA 94188

Robert Dickinson makes mustard in very small batches in his own kitchen. An old-world recipe combined with fresh California ingredients makes for a mustard to remember. Robert uses two kinds of whole seeds: *Brassica alba,* a large yellow seed, and *Brassica junicea,* a smaller, spicier variety. The mustard seeds are left whole, combined with white-wine vinegar from Napa Valley, Sierra Nevada honey, and pure spring water. This crunchy brown, German-style mustard, with no salt, sugar, artificial colors, flavors, or preservatives, is a natural with cold cuts. It comes packed in a great-looking earthenware crock.

CANADIAN CONDIMENTS

Sable & Rosenfeld   phone orders: yes
89 McCaul St., Ste. 225   416-595-1727
Toronto, Canada M5T2X7   visa/mc through
                           I. Magnin, Macy's Cellar,
                           or Neiman's only

Up in Canada, Myra Sable has the same formidable reputation you'd find here from Silver Palate. Using home recipes, no preservatives, and high standards, she's

---

Carrol Norman's Barbecue Sauce

Makes 1½ cups

¾	cup catsup
½	can beer
¼	cup Norman-Bishop garlic mustard
1	small onion, diced
4	drops Liquid Smoke (optional)
1	teaspoon Worcestershire sauce

Blend ingredients together, cover, and let stand overnight. Store in refrigerator up to two weeks. Excellent with baked chicken or spareribs.

Myra Sable's Broiled Russian Mustard Chicken

Serves 4 in 40 minutes

1	3-pound fryer, quartered
4	tablespoons sweet butter
4	tablespoons Russian Style Mustard
½	teaspoon cayenne pepper
2	scallions, finely chopped
3	cups fresh bread crumbs

Pat fryer dry. In a large skillet, heat butter until foaming, then sauté chicken pieces, turning frequently, until almost done—10 minutes or so. Set aside. Mix cooking butter and pan juices with mustard, cayenne, and scallions, and whip into a creamy mayonnaise. Spread liberally all over chicken, then roll in bread crumbs, pressing to adhere. Broil 3–5 minutes each side under preheated broiler, or until coating is toasty brown. Drizzle with any remaining mustard-mayonnaise and serve hot or cold.

created a line of fine condiments good as homemade and put up in attractive packages. Mail-order through the closest American retailer you see listed above.

Of a half-dozen mustards and sauces, preserves, jams, and toppings, two things we liked best were the mustards and mayos: Russian and Tarragon. Both are sweet and silky, good as a béarnaise for steaks or as a basis for a Russian salad dressing.

VERMONT STYLE MUSTARD SAUCE

The Vermont Shop   phone orders: yes
Box 83   802-253-8338
Stowe, VT 05672   visa/mc

This old Vermont recipe makes a sweet-sour mustard that's good with deviled eggs, game, or cold cuts. Made from imported mustard seeds, apple cider vinegar, herbs, spices, whole eggs, and a touch of sugar, it contains no salt, no colorants, no additives or preservatives of any kind. Made in small batches, it belongs on hot dogs at the ball game.

DUTCH-STYLE MUSTARD

Boetje Foods, Inc.   phone orders: yes
2736 12th St.   309-788-4352
Rock Island, IL 61201

This 96-year-old, three-person company has been making brown Dutch-style mustard the same way, the whole time. This is best-quality light brown, nonsweet mustard with whole mustard seeds visible. If you just smear this over thick fish filets and then dip them in flour and pan-fry, you'll have an old American standby that's delicious. The Boetjes are used to getting desperate letters from people who have moved away from their small selling range, and so they offer a six-pack of Boetjes for under $10.

CALIFORNIA FLAVORED MUSTARDS

Helen Harmon's Gourmet   phone orders: yes
4226 S. Produce Plaza   213-589-1616
Vernon, CA 90058   visa/mc

Helen Harmon makes a smooth, sweet mustard that begins with mustard powder, white-wine vinegar, and eggs. She then seasons it 10 different ways: sweet-hot, dill, onion, horseradish, jalapeño, champagne-honey, wheat germ and honey, toasted sesame, teriyaki, and pepper-hot. As you can imagine, these mustards are useful as marinades as well as salad dressings.

See also: To Market To Market for a do-it-yourself Sweet and Saucy Mustard sauce that's at least as good as any you can buy.

NAPA VALLEY SWEET HOT MUSTARD

Napa Valley Mustard Co.   phone orders: yes
PO Box 125   707-944-8330
Oakville, CA 94562

This mustard has the texture of fine, creamed honey given a hot mustard bite. Mixed with curry powder and thinned with a little cream, it makes a wonderful dip for prawns. It is also outstanding for deglazing the pan after you sauté chicken breasts. Of all the prepared mustards I've seen, this one is my favorite. (Although I do love to make my own, using To Market To Market's mustard and recipe.)

CAJUN/CREOLE SAUCES

Evangeline Pepper &   phone orders: yes
   Food Products   318-394-3091
PO Box 798
St. Martinville, LA 70582

No self-respecting Cajun would dream of setting up house without a bottle of Louisiana hot sauce on the shelf. Begin-

Evangeline Grillades

A classic Cajun dish, these are generally served with grits, although rice will do in a pinch.

Serves 4 in 1 hour

1	pound round steak
½	cup cooking oil
1	large onion, sliced thin
1	large green pepper, chopped
1	tablespoon Evangeline hot sauce
	Salt to taste

Cut round steak into small pieces, about 2-inch squares. Heat oil in skillet until very hot. Add meat. Do not turn meat until you can see it brown from the sides; then turn and brown other side. Add onions, green peppers, and hot sauce. Cover tightly, lower flame to simmer, and cook until meat is tender, about 30–40 minutes. Add salt to taste. Serve with grits or rice.

ning with crushed cayenne and Tabasco peppers, the Evangelinists age the mash in wood casks, then mix with distilled vinegar, this being one case where the vinegar is swallowed up by the hot peppers. It comes red or green.

Another Cajun staple is a bottle of Tabasco peppers with vinegar. Buy it once and you get a lifetime supply. All you have to do is add more vinegar as you shake it out. If you like your pot of beans, you ought to have this on hand to shake over the beans. I grew up on this stuff. Delicious. You can also get three kinds of Louisiana long-grain rices: Regent, Evangeline, and Chinito. Ask for their recipe booklet. It will start you on your way to cooking Cajun.

CHAPTER 5

THE CONFECTIONERY

I. Fudge
II. Toffees
III. Caramels, taffies, and pralines
IV. Hard candies
V. Truffles and other chocolates
VI. Ice cream toppings and dessert sauces
VII. Belgian chocolates

Good, fresh candy made with pure, whole ingredients and no preservatives is not as easy to find as one would hope. I tried a lot of different candies for this chapter and soon got absolutely ruthless in rejecting second-rate ones. You can overdose on sugar in a hurry. The candymakers chosen for this chapter ship just-made fresh candies direct to customers with no warehouse standing between the cook and the candy lover, and no preservatives inserted to extend shelf life. Most chocolate makers and many other candymakers will not ship in hot weather. Forget it. Eat ice cream in the summer. Save the candy for fall.

FUDGE

Fudge, that homiest of candies, is made from cream, butter, sugar, and flavoring. Anything else and you're getting some sort of *faux* fudge. But the techniques for putting those ingredients together make for remarkably different results. These are the best.

HEAVENLY FUDGE

Briggintine Monks   phone orders: yes
23300 Walker Lane   503-835-8080
Amity, OR 97101   visa/mc

Did you ever use that kind of fudge recipe that began, "one jar Hippolite cream"? That was a kind of prepared marshmallow cream known to candymakers as mazetta. The Amity monks have mastered the process for making homemade marshmallow cream without the chemical undertones of preservatives, and from that they make a fudge so creamy, so long-lasting it doesn't turn to sugar shards after a week, and so delicious that some say it's the best fudge in this world and maybe the next. Care for ingredients as well as the process makes the difference. Beginning with Guittard chocolate, real cream, and that homemade mazetta made from both brown and white sugars, this is a really good fudge.

Nearly a dozen flavors can be mail-ordered, available at under $10 a pound postpaid, ranging from traditional chocolate fudge with nuts to divinity with nuts, peanut butter, pecan praline, lemon crème, and butterscotch. They've recently added giant truffles and chocolate barks to their product line. All creamy-smooth and delicious, heavenly concoctions to satisfy earthly desires.

CARAMEL-BASED FUDGE DROPS

Chapin's Fudge   phone orders: yes
PO Box 285   503-643-1757
Beaverton, OR 97075

When Ceac Chapin and Anne Collier first tried to increase their home recipe for a prize-winning fudge to commercial proportions, donning hair nets and aprons and entering a state-approved kitchen with nothing but their recipe times 10 and 100 pounds of ingredients, they wound up with 84 pounds of failure in the pans, and 16 pounds on the floor. They were glad that Grandpa Bill wasn't around to see. It was his recipe, and he'd operated a candy kitchen in Portland early in the 20th century made famous by Bill's Rocky Road and this fudge. But after trial and error—as Ceac says, much error—the two got the candy back to the fine version they remembered.

This is the kind of fudge made from a caramel base of sugar, butter, whipping cream, salt, and condensed milk, to which they add chocolate, vanilla, and walnuts. Then they enrobe the soft fudge in milk chocolate *couvertour.* These fudge drops are soft, sweet, and light on the inside, with a crisp chocolate cover. They melt in your mouth. Perfect.

MACKINAC ISLAND FUDGE

Marshall's Fudge   phone orders: yes
308 E. Central Ave.   616-436-5379
Mackinaw City, MI 49701   ae/visa/mc

Most tourist stops offer more local color than good quality, but this is an exception. Mrs. Marshall and son Dean have been making 16 flavors of fudge and other candies for the tourists and have developed a mail-order business out of necessity—they keep getting letters pleading, "I've got to have more of this candy!" Their pecan roll is positively addictive. They make your classic homemade-type fudge; creamy, smooth, made with good, pure ingredients, and orders are shipped the same day they're received. Of the 16 flavors, we particularly liked the white fudge with peanuts. The Marshalls close from December 10 to May, but other than that, they ship just-made candy every day and do a land-office business of Christmas mail order.

TOFFEES

You wouldn't think there could be much variety here, but believe me, there is. And I must say, there is life after a Heath bar. A good afterlife, indeed.

SOUTHERN-STYLE TOFFEE

Buckley's English Toffee,
  Inc.
PO Box 14119
Baton Rouge, LA 70898

phone orders: yes
504-642-8381
visa/mc

Butter, sugar, almonds, and a little margarine, all cooked together to just the light crack stage, then poured out thin and cut into 1-inch squares. These thin, rich, buttery, golden squares of hard toffee come to you in a 2-pound tin that I swear you'll want to hide from everybody else. Spurgeon Buckley first made it to raise money for his Newton, Mississippi, church bazaar. After somebody shipped a can of it to Atlanta, Buckley got his first mail order. He soon moved his candymaking venture to a greenhouse in his backyard. For a long time he used a Rube Goldberg–type candy machine that he designed and built to fill his own needs, making candy only during the fall for Christmas mail orders. But now his daughter Beverly has taken over, moved the venture to her home-town, and sells year-round.

WORLD-CLASS TOFFEES

Enstrom Candies, Inc.
212 S. Seventh St.,
  PO Box 1088
Grand Junction, CO 81502

phone orders: yes
303-242-1655
visa/mc

During the summers when I used to visit my Aunt Jamie in Grand Junction, the talk around town was of the coming riches of uranium. But the undiscovered treasure was made by another Jamee, and that was toffee, rolled in chocolate and almonds, a toffee of such quality that one *New York Times* reporter said, "Honestly, I suggest you skip this paragraph because if you read on, and if you order, you'll be hooked." If you have ever had traditional English toffee rolled in almonds and chocolate, you'll know this is it. Perfect, buttery, rich with California almonds and fine chocolate. This little candy store in this fair-sized town has made a worldwide reputation from this one product.

RUSSIAN-STYLE SUGAR ON SNOW WITH CHOCOLATE

Chocolate Lace   phone orders: no
8 South St.   203-792-8175
Danbury, CT 06810

What happens when a Stanford Business School gradu-
ate who started out pushing breath control—Listerine, that
is—buys an obscure machine called "the dancing dish"
and a recipe for a Russian confection? You get a very
exclusive, high-quality product, aimed at a narrow market, he says. This is how Stephen Bray describes his entry
into the candy business.

What Stephen Bray calls Chocolate Lace originated
in Russia and is a cousin to Vermont's sugar on snow. After
the first snow, a boiling sugar syrup was streamed over
snow to make a lacy pattern. When cold and crisp, it was
then dipped into chocolate. A woman named Eugenia
Tay came to America from Russia early in this century, and
after making small batches and waiting impatiently for the
first snow to arrive, she invented and patented this little
machine. It wiggles back and forth, squeezing out trans-
parent strands of sugar syrup into designs—no two alike,
just like snowflakes, says Bray. He dips it into first-quality
dark chocolate that he buys from Mercken's in Boston.
Then, Bray and his three helpers—standing on a floor
made sticky from that dancing dish's zealous splashing of
candy on the floor, the wall, one's shoes—pack and ship
the lace directly to customers in 7-ounce and 14-ounce
sizes. As delicate as the sugar glass in the old Saturday
Westerns, this candy has a rich toffee flavor under the
thick dark chocolate coating. You won't see this anywhere
else. The Stanford man has cornered the market.

AMERICAN TOFFEE

Eisenhower Candies, Inc.   phone orders: yes
686 S. Arroyo Pkwy., #102   818-441-3711
Pasadena, CA 91105   visa/mc

Lyn Eisenhower calls her version "American" toffee. But
it seems to me to be the classic English toffee; pure butter,
delicate and rich, thin, with a little crunch to it. Lyn covers

her toffee with chocolate in three versions—dark, light, and white—then sprinkles the chocolate with paper-thin slivers of fresh nuts. She offers the candy in the breakup sheet, or cut into squares.

CARAMELS, TAFFIES, AND PRALINES

These soft, rich candies made from sugar, butter, and cream are either pulled as taffies, or poured and cut as caramels and pralines. This category is one in which the big candymakers take a lot of shortcuts because these are fragile candies, with a short shelf life. The very best ones are shipped as soon as they're made. Here are the best we could find in America.

HONEY CANDIES

Queen Bee Gardens
1863 Lane 11½
Lovell, WY 82431

phone orders: yes
307-548-2543

Clarence and Bessie Zeller raised three boys on the proceeds from pure, unfiltered mountain honey they gathered from clover and alfalfa fields. But what the boys liked best was the candy their mother made using her old Scotch grandfather's recipe for honey taffy. So when the boys grew up, they decided it was time to expand beyond their local honey market. Nobody thought you could produce candy using only honey—too sticky, too liquid, too messy—but the Zeller boys worked at it and now make the only honey taffy in the world.

I'll tell you, this taffy is delicious. Soft, redolent with the aroma of mild honey, it comes in several flavors from vanilla to licorice; the peanut butter flavor is outstanding. Just to show they weren't a one-shot wonder, the boys went on to invent a candy they call Pecan Pearl, a praline made from pure honey, dairy cream, butter, pecans, vanilla, dry milk, lecithin, and algin. This is a melt-in-your-mouth praline. They also invented a fudgelike candy they call Stasia; a mint; pollen drops; a super honey peanut brittle they call Hoo Doo; suckers; and, of course, just to please Dad, they still sell Zeller's unfiltered, raw Wyoming clover and alfalfa honey.

SALTWATER TAFFY

Phillips Candies   phone orders: yes
217 Broadway   503-738-5402
Seaside, OR 97138   visa/mc

Steve Phillips's family has owned this seaside candy shop since 1939, when they bought out the original owners who had made candy here since 1898. Although this is a full-line shop that makes good, fresh candies and chocolates in hundreds of varieties, they have made their reputation with two products: saltwater taffy and Rocky Road.

The taffies, made from original recipes dating back to the 19th century, are a far cry from the mass-produced, rocklike, oversweet taffies one sees in most airport shops. These taffies are soft, sweet, and laced with butter and cream. My personal favorite is the butter one, a translucent yellow, which blends the very best of butter's natural taste with that of caramelized sugar into a soft, chewy bite that is unforgettable. There are a dozen flavors you can order, either separately or mixed.

Of all the American candies that have been maligned, maltreated, and mass-produced to no good ends, Rocky Road stands as the candy most in need of having its past glories revisited. Steve Phillips has done it. He makes his own mazetta—marshmallow cream without the preservatives—and adds to it fresh walnuts and pure, first-quality milk chocolate in the combination that first made Rocky Road famous. This is the real McCoy, folks. Don't ever order it unless you are prepared to order it again. Delicious.

BUTTER-RICH SOFT CARAMELS

My Sister's Caramels   phone orders: yes
1884 Bret Harte   Carmel Bay Co.
Palo Alto, CA 94303   800-345-0040
                             visa/mc

Hilary Donahue says her caramels are the closest to homemade you've ever tasted. Well, Hilary, I don't know anybody who can make caramels like this at home. This recipe of her sister's is soft, pure, translucent butter-colored caramel made from pure Knudsen's whipping cream, Darigold grade AA butter, and C&H sugar. That's all. But, if you ever taste these, you will never forget them. Of all the taffies I tasted, these were my favorites. The absolute best.

Hilary first made them for sale from her kitchen, but this is one of those stories where the orders quickly jumped out from under her, so she now has them made professionally in a candy kitchen, in small batches. She also makes chocolate caramels, which I think are not nearly as good as the original butter flavor. She also has a great new flavor called Praline Cream, made with dark brown sugar and pecans. Now, that is delicious. The packaging done for Hilary by The Carmel Bay Company is gorgeous and changes with the season. Send this as a gift and the recipient will love it even before tasting.

SAVANNAH PRALINES

Gaston Dupre, Inc.　　phone orders: yes
6201 Johns Rd., Ste. 11　813-885-9445
Tampa, FL 33614

Lucky for us Sophie and Emmanuel Roux stumbled onto this old, authentic French recipe for pralines, which are named for the Duke of Praslin, who used to present these crisp, glazed nuts to the ladies of the court of Louis XIII. The original pralines differ from the New Orleans or Texas evolutions in that they are simply crunchy, heavily sugared grilled nuts. The Rouxs make these old-world pralines with pecans, almonds, macadamias, and now hazelnuts. *Connoisseur* magazine called them one of the 16 most delicious regional specialties in America.

The Roux family has had such success with pralines that now they've branched out. You may also order from them award-winning pasta (try the delicious three-color confetti) or their very own French vinaigrette.

NEW ORLEANS PRALINES

Creole Delicacies Co., Inc.   phone orders: yes
533 Saint Ann St.   504-524-7429
New Orleans, LA 70116   ae/visa/mc/dc

The famous New Orleans-style praline is made here using only sugar, butter, cream, and pecans. It has a fudgelike texture and is loaded with nuts; the closest you can come to homemade comes from this French Quarter shop, which has been selling them to tourists for 30 years. Besides the original, they also make rum and chocolate flavors in the big copper kettles from which they hand-pour their candies. Each praline is wrapped in a sealed bag for freshness. Besides these melt-in-your-mouth candies, they sell other Creole specialties: remoulade sauce—a must for a genuine oyster loaf sandwich; hot-pepper jelly; and Creole dry seasonings—spicy, gumbo, omelet, herb blend, and seafood seasoning. With each spice blend, you also get a gen-u-wine Creole recipe to boot.

TEXAS PRALINES

Lamme's Candies   phone orders: yes
PO Box 1885   512-835-6791
Austin, TX 78767   visa/mc

Anybody who went to the University of Texas learned at least two things: to sing "The Eyes of Texas" and to love Lamme's pralines. This Austin establishment makes a Texas kind of candy: chewy, with more native pecans than anything else, and each individually wrapped in cellophane to save you from the inevitable sticky fingers. The candy has been made by members of the Lamme family since the late 19th century. Today, walking through their plant, you still see ladies hand-dipping hot praline spoonfuls onto a belt that travels through a cooling chamber and out the other side, where more ladies pick up the candies and individually wrap each one. Why don't they automate? Fourth-generation owner David Lamme Teich

Tips from David Lamme Teich for Making Candy at Home

■ Use high-quality ingredients only.

■ Buy a good candy thermometer.

■ Water is chocolate's worst enemy. If you have sweaty palms, wear gloves to dip chocolates.

■ Keep chocolate away from other foods. It will absorb stray odors and flavors.

■ Candy should be kept cool but not in the refrigerator: too humid.

■ Most candy can be frozen. Double-wrap in foil, then plastic.

(say *tice*) says, "I like to dance with the girl I brought. When you automate, you usually have to change the product to fit the machine." As a 20-year fan of Lamme's pralines, I can tell you that if they changed this candy, the Longhorns would hook 'em for sure. We like this candy just as it is: native pecans, sugar, corn syrup, milk, and butter. Nothing fancy.

In the spring, Austin residents participate in a rite of passage that's exclusive to Lamme's. For three days a year, the Lammes bring in strawberries and hand-dip them in milk chocolate. They sell these only to customers in the store, and you'll have to call around the first of March just to see when the berries will peak. Besides the famous chewy pralines, Lamme's also makes nonpareil taffy and good chocolates.

ALABAMA PECAN CANDIES

Priester's Pecans   phone orders: yes
227 Old Fort Dr.   800-633-5725
Fort Deposit, AL 36032   visa/mc/dc/cb

Although these folks call themselves a nut company, they're really best known for their candies. Their pralines, the fudge kind made from pure ingredients and good Southern Alabama pecans, are famous, as are their glacéed pecans, frosted pecans, Cajun Bits, and Fiddlesticks, which are a caramel and pecan candy they recommend to "every Southern Gentleman and Yankee-Doodle." They've put pecans into every kind of mouth-watering candy: divinity, fudge, brittle, and bark. They also sell roasted and salted pecans—Schley, Stuarts, Desirables, and Azalea hybrids in halves and in the shells.

HARD CANDIES

According to confectioner Sonny Schimpff, hard-candy making began in England in the early 1800s and was introduced worldwide at Prince Albert's London Industrial Exposition in 1851. Hard candies today are out of favor with many candy lovers. Those commonly available are just too sweet, too insipid, or artificially flavored. According to Schimpff, this is because hard-candy making is one of the most difficult crafts for the candymaker to learn, and there are simply few people around anymore who know their craft. Natural flavors are the best but require a dedication on the part of the candymaker that is hard to find when the company becomes some big division of a multinational. And that's too bad for us because the object in any hard candy is flavor, not sweetness—flavor that stays with the candy from first taste to last. Schimpff, for example, raises horehound in his garden so that he can harvest the herb at just the right moment to get that pure, distinctive myrrhlike flavor.

Within the hard-candy category, one finds stick candy, lemon drops, lozenges, suckers, mints, ribbon candy, sour fruit balls, peanut brittle, anise drops, as well as the more exotic peanut butter krumbles, jackstraws, chicken bones, and various chips. One of the few oldtime candymakers to know how to make all of these is Sonny Schimpff. He ought to be one of our national treasures. Almost single-handedly he is keeping a vanishing craft alive.

OLD-FASHIONED HARD CANDIES

Schimpff's Confectionery   phone orders: yes
347 Spring St.   812-283-8367
Jeffersonville, IN 47130   visa/mc

Those big box candymakers, Whitman, See's, Pangborn, you know the brands, they all started out in the same way that Schimpff's did, but over time they've automated and added so many preservatives that about all you get from them is a bare hint of what really good confections can be. Sonny Schimpff makes hundreds of candies in his store and boxes them up to look like the candies you see at the drugstore. But there the comparison fails. For Schimpff's candies are in a higher league.

His skills with hard candies especially set him apart. According to production records he found, his great-grandfather was making red-hots as early as 1876. Now, these aren't what you get at the 7-11 but are a clear red, hard, square pillow of pure cinnamon flavor that tastes *good.* Sonny first tried his hand at this skill in the 1920s under the training of his father and grandfather.

It took years before he was able to make such candies as peanut butter krumbles, a hard candy softened by the addition of peanut or other nut butters; and peppermint-filled jackstraws; and walnut chips—these candies are a marvel, all 25 kinds. According to Schimpff, caramels are really hard candies made soft by the addition of butter or cream. One of the most interesting caramels he makes is called Modjeskas, after an actress who came through Louisville, Kentucky, about 1883 and entranced a Mr. Anton Busath, who was in the candy business there at the time. The Modjeska is a cream caramel-covered pure egg-white marshmallow about an inch square and a half-inch thick. This candy is to die for.

You've seen so-called turtles before. But Sonny's turtles are really turtles, molded chocolate with a caramel center and pecans for feet. If you ever try these once, you'll see what those drugstore candies are imitating and what a poor imitation they are, compared to Sonny's.

If I were planning a wedding, I'd be sure to order the wedding mints from Sonny. Real Swedish mints have to ripen in a special high-temperature controlled environment, and Sonny still knows how to do this. The result is a hard candy that has a kind of fudged texture from the careful tempering and is absolutely delicious. Not to mention beautiful.

One of the great things about ordering from Schimpff's is that you can get truly custom-made candies. This is a man doing exactly what he wants to do, and he loves nothing better than to help somebody fill a special order—say, mints with your initials on top for a wedding. Or bonbons decorated with Santas and holly wreaths. This man is an artist. Even if you just order a box of candy, for no special occasion, but mixed to your special requirements, the candies will be absolutely fresh; if Sonny doesn't have everything you want, he'll make it after he gets the order and still have it on its way to you in 24 hours.

Another fun thing is to get on the mailing list for his quarterly newsletter. The candy information that I'm passing on to you, I learned from the newsletter. All you have to do to get on the list is send him your address. You'll get the newsletter for a year. As long as you purchase Schimpff's candy at least once a year, you'll keep hearing from Sonny. You'll enjoy the information as much as the candy.

NUT BRITTLES

Grandpa Buswell's Candy   phone orders: yes
26860 Salmon River Hwy.   503-879-5377
Willamina, OR 97396   visa

"Grandpa" in this case happens to be a comely young woman who makes old-fashioned brittle and sells it through her family's fruit stand. Judy Buswell's most popular flavor is hazelnut, and it has received favorable mention from as far away as *The Washington Post*. She also makes brittle using peanuts and almonds. This is made the way Grandpa would do it, using pure ingredients and in small batches. In fact, Judy and her two helpers stir brittle for seven hours a day in a 80-year-old farmhouse. To keep from going stir crazy, they used to read mysteries aloud to one another, but as the plot thickened so did the candy. After a few instances of having the pages stick together at the crucial moment, the brittlers switched to books on tape. Now you can find them, staring at the bubbling brew, a distant look on their faces, as the tape whirs on, finally telling whodunit.

CRANBERRY CANDY

Cranberry Sweets Co.   phone orders: yes
PO Box 501   503-347-2526
Bandon, OR 97411   visa/mc

This wonderful sour/sweet cranberry candy laced with walnuts is more a gel type than anything else, but the texture comes only from the natural pectin in the cranberries, which come from the bog next door. Cut into small rectangles and rolled in sugar, these are a fabulous, fresh-tasting sweet. Using the same method, these candymakers also make an outrageous wild blackberry confection and, believe it or not, a delicious beer candy made from Henry's Blitz Weinhard. One of their best is called lemon-pie candy. A rectangle of filling that tastes like a fresh lemon pie is dipped in white chocolate. This is too much! All candies here are made in small batches using no preservatives, no starch, no food colorings or artificial flavorings.

TRUFFLES AND OTHER CHOCOLATES

According to Sonny Schimpff, a truffle is a French cream type of chocolate, traditionally flavored with nuts, liqueurs, or liquors. The center, known as ganache, is made from chocolate, whipped cream, and butter. Since the cream and butter are not cooked, the truffle is considerably more fragile than other cream chocolates, which have a center made from sugar and egg whites. With the truffle, more than any other kind of candy, freshness is a must. Truffle shops have sprung up around this country like the fungi from whence they derived their name. While you may be able to get a decent truffle locally, not just anyone can be relied on to ship them properly. As a general rule, truffles should be shipped by air, kept cool, and stored in a cool place to be eaten within a week. The refrigerator may make them sweat or take on other odors. It's best not to order more than you can consume in a brief time—but I'd hate to tell you how many of these things a chocoholic can put away in a brief time. In selecting truffle makers for this chapter, I have graded not only for taste but also for shipping expertise. These are the best I could find in America.

Storing Chocolates

Light and heat are detrimental to the quality of chocolates. Store in a cool, dark space. If they are kept in the refrigerator, remove them at least an hour before serving, but do not open the box until the temperature adjusts to room temperature. Fast changes in temperature bring about condensation and loss of shine. Chocolates should be eaten fresh.

KANSAS CITY SWISS CHOCOLATES

Andre Bollier, Ltd.   phone orders: yes
5018 Main St.   800-892-1234 (national)
Kansas City, MO 64112   816-561-3440 (MO)

The next time Calvin Trillin flies to Kansas City for dinner, I can tell him where to go after the doughnut and barbecue stops: Andre's Confiserie Suisse for chocolates. Oh, I know, Andre is not a native like Calvin. But he did choose Kansas City when he came to the States from his apprenticeship in his home country, Switzerland—which is more than Trillin can say, despite his protestations that Kansas City has the best food in America. Now that I've come to know Andre Bollier, I think there may be some truth to this claim. Even if Andre Bollier is—dare I say it—really Continental. Eat your words, Calvin Trillin. Try a truffle, too.

These are among the best domestic truffles and chocolates you can find. Small, dense, intensely flavored, they come enrobed in light or dark chocolate convertour or rolled in best-quality cocoa. You can order them in the variety of your choice. The Truffe Madame, a milk ganache with powdered-sugar covering, and the Truffe Monsieur, a bittersweet chocolate ganache dusted with cocoa, make a wonderful pair. In addition to the authentic Swiss-style truffles, don't miss the pistache, a bittersweet chocolate ganache on pistache marzipan; or the Aida, marzipan with pineapple pieces. Andre also offers a Mondavi-labeled wine bottle molded of the highest-quality chocolate and filled with California almonds carefully roasted and covered with fine chocolate. The postpaid charge for these superior candies—shipped only from October 1 to April 15—is a very reasonable $20 per 18 ounces as we go to print.

MICHIGAN TRUFFLES

Minerva St. Chocolates	phone orders: yes
1052 Olivia	313-998-4090
Ann Arbor, MI 48104	visa/mc

Judy Weinblatt, who has been making and selling truffles a mere five years, has seen her business mushroom (pardon) from that of a purely local one serving the college kids to a national market with praise from everybody who counts in the food business. One critic even named her truffles along with some of the best available from Europe. She has given these tender, intense chocolate morsels her own American touch. While still hand-dipping each and every one, she produces fresher, finer, creamier, more perfumed truffles than one can get from most import places. She fills her truffles with flavored cream, butter, and egg yolk mixtures that have no added sugar. The flavors include vanilla bean, praline, rum, brandy, orange, mocha, and dark chocolate. The one I liked best was rolled in crushed pistachios over an intensely bitter chocolate shell and a solid white chocolate ganache studded with more pistachios. Can you believe it? Too good. Judy Weinblatt's truffles are as good as they get.

> Judy Weinblatt's instructions for eating a truffle: Take a small bite. Roll it around your tongue and let the flavors loose, as you would with a fine wine. Now swallow. You may not have found paradise, but until the real thing comes along, this comes awfully close.

CHAMPAGNE TRUFFLES

Teuscher Chocolatier   phone orders: yes
9548 Brighton Way   213-276-2776
Beverly Hills, CA 90210   ae/visa/mc

If you think a champagne truffle is a case of gilding the lily, think again. Swiss chocolatier Teuscher made his American reputation by hand-dipping a champagne ganache in a mild milk chocolate. Although there are those old enough to say these aren't as good as they used to be, I dare say if you try one for the first time you will be impressed enough to feel a little stunned with the sheer pleasure of this soft, creamy champagne taste enrobed in Swiss chocolate. These are flown over to New York and Beverly Hills twice a week from Switzerland. Don't buy more than two or three. They really should be eaten within a day or so of the time you buy them, having spent most of their short lives in airports.

BLOOMINGDALE'S TRUFFLES

Adrienne's   phone orders: yes
Bloomies/1000 Third Ave.   212-705-2953
New York, NY 10021   ae/dc

The East Coast champion of the truffle makers is Adrienne Welch, who makes a dozen flavors, from a deep coffee-cinnamon to a pale white chocolate-vanilla bean. She hand-makes and ships daily by Express Mail during cool months only. Once you've tasted these, there's no turning back.

CLASSIC TRUFFLES

Fran's Patisserie and   phone orders: yes
  Chocolate Specialties   206-322-6511
2805 E. Madison St.   visa/mc
Seattle, WA 98112

In no other field that I know of is there such xenophobia as in the truffle-making art. Everybody thinks his or hers is the best. One Seattle reporter even went so far as to engage a native Seattle chef, en route to France, to truffle across the United States, just to prove that Fran Bigelow's truffles were the best. Guess what the expert wrote back? They were.

Fran Bigelow does make good truffles. She was trained at the California Culinary Academy and in Europe. She has great local chocolate available to her as well as the Belgian kind. She understands the technique. From Fran Bigelow you can get classic truffles that are wonderful. Beyond the pure Belgian chocolate one, she offers Grand Marnier, amaretto, Kahlua, Chambord, and a white chocolate that melts in your mouth.

I'll tell you what I think this truffle business boils down to: Eliminating the big blob comfort food truffles from the running, the best thing you can do is pick the truffle maker nearest you. If you live in the Northwest, call up Fran Bigelow. If you're in her area, stop by. Her reputation for pastries in Seattle is sterling. This is one woman who knows how to cook.

SWEETHEART BOXES OF CHOCOLATES

Crand's Candy Castle　　　phone orders: yes
PO Box 3023　　　　　　　203-623-5515
Enfield, CT 06082　　　　visa/mc

Bob and Thomas Crand don't claim to make truffles. They just say they make "the best in homestyle candies." Out of what home, I'd like to ask? When I opened up this box of assorted chocolates, the perfume of chocolate, raspberry, and nuts wafted up even before I had the inner box open. No home candymaker that I know of can even come close to this.

Like so many other master chocolatiers, the Crand brothers learned their craft from their father and still operate the business that he began. And keeping the same hours: 9 to 9, seven days a week. Oh, that Yankee work ethic. For the natives, a visit to the candy castle, which looks like your standard New England saltbox house with candy-striped awnings over the lower windows and big letters announcing the name, is a ritual of Christmas.

The Crands make candy using old recipes and old techniques. They do not use assembly-line machines, artificial flavors, or preservatives. Emma Rousseau has been hand-dipping chocolates for over 50 years and can artistically drip a distinguishing letter in chocolate on each candy—r for raspberry, p for pineapple. Ever try to do that? Nigh onto impossible. Their package is modest, nothing fancy. Their prices are so low, I hate to let on. But if you want to know what the original "Sweetheart" box of candy was supposed to be like, order here.

SWEET SLOOPS AND OTHER SURPRISES

Harbor Sweets
PO Box 150
Marblehead, MA 01945

phone orders: yes
617-745-7648
visa/mc

Ben Strohecker says he scientifically conducted market research before plunging into the cold waters of commerce. He stopped everybody he saw on the street and asked them this question: If you were going to die in the next 10 minutes, what is the last piece of candy you would choose to eat? Now Ben Strohecker tells this story with a perfectly straight face, and he swears that the majority answered thoughtfully: "I'd like a chocolate-dipped toffee crunch." OK, Ben. Whatever you say.

But I will say this. Ben Strohecker's four candies, headed up by Sweet Sloops—triangular-shaped toffee crunch dipped in white chocolate with the hull dipped in chopped nuts—are the best. Besides these wonderful morsels, he makes Sand Dollars of molded chocolate that enrobe soft, creamy butter caramel centers studded with fresh pecans. His Marblehead mints are deep chocolate coins with sailboats embossed in their peppermint chocolate bodies. Sweet Shells are shaped like scallop shells and are made of dark sweet chocolate with a hint of orange crunch.

As you can see, Ben has an eye for looks as well as taste. His candies are expensive but are totally hand-made from fresh ingredients and individually foil-wrapped to retain the maximum flavor and aroma. Ben will even custom-design chocolates for you, creating a mold using your

---

You can make your own truffles with about any thick hot fudge sauce. Just shake some cocoa powder out onto waxed paper; using a demitasse spoon, scoop out a little blob of chocolate and roll it around in the cocoa. Store, covered, in the refrigerator. You can press a pecan into the top, or a nonpareil candy, or whatever strikes your fancy. You can roll the whole thing in ground hazelnuts, pistachios, or roasted almonds. All delicious.

To heat any hot fudge or other thick dessert sauce, remove the metal lid of the jar and place jar in the microwave set on low. Check every 15 seconds. Doesn't take long. Otherwise, place jar in hot water on stove and be patient for about 15 minutes.

logo, and make a custom chocolate coin for your company or charity. Public relations people, pay attention. Here's the best source I know for one-of-a-kind giveaways that will keep your clients' names in the sweet memories of their customers. Who wouldn't feel kindly toward the person who'd just sent them one of Ben Strohecker's mouth-watering chocolate coins?

ICE CREAM TOPPINGS AND DESSERT SAUCES

You'd think when you'd seen one hot fudge sauce, you'd seen 'em all. But not so. In the fancy food business, where ice cream sauces are a not uncommon first product for kitchen entrepreneurs, there is considerable variation in these sauces. This was one category where we were able to ruthlessly eliminate those that were (a) just cloyingly sweet, or (b) not even as good as the Hershey's syrup you see at the supermarket—which is, to my mind, still a decent standard against which to measure.

Just as you might imagine, there is a direct relationship in this category between what goes in and what comes out. The more butterfat and Belgian chocolate that's infused into the sauce, the silkier the texture, the heavier the perfume, the better it's going to taste.

BUTTERCREAM BEST

Grand Finale phone orders: yes
200 Hillcrest Rd. 415-655-8414
Berkeley, CA 94705 ae/visa/mc/dc/cb

Lucky for us somebody tipped me off about this, the smallest licensed candy manufacturer in the state of California. Barbara L. Holzrichter has made the best buttercream confections on the face of the earth for the past five years, working from the basement of her house and using a Willy Wonka candy machine invented and built by her physicist husband. I'm not kidding.

Beginning with buttercream caramels in five flavors (which *New York* magazine called the "Sweet shock of astonishment—the ultimate caramel!") and half a dozen

---

Basic Chocolate Sauce

1 cup whipping cream
8 ounces best-quality semisweet chocolate (I like Guittard)
1 tablespoon liqueur or liquor of your choice, or good vanilla

Combine cream and chocolate in heavy saucepan and raise slowly to a boil, stirring constantly. Boil gently about 5 minutes to thicken. Remove from heat and stir in flavoring.

Chocolate Shell

(Hains sells coconut oil in most health food stores. It comes in a solid bar. You can melt it over hot water, or in a microwave set on low within 15 seconds.)

6 ounces best-quality chocolate of your choice, grated
6 tablespoons melted coconut oil

Stir together over hot water until completely blended. Should be thick but still pourable. Will form a hard shell on ice cream within 30 seconds.

ice cream sauces that will turn you into a faithful sundae worshipper, here's what you have to choose from. The caramels, which are shipped only in cool weather, include: classic vanilla and buttercream caramel, almond, mocha, chocolate, and—last, but great God, not least—bourbon pecan, made with Kentucky bourbon and fresh pecans. For hot weather, she figured out a way to put this melt-in-your-mouth-as-well-as-your-mailbox caramel flavor into a jar and sells it as ice cream topping. Using the cream caramel base, Barbara makes mocha caramel, cream caramel, and bourbon pecan caramel ice cream sauce. Lately she's taken a fancy to chocolate and has added triple chocolate fudge, Grand Marnier, chocolate caramel sauce, and, finally, white chocolate framboise sauce. How can I possibly tell you which one is the best? They're all the best. Drizzle the pecan over a poached pear and watch the shock of delight ripple across your dining table as your dinner guests take their first bite.

The reason all this stuff is to die for is that Barbara uses only sugar, fresh cream, and real butter, enhancing the basic caramels with natural flavors including Madagascar vanilla, California almonds, real coffee, and best-quality dark chocolate. What she doesn't use is condensed milk, or coconut oil, or chemical additives or preservatives. No wonder everything is so fresh and good. Should be stored in the refrigerator like the fine dairy product it is.

Fancy Sundaes from C. C. Brown's

Buster Brown: banana, scoops of vanilla and chocolate high-butterfat ice cream, fresh chopped roasted almonds, whipped cream, and a pitcher of bubbling hot fudge

French Nougat Sundae: vanilla ice cream, marshmallow, fresh raspberries, chopped roasted almonds, and whipped cream

Royal Mocha: mocha ice cream, mocha syrup, crunchy peanut topping, and whipped cream

Cinderella: layered in a tall glass, a sliced fresh peach, vanilla ice cream, sliced strawberries, lemon sherbet, chopped pineapple, roasted almonds, and whipped cream

Golden Mocha Sundae (designed for the 50th anniversary of the confectionary): three scoops of ice cream, roasted almonds, whipped cream, and a pitcher of smoking-hot mocha sauce

HOLLYWOOD HOT FUDGE

C. C. Brown's of
  Hollywood
7007 Hollywood Blvd.
Hollywood, CA 90028

phone orders: yes
213-464-9726
visa/mc

Since 1929, the kids from Hollywood High have been coming to C. C. Brown's for his famous "last act" sundaes. Sitting in high-backed booths and inhaling the intoxicating perfume of cream and chocolate, they've ordered countless hot fudge or hot caramel sundaes. Brown makes only 35 gallons of hot fudge and hot caramel sauce a day. Some he serves in the store, some he sends out in hot cups with liveried chauffeurs to waiting stretch limos out in front. But now, in cans that look like Campbell's soup, he also sells his hot fudge and caramel sauces for the home larder.

The sauce is thick, dark, rich caramel flavor, either chocolate or vanilla. Brown worked 20 years to perfect the hot fudge recipe; the secret, he says, rests in just the right blend of cane and corn sugars. To this he adds chocolate, cocoa, whipping cream, dairy butter, egg whites, salt, and pure vanilla. Place the can in boiling water until it heats through, pour over ice cream, and just pretend—for a minute—that you went to Hollywood High. This is the sweet stuff dreams are made of.

HOMESTYLE HOT FUDGE SAUCE

R&R Homestead Kitchen   phone orders: yes
803 Morning Glory Lane   414-336-7574
De Pere, WI 54115   visa/mc

Getting to know Ruth Roffers is kind of like rekindling an old relationship with your favorite aunt, the one who used to send boxes of chocolate chip cookies to you at camp. Ruth makes hot fudge sauce. This is not some fancy gourmet hotsy-totsy Belgian chocolate confection; this is good all-American comfort food that will make your heart swell (if not your thighs). Made from cocoa, sugar, evaporated milk, soybean oil, corn syrup, and vanilla and put up in honey jars. Ruth began in her basement five years ago. Within six months, she couldn't keep up with demand and hired her first helper.

Within a year she'd outgrown the basement and moved to a rented kitchen, where she not only makes the fabled hot fudge sauce but also sells good glazed walnuts (also put up in the honey jars), fudge, and various baked goods: a decent homestyle fruitcake, stollen, and pound cake. One of the items she sent me is a sentimental favorite in her household and may well become one in ours: a Grapenuts bread she calls Granny Dittman's Holiday Loaf, with fruit, straight out of the Depression and made for her family by a neighbor they all loved. It's a tight, sweet, dense little loaf; eating it, I got sentimental about the Depression, and I wasn't even born then! All Ruth's products are homemade without preservatives.

Ruth Roffers's Hot Fudge Brownies

Makes 36 brownies in 1½ hours

½	pound butter
1¾	cups sugar
4	eggs
2	teaspoons vanilla
1	13.5-ounce jar hot fudge topping (plus additional topping for frosting—optional)
1½	cups sifted flour
5	tablespoons cocoa
¼	teaspoon baking powder
2	cups chopped nuts (walnuts or pecans preferred)

Beat together first four ingredients. Stir in fudge topping. Add remaining ingredients. Pour batter into a greased and floured 9-by-13-inch pan. Bake at 350° F. 55 minutes. If desired, frost with additional hot fudge topping right from the jar.

Serving Ideas for Paradigm Sauces

■ A spoonful of Vanilla Caramel sauce over Irish oatmeal with buttermilk and toasted hazelnuts for breakfast.

■ Brush top of apple pie with caramel sauce 5 minutes before end of baking time for a luscious glaze.

■ Unmold baked custard into a pool of Gingered Caramel sauce with fresh strawberries.

■ Drizzle white chocolate cream over pistachio ice cream.

■ Stir Bailey's Haute Fudge into coffee and top with whipped cream and chocolate shavings.

Carrol Norman's White Chris-Mousse

Adapted from *The First Real Chocolate Sauce Cookbook for Teddy Bears and People*, from Norman-Bishop.

Serves 8 in 30 minutes (4 hours to chill)

1   10-ounce jar White Chocolate Truffle Sauce, softened over hot water
4   egg whites, room temperature, beaten to stiff peaks
1½ cups heavy cream, beaten to soft peaks
    Raspberries and

CONTINUED ON PAGE 195

HOMEMADE DESSERT SAUCES

Paradigm Chocolate Co.   phone orders: yes
3438 S.E. Radcliff Court   503-648-5139
Hillsboro, OR 97123   visa/mc

Lynne Barra and her husband make 11 dessert sauces, all by hand with no copacker and no compromise about ingredients. They use the best chocolate they can lay hands on and their own recipes with no salt, no preservatives, no artificial flavors; these sauces aren't too sweet but are terminally rich. Frangelico is chocolate with hazelnut —smooth, velvety, and chock full of nuts, as they say. Also fabulous are Jamaican Praline; Gingered Caramel; Vanilla Caramel; Amaretto; Bailey's Irish Cream; Deep Dark Fudge; Grand Marnier; Kahlua; and Peppermint Schnapps. These sauces are so thick a spoon will stand upright in them until doomsday.

TRUFFLE DESSERT SAUCES

Norman-Bishop   phone orders: yes
111 W. Saint John St.,   408-272-1763
  Ste. 666-G
San Jose, CA 95113

Putting a truffle in a jar may be the best solution yet to the difficulty of preserving the perishable confection. Carrol Norman makes thick, deep, rich dessert sauces that do taste like truffles that have been poured into a jar instead of rolled into a ball. In addition to the regular chocolate, she blends natural essence of raspberry, Kahlua, amaretto, orange, or hazelnut with the deep, triple-dark chocolate. She also makes milk chocolate and white chocolate as well as a caramel pecan.

Along with her partner, Louise Wright, she has written a handy chocolate sauce cookbook that will show you how to use chocolate sauces in everything from chafing-dish appetizers and Mexican crêpes to (are you ready?) chocolate fettuccine and a royal raspberry bombe. You can even learn to make trouble-free truffles at home using the thick, solid sauces. I recommend you order this handy spiral-bound cookbook from Carrol if you love chocolate even a little.

DESSERT SAUCES AND TRUFFLE KITS

Dearborn   phone orders: yes
1 Christopher St.   212-691-9153
New York, NY 10014

Lisa Goldberg, 35-year-old owner of Dearborn, had a childhood to rival Eloise's at the Plaza. Her mother presided over Maxim de Paris in Chicago, and for 20 years Lisa observed and tasted in a great kitchen frequented by the giants of haute cuisine. So it isn't surprising that when she began her own food venture, the products tasted great. Lisa sticks to what she likes: dessert. To that end she makes only four flavors: chocolate, maple, butterscotch, and white chocolate with hazelnut. I wish you could have seen us here at noon tasting these, trying to decide which we liked best. After so many tastes that our eyes had glazed over, we decided we liked the butterscotch best . . . provided you tossed in a few fresh pecans, as we'd just done. But, no, maybe the white chocolate and hazelnut was the best after all. And the pure, deep, rich double chocolate so thick it's just like a truffle's ganache. Well, who can say? This is first-quality stuff.

Lisa also sells a truffle kit that consists of a large jar of the chocolate sauce, cocoa powder, and truffle tools, including a supply of violet and foil candy cups and a little truffle spoon that may soon be seen worn around the necks of truffle-crazed addicts. Sometimes I think this kind of thing ought to be against the law.

BEST BELGIAN CHOCOLATE

Neuhaus   phone orders: yes
97-45 Queens Blvd.,   718-897-6000
   Ste. 503   ae/visa/mc
Rego Park, NY 11374

Neuhaus of Belgium is the oldest chocolatier still making chocolates by hand, in business about 128 years. With more than 120 locations in the United States, they fly in their precious morsels weekly, *never* storing the chocolates, and holding them under scientifically controlled

CONTINUED FROM PAGE 194

peppermint leaves as garnish

Stir softened sauce until smooth, then fold into beaten egg whites. Fold mixture into whipped cream. Pour into an oiled 1½-quart soufflé dish. Chill 4 hours. Turn out and serve with fresh raspberries and peppermint leaves to garnish. Merry Chris-Mousse to you, too.

Dearborn Maple-Whiskey Cake

By threatening the panel of tasters, I did manage to save enough dessert sauce to make this cake. Too good to be true.

Serves 10 in 1½ hours

⅔	cup raisins
½	cup whiskey
½	cup sweet butter, softened
1	jar Dearborn maple sauce
1¼	cups packed brown sugar
3	eggs
2¼	cups flour
1	teaspoon baking soda
⅓	teaspoon salt
1	cup sour cream
⅔	cup chopped walnuts
1½	tablespoons grated orange rind
	Powdered sugar (optional)

Preheat oven to 350° F. Soak raisins in ¼ cup whiskey.

CONTINUED ON PAGE 196

CONTINUED FROM PAGE 195

Grease a 9- or 10-inch bundt pan. Cream butter, then add maple sauce, then brown sugar. Mix. Beat in eggs one at a time. Combine flour, baking soda, and salt. Add the flour to the butter mixture in three additions, alternately with sour cream. Beat well after each addition. Fold in chopped nuts, remaining whiskey, grated orange rind, and raisins with their liquid. Pour into prepared pan and bake an hour or until toothpick comes out clean.

Cool in pan 10 minutes. Invert pan onto cake rack. Do not remove from pan until cake reaches room temperature. Dust with powdered sugar or serve plain. A good keeper—if you can keep people away from it, that is.

What to Look for When You Shop for Fine Chocolates (Suggestions from Jean Neuhaus)

1. Never purchase chocolates with any sign of moisture on them.
2. Make sure chocolates are shiny. A dull finish means they might not be fresh.
3. Avoid broken chocolates.
4. Make certain chocolates are kept in a cool place. Never ac-

CONTINUED ON PAGE 197

heat- and humidity-maintained cases. The phone number above will simply guide you to the Neuhaus outlet nearest you so that you can be assured of utmost freshness.

Besides chocolates that are better than anything Godiva ever got attention for—including the famous horseback ride—Neuhaus makes a dessert sauce with a most unlikely name: Chocopaste. Now this is something like calling heaven PAIR-O-DIZE in flashing red neon. Chocopaste is a heavenly smooth Swiss chocolate infused with hazelnuts into a paste that's about the same consistency as Hershey's kisses you've held in your hot hand too long, but aromatic with the scent of fine chocolate and filberts. Sold in a big 14-ounce jar, this luxury will keep well in your refrigerator for weeks and is so far superior to any other chocolate product, you won't believe it. Use it on croissants for breakfast, over ice cream, or spread on a raspberry bread. Really the very essence of chocolate.

The original Neuhaus was a Brussels pharmacist who believed chocolate had healing powers. He sold chocolate tablets that he prescribed for everything from fatigue and depression to digestive disorders. Soon he and his wife began dipping chocolates and using only the best ingredients: Belgian beet sugar, milk, butter, natural liquor extracts, whole nuts. The finest chocolates Belgium had ever seen began appearing in this Brussels pharmacy. Now down through four generations, the Neuhaus family makes over a hundred flavors and still adheres to hand methods that begin with a 72-hour period of "conching" (stirring) of cocoa beans and sugar to smooth down the chocolate particles and homogenize the mixture. Neuhaus chocolates are among the most expensive in the world, but when you taste them you'll see why.

FONDUE AU CHOCOLAT

Sahagian & Associates, Inc.
115 N. Oak Park Ave.,
  PO Box 997
Oak Park, IL 60303

phone orders: yes
312-848-5552
visa/mc

At the San Francisco Gourmet Food and Wine Show, participants became so jaded by the embarrassment of riches that few items got special attention. But one particular item drew a crowd no matter who was selling it: Belgian chocolate. It is without peer. For eating, for cooking, there's nothing that comes close. This Belgian chocolate, which is routed to us through Montreal and into Sahagian, is just heaven in a bar. All you have to do is melt it in a chafing dish—either light or dark chocolate, whichever you prefer—pass the fresh fruit, some long-handled forks, and you will soon see the peace that passeth understanding on the faces of all who try fruit chocolate fondue. A big, luscious strawberry dipped in dark Splendid chocolate from Belgium is, quite simply, to die for. You can keep this in your pantry for up to two years and have on hand a dessert to satisfy the gods in the time it takes to heat chocolate and spear fresh fruit.

CONTINUED FROM PAGE 196

cept chocolates that have been stored near heat.

5. Like precious gems, fine chocolates should be displayed under the cleanest conditions.

How to Serve Fine Chocolates at Home

1. Serve chocolates as soon after purchase as possible.

2. When arranging chocolates on a tray, use tissues or gloves to handle them. Fingerprints are unappealing, and tongs will break the candies.

3. Truly luxurious chocolates are filling. No more than three per guest.

4. If you're planning to serve champagne with chocolates, choose pure chocolates rather than filled ones. Neuhaus chocolates are also great with cognac.

5. As with asparagus, it is considered perfectly polite to pick up pieces of chocolate with your fingers. Lick any traces of chocolate from one's fingers. (Don't you love the tone of these instructions?)

CHAPTER 6

HIGH TEA

In traditional England, high tea is served about 6:00 P.M. and is as substantial as a regular meal, being comprised of both savory and sweet foods, including the ubiquitous cucumber and watercress sandwiches. In addition to the tea, flavored cocoas, fine sherry, port, or champagne may also be on the menu.

The English actually adopted the idea of tea parties from the Dutch in the 1600s. Naturally, the teas began in the great country houses and were a marvelous excuse to haul out the silver tea service, the starched linens, and the thinnest china. Great God. Do you suppose the renewed interest in high tea means that brides are going to want those quick-to-blacken teapots for wedding presents again? I doubt it. A good ceramic teapot, perhaps resting in a quilted calico tea cozy, actually works better than silver anyhow. Ceramic keeps the tea warm and it never tastes of tarnish or silver polish.

For entertaining at home, the late-afternoon tea that may include some sort of alcoholic beverage as well—say, a hard cider or champagne—is a good weekend choice for the working person who wants to see friends but just isn't up to throwing a full-blown dinner party.

Remembering that tea can well stand in the place of a late, heavy dinner, choose both savories and sweets. A 12-inch round of peasant bread, spread with ricotta, then trimmed in concentric circles with black olives, red and green bell peppers, green onions and tops, chives, and tomatoes, then cut into pie wedges, is both delicious and low-fat filling. Now is the time to dust off that footed cake stand and place on it either a whole cake—boy, have we got some good ones to recommend that you can just keep on hand in a tin—or individual cookies, biscuits, or tarts. Refer to Chapter 1 for suggestions for a wedge of really outstanding cheese, include Armenian cracker bread or Vermont common crackers, some good sweet butter and jam, and you've just laid out a meal that is both dazzling to look at and delicious. And there's really no cooking at all. You can also add smoked salmon, caviar, pâtés, and sausages (see Chapter 2). Now you won't even need to eat breakfast the next day.

How to Make a Proper Pot of Tea

I hate to repeat the oft-printed instructions, but just in case no one ever told you about making a proper pot of tea, here's how. Begin with a kettle full of cold water and raise it to a boil. Meanwhile, run hot tap water into the teapot to heat the pot. When the water in the kettle reaches a furious boil, dump the warm water from the teapot, add *loose tea* to the pot at the rate of a scant teaspoon per cup of tea you are making, then pour the boiling water over, cover, and let steep about 5 minutes. Strain into cups. Serve with sugar, thin lemon slices, and milk—never cream.

TEAS, COFFEES, AND FLAVORED COCOAS

Tea can be as simple or as elaborate as you care to make it. From a simple pot of freshly made tea, flavored cocoa, or coffee, a pot of jam, and a decent bread, all the way to a dazzling five- or six-choice spread, it's a wonderful respite from the pressures of life when an hour of quiet repose becomes the real luxury, regardless of what there is to eat.

ENGLISH-STYLE TEAS

Upper Canada Coffee Works & Tea Mill
534 Gordon Baker Rd.
Willowdale, Ontario
M2H 2S6 Canada

phone orders: yes
416-494-9700
visa/mc

The mother of one of my friends always takes a turn through Harrod's in London for tea on her way home from

Europe. When I first tentatively offered her the teas I had gotten from Canada, she put her cup down with a decided clunk and said, "This tea is as good as any I ever bought at Harrod's." And well it may be. Many Canadians came from England, and they simply demand first-quality tea. And such choices. Hundreds imported from their country of origin. Sixty flowered teas ranging from China lapsang to Earl Grey to Turkish to Winter's Dream to Garden of Eden. Forty fruit flavours (as they spell it), including passion fruit, Japanese cherry, elderberry (really terrific), and Tropic Fire. They also have nut/spice/mint/spirit teas including aniseed, chocolate mint, cinnamon, walnut, and whiskey. Herbals include chamomile, comfrey, ginseng, rosehip, and skullcap. Some are available decaffeinated. The mail-order list is so long it takes two sides of legal-length paper just to list all the choices. And we haven't even mentioned the coffees, which are 100 percent pure Arabica beans of nearly 50 types, roasted at their Toronto facility.

I would recommend that you pay using Visa or Mastercard if you can. Due to the confusing and ever-changing exchange rate between American and Canadian dollars, they add a $2 service charge for "U.S. cheques written on U.S. banks in U.S. funds," and they don't accept checks marked "payable in Canadian funds."

CHINESE TEAS

Ten Ren Tea Co.	phone orders: yes
949 Grant Ave.	800-292-2049 (national)
San Francisco, CA 94108	415-362-0656 (CA)
	ae/visa/mc

This 30-year-old Taiwanese company, with shops in Chinatowns in New York, Los Angeles, and Toronto as well as San Francisco, not only imports fine-quality Oriental teas but also operate their own tea farms and factories. They offer 30 varieties of teas in six grades from about $6 a pound to over $100.

According to Mark Lii, who operates the New York shop, the drying, rolling, fermentation, blanching, cutting, and storage determine the value of the tea. The tea connoisseur looks for four things: color, aroma, taste, and the appearance of the leaves themselves. Oolong, for exam-

Tea Money

The Chinese are credited with one of the earliest systems of banking, with the circulation of bank notes and coins. But in commercial transactions with far-inland tribes in China and Tibet, paper money had little value. The Chinese formed tea bricks for trade, the value of which increased with every mile they traveled away from the tea gardens. Over time, they were improved until they became hard bricks of considerable beauty with designs impressed onto the front and back surfaces. These bricks were still used for trade until rather recently in parts of Outer Mongolia and Northern Russia.

You can buy from Upper Canada a real tea brick that you can even use for tea. Now, if you really want a new experience at teatime, you can try the Tibetan treat, tea boiled with yak butter. The tea brick is made from fine China congou tea and, if lacquered, will be a fine conversation piece for years—should the subject of yak butter come up at your house from time to time.

Black teas are fermented, standing in a fairly raw, moist state until bacteria and enzymes change the chemistry of the tea leaves. Fermentation reduces pungency and intensifies flavor-producing oils, creating strong but mellow teas. Green teas are unfermented and dried carefully to avoid fermentation. These teas brew up light and are delicate yet brisk and astringent. Oolongs, known as semifermented, are an attempt to strike a balance between the two types.

ple, should brew into a bright golden color, have a fragrant aroma and a taste that strikes a balance between richness and delicacy. The leaves themselves should be curled and dark green.

Should you visit one of the Ten Ren shops, you'll be offered a taste of any tea you'd like to consider. That way you can decide whether you really want the King's tea, a combination of top oolong and ginseng, which goes for $108 a pound, or whether you'd be happy with one of Lii's personal favorites, Roselle, a black tea blend that incorporates dried hibiscus, creating a spicy, lemon taste. It's a mere $23 a pound. If you call the 800 number, they'll send you a price list and tea descriptions.

LOUISIANA COFFEE ROASTER

See also: Community Coffee Co.

Roland Suarage is carrying on a family business that offers, through the Gulf ports, fine coffees roasted in Louisiana and shipped promptly to mail-order customers. You can purchase not only Colombian and French roast but also Evangeline, Kenyan, and other fine private-reserve roasts. The 4-ounce tin of mulling spices they offer for the drip pot would make flavored coffee a good option for teatime. Chocolate spice contains sugar, chocolate, cinnamon, orange peel, cinnamon oil, and orange oil. Just put a spoonful over the coffee grounds and let the water drip through. *Voilà!* Perfumed coffee.

One good reason to order from Roland Suarage is to get his catalog, which offers everything from beignet mix (delicious, let me tell you) to Cajun-style cheese grits to fine flavored cocoas. If you've ever seen a Williams-Sonoma catalog, this one's a dead ringer for that except it focuses on Creole and Cajun specialties. (See Mail-Order Grocery Stores, Chapter 9.) You can even sign up for the Suarages' gourmet coffee course, which gets you a new brew every month along with a description of the coffee's origin, how it was grown, and a comparison to other coffees. They have similar clubs for teas, preserves, dessert sauces, and—can you believe this?—truffle service. Real Belgian truffles in six flavors from praline to raspberry, served to you on a regular, prearranged schedule. The Suarages have high standards and are a reliable source for fine foods and kitchen hardware, too.

Cafe Brulot

Makes 8 demitasses

    Peel of 1 medium orange
1   cup fine brandy
6   whole cloves
4   whole allspice
2   cinnamon sticks
3   tablespoons sugar
3   cups freshly brewed
    strong Evangeline
    coffee

Cut eight very thin curls or flowers from orange peel, and place one in each demitasse cup. Set aside. Reserve remaining peel. In a medium saucepan or chafing dish, heat brandy, cloves, allspice, cinnamon sticks, sugar, and remaining orange peel until very hot. Remove from heat and strain to remove solids. Replace in pan. Carefully ignite and flame for a minute. Pour hot coffee into flaming mixture. Ladle into cups. Serve immediately.

QUALITY COFFEES, TEAS, AND SPICES

The Kobos Co. phone orders: yes
5620 S.W. Kelly 503-222-5226
Portland, OR 97201 ae/visa/mc

Of all the mail-order coffees I tasted, these were the freshest and highest quality. Dave and Susan Kobos were teaching school in the Portland area after graduation from Harvard in the early 1970s. They missed the little neighborhood shops in the East that offered fresh roast coffees and quality herbs and teas. So, taking a deep breath, they opened their own store. Now, 15 years and several stores later, they are still enthusiastic about cooking and brewing. Every day they freshly roast a couple of dozen flavors of coffees, which they then vacuum-seal and ship the same day they receive the orders. They also offer good teas and a staggering number of carefully chosen herbs and spices. For sheer reliability, this is it.

They also have a full array of "hardware" to go with the beans and leaves. Call David and he'll advise you what coffee maker or teapot to buy. If you're in Portland, do stop by their stores. They teach well-respected classes in all sorts of cooking. You can take the teacher out of the classroom but you can't take. . . .

SPICED COCOAS

Rainbow Tea & Spicery phone orders: yes
PO Box 293 503-657-3055
Clackamas, OR 97015 visa/mc

Not only are teas and coffees delicious for teatime, cocoa is a perennial favorite as well. Pat McCormick has taken cocoa one better. She has created spicy flavored varieties: amaretto, orange, mint, cherry, and spice. For a blustery winter day, the combination of hot, steamy cocoa and spice is a real winner. The cocoa is available in regular and instant types. She also offers hot cider spices that you can combine with apple juice and/or red wine for a winter warmer. She also sells flavored teas from apple to lemon spice in a couple of dozen varieties, as well as several blended herbals.

Susan Kobos's Dutch Baby

Serves 4 in 40 minutes

- ¼ cup butter
- 3 eggs
- ¾ cup *each* milk and flour
  Ground nutmeg
  Powdered sugar
  Lemon wedges

Place butter in a 2- to 3-quart ovenproof saucepan and set inside a 425° F. oven. While butter melts, quickly mix batter: Put eggs into food processor and whirl at high speed for a minute. With motor running, gradually pour in milk, then slowly add flour. Continue whirling for 30 seconds. Remove pan from oven and pour batter into the hot, melted butter. Return to oven and bake until puffy and well browned, 20 to 25 minutes. Dust with ground nutmeg and serve with powdered sugar and lemon wedges.

CRACKERS AND BISCUITS

Alongside some fine cheeses—say, a Maytag blue, Vermont cheddar, or Blue Heron brie—and perhaps a slice of Les Petites Trois Cochons (3 Little Pigs) pâté (see index), here are some good savory choices for the tea table.

SEA BISCUITS

G. H. Bent Co.   phone orders: no
7 Pleasant St.   617-698-5945
Milton, MA 02186

The Bent water cracker has been made continuously by this company since 1801. Originally, it was sold town-to-town by Josiah Bent from saddlebags. It is nothing more than flour and pure spring water, hand-formed and baked in a Dutch oven, somewhat similar to the hardtack that was a staple on sailing ships. Primarily, it is valuable as a backer to cheeses because of its neutral flavor, and for the fact that it will keep in the pantry until hell freezes over. It has traditionally been used crumbled and mixed with sweet clams and salt pork to make the original New England clam chowder.

I read an interesting history of the water cracker when it was already old—this was written in 1914—which claimed it as "the cracker for after-dinner incentives to good digestion." The history closed with these solemn words: "The girls with nimble fingers, whose personal appearance can be safely scrutinized by the most critical connoisseur, mold, roll, dock, and, in fact, are fully competent to keep the pace with the men in doing any part of this work, just as my aunts did in 1801 for their father, Mr. Josiah Bent." Boy, that's a relief, to know that mere girls can make crackers. I'm sure glad to hear it.

COMMON CRACKERS

The Vermont Country Store   phone orders: yes
PO Box 1108   802-362-2400
Manchester Center, VT   visa/mc
    05255

The Vermont common cracker is so freighted with meaning to New Englanders that to discuss it is akin to discussing the flag. To a New Englander, the cracker symbolizes a traditional philosophy that encompasses the measure of a man: from stingy to generous, on a sliding scale based on his posture toward crackers. This is the cracker of the cracker barrel, around which the old coots sat and hatched their philosophy. They measured the storekeeper by the lid on his cracker barrel. If he kept it locked, he was stingy. If he kept it just laid on, he was frugal. If he kept it cracked so that customers could help themselves, he was generous. The customers were also judged by their posture toward the crackers. A man was considered stingy, frugal, or reasonable depending on how many free crackers he grabbed to go with his hunk of rat-trap cheese. If you ask me, those old boys would have done better to be home helping the missus put out the wash rather than eyeing one another over crackers.

These crackers are simply flour, water, lard, salt, potato flakes, lecithin, yeast, and baking soda, baked plain to become round, unflavored puffs that serve not only as a foil for cheese (Vermont cheddars being the traditional choice) but are also traditionally used crumbled in everything from turkey stuffing to meat loaf. If you want to see a New Englander go all gooey and sentimental, just serve him some milk and crackers at tea. Don't be surprised if he breaks into song.

You can still buy a barrel of crackers as the New Englanders once did, 1,200 crackers in a wooden barrel to last the year, or you can get a good-looking green tin that holds enough to last non-Yankees through the winter. You ought to order these crackers at least once, just so you get on the list for Vrest Orton's catalog for The Vermont Country Store. Here you can order anything from bag

Josiah Bent's Common Cracker Pudding (1801)

Here's a surprise for teatime, in Josiah Bent's own words. See if you can figure out how to do this with a Cuisinart and a Jenn-Aire.

Serves 8 in 3½ hours

    2   cups cracker crumbs,
        soaked in:
    3   pints milk
    1   cup sugar
    ½   teaspoon cinnamon
    1   teaspoon salt
    1   tablespoon butter
    1   cup raisins

Butter a deep-dish earthenware container. Bake 3 hours (maybe less). Puff up the raisins over steam before adding. After thirty minutes, stir in the raisins. Pour additional milk around the edges, not in the middle.

Don't forget the breads from Chapter 1: Wolferman's English muffins, crumpets from The English Tea Shop, or the Valley Bakery's Armenian cracker bread. Any of these will do well on the tea table. Just today, we had a Wolferman's blueberry muffin, toasted, slathered in sweet butter and brie, with a dollop of Pan Handler Products' Vermont Harvest Blueberry Bourbon Conserve atop and a pot of Monk's tea from Upper Canada Coffee Works and Tea Mill. Yum.

balm (good for chapped lips) to reconditioned Electroluxes (still the best, says Vrest) in one of the truly eccentric catalogs representing the strongly held beliefs of one man. Read this catalog and you'll see what moves in Vermont. You can even find a classic white enamel steel breadbox here, or a lady's English purse knife, known as the Dinkie knife, with a genuine pearl handle. MacIntosh apples, maple-leaf candy, cider jelly—104 pages of all things Vermont.

COOKIES, SHORTBREADS, AND BISCOTTI

A tin of melt-in-your-mouth cookies, on hand and ready for tea at the drop of a hat, is a wonderful luxury. To be able to simply pop open a container that holds cookies unlike any you can buy at the store can make your day. We have honed the choices down to cookies that just plain can't be bought in local markets, that have no preservatives, and that taste so good you'll wish you could say you made them yourself.

OREGON WINE COOKIES

Taste 1
3101 N.E. Barkerbrook Rd.
Portland, OR 97230

phone orders: yes
503-254-5309
visa/mc through
Norm Thompson only

The Oregon wine cookie came about because Lynda Nestelle liked the European idea of dip and sip. She invented these small, crisp, firm, spicy cookies made from a reduction of local wines to be dipped into or eaten alongside a glass of wine or sherry. Three flavors, Riesling, Pinot Noir, and loganberry, are now available. She buys wine from Sokol Blosser, reduces it, incorporates it into a spiced dough, glazes it with a wine/honey mist, then bakes it crisp. The Riesling is Nestelle's favorite, having just a hint of cardamom to spice it, cardamom in this case living up to its nickname "grains of paradise." Most popular with buyers is the Pinot Noir, a spicy, lively, gingery cookie.

You can buy them direct from Lynda or you can order them through the Norm Thompson catalog.

MELT-IN-YOUR-MOUTH SHORTBREADS

Simply Shortbread
1941 Ocean Ave.
San Francisco, CA 94127

phone orders: yes
415-333-2400

Jay Kanika began making cookies when she was 13. After she was grown, she began taking her filled shortbreads to work with her, and people simply fell on them. One day a woman in the office asked Jay how much she'd charge for a dozen. One thing led to another, and eventually she got a call from Saks Fifth Avenue. That's when she got serious about it. Now, some three years later, she has a booming retail business, more catering orders than she can handle, and a mail-order business that's growing. What is this one product that put her in business?

The aroma of purest caramelized butter, a texture that crisply melts in your mouth, the taste of sweet, buttery, moist cookie packed with nuts enrobing a thin layer of fine-quality jam, this little 1-by-2-inch rectangle, individually cut and wrapped, is simply divine. Made only of flour, butter, sugar, walnuts, egg yolks, and jam in one of 15 flavors, these cookies are so good they stay in your memory forever. To maintain that ultimate freshness, outside of California they're shipped only second-day air. They come in a box tied with a violet satin bow, the cookies inside resting on violet tissue paper. They're as fragile as a dozen long-stemmed roses.

BUTTER PECAN BARS

Texas Toffee, Inc.
9633-B Fondren St.
Houston, TX 77096

phone orders: yes
713-988-3760
visa/mc

When I received a tin of these pecan-studded butter wafers in the mail, they seemed vaguely familiar. After thinking about it awhile, I knew where I'd seen them. The recipe came from my own first cookbook, *The Only Texas Cookbook.* What goes around, comes around. Susan Vogelson is now making for sale this old Texas recipe. I got the recipe from an 80-year-old woman named Martha Kavanaugh, who served them in the landmark cafeteria she owned in Houston for 50 years. Simply made from butter, sugar, a pinch of salt and cinnamon, flour, and a lot of good Texas pecans, these are nice, thin bar cookies, more taste than sweetness and ideal for afternoon tea. They're even for sale in the Smithsonian Shop, representing Texas. Right this very minute, I'm writing Martha Kavanaugh a note to tell her. She's such a Texan, I know she'll be pleased.

CRISPY CUT-OUT COOKIES

Mrs. Travis F. Hanes   phone orders: no
Rte. 2, Friedberg Rd.   919-764-1402
Clemmons, NC 27012   visa/mc

Evva Hanes began helping her mother, Mrs. Travis F., make Moravian sugar crisps back in the 1950s when people drove to the Hanes farm to pick up these thin, flavorful, crisp cookies, the recipe for which originated in the part of Czechoslovakia known as Moravia. Evva's husband remembers mixing cookie dough in a baby bathtub. Now, 30 years and no advertisements later, Evva, Travis, and their grown kids Mike and Mona have to employ a virtual army of grandmothers to keep up with the demand. Travis mixes up to 5,000 pounds of dough every week. Yet every cookie is still rolled by hand and cooked precisely. Then stacks of cookies are hand-wrapped in white napkins and placed in tins or cardboard tubes for mailing.

They don't hold to old-fashioned ways just for the heck of it. These cookies are simply too delicate to withstand machine handling. But watch those well-muscled women working over the dough with rolling pins and you'll believe it when Evva Hanes says that they get their cookies to come out so thin and crisp by one means: elbow grease. These crisp and delightful cookies come in five flavors: sugar, lemon, chocolate, butterscotch, and the most popular, ginger, made with the traditional Moravian blend of cinnamon, nutmeg, ginger, and cloves.

COOKIES LIKE MOTHER USED TO MAKE

Neal's Cookies by Mail   phone orders: yes
423 Southwest Freeway   800-847-0096
Houston, TX 77002   ae/visa/mc

Neal Elinoff dropped out of medical school to make Italian ices, then cookies, full time. He offers plain old, top-of-the-line, homemade chocolate chip–type cookies in several varieties: chocolate chunk, pecan chocolate chunk, white chocolate macadamia nut (can you stand it?), chocolate walnut chocolate chunk, peanut butter chocolate chunk, milk chocolate with pecans, and oatmeal raisin. If you had time to stay home and cook, had a good recipe and the best ingredients, this is what you'd get. Almost. Except that Neal even makes his own chocolate (move over, Willy Wonka), and he can honestly say chunk instead of chip. These cookies drip with the best chocolate I've seen. He has mastered shipping, no small item in a cookie as fragile as this one, so that even Mrs. Fields had better worry—her cookies being delicious but with a shelf life of 20 minutes.

One thing you can buy from Neal is cookie dough by the tub, at about $4 a pound. Same flavors as listed above. This way, you can bake only what you want for the moment. He also sells the dough in great huge tubs for places that want to sell hot cookies. You wouldn't really want that much. Would you? Tempting. He also sells his chocolate, dark, milk, and white, conched 72 hours just like the best European chocolates. He only uses pure cocoa butter. And still charges less than $4 a pound for any flavor.

Frozen Pistachio Custard

Just the right accompaniment to Neal's cookies and tea.

Serves 6 in 4½ hours with only 20 minutes preparation time

- 2 cups milk
- 3 beaten eggs
- ¾ cup sugar
  Few grains salt
- 1 cup heavy cream, whipped
- 2 teaspoons vanilla
- ¼ teaspoon grated nutmeg
- ¾ cup chopped pistachios

Scald milk either in double boiler or microwave set on low. Mix eggs, sugar, and salt. Gradually stir in hot milk. Cook over simmering water or in microwave until you've made a custard that coats the back of the spoon. Place pan in an ice-water bath and paddle custard until ice-cold. Fold in whipped cream, flavorings, then nuts. Pour into refrigerator tray. Freeze until firm, about 4 hours.

BITE-SIZED COOKIES IN A JAR

Miss Chippy's Spirited   phone orders: yes
  Confections   209-686-3636
501 S. L St.   visa/mc
Tulare, CA 93274

Sold in a quart mayonnaise type jar, these quarter-sized cookies are good dippers for sherry or tea. The crisp sugar cookies come in Tequila Sunrise, Old Irish Coffee, Mint Julep, Black Russian, Rum Runner, and Shirley Temple flavors, with just a hint of liquor and liqueur tastes. The jar keeps them crisp, and the size is just a good, delicious bite. These are good to have on the shelf.

PANFORTE AND BISCOTTI TOSCANI

La Tempesta   phone orders: yes
PO Box 955   415-573-7938
Millbrae, CA 94030

When you meet Bonnie Tempesta, owner of the bakery in South San Francisco that bears her name, you will begin to understand why Shakespeare liked to set plays in Italy. Bonnie is young, beautiful, with a shock of blue-black hair and a temperament that goes with her name. She also offers for sale some traditional Tuscan pastries.

Panforte is a confection from the Middle Ages, used by the Crusaders the same way modern hikers might use trail mix. One little reminder that all is not progress, because panforte is vastly superior to any modern nibble that I know of. A flat, dense cake, it contains honey, candied orange and lemon rinds, whole almonds and hazelnuts. You can buy it plain or enrobed in bittersweet chocolate and dusted with cocoa. Just the thinnest sliver served with espresso and cognac—what a dessert. Bonnie also bakes a splendid example of biscotti, a light, crunchy, almond-stuffed biscuit that makes for a lighter dessert. Bonnie Tempesta uses only the finest California-grown fruits and nuts, no preservatives or artificial ingredients. Her products are great.

ITALIAN BISCOTTI AND OTHER SWEETMEATS

Di Camillo Baking Co.,   phone orders: yes
  Inc.   716-282-2341
811 Linwood Ave.   ae/visa/mc
Niagara Falls, NY 14305

This full-line Italian bakery, in place over 60 years, has gained a national reputation for biscuits both sweet and savory. Wine sticks, champagne cookies, Italian cheese crisps, butter cookies, apricot tart cookies—there is nothing the De Camillos sell that isn't first-rate. As Clark Wolf says, "If you have to go over Niagara Falls in something, let it be a canister of focaccia from the De Camillo Bakery." Perfect also for late-afternoon tea, this flat savory bread is made with extra-virgin olive oil, fresh herbs, and spices. The *New York Times* calls them Torta di Frutta, an Italian fruitcake with neither citron nor raisin, the best fruitcake there is; one that will age like a fine wine. My own personal favorite—and this was a hard decision to reach—is their Biscotti Angelica, an Italian crisp bread saturated with pure butter and double-baked; perfect with a slice of pâté from 3 Little Pigs (see index).

FRUITCAKES

I don't actually hate fruitcake, but I wouldn't really go out of my way to buy one and I would never, never make one. On the tour for my first book, some ad agency whiz who never cooks anything messier than Top Ramen conned me into making Texas plum puddings, which have those same sticky fruits. You know, don't you, that they plan those book tours for cooks so that the demonstration station is at the opposite pole in the store from running water? I'm sure they pay somebody big bucks just to figure out how to separate the cook from hot water and soap—which are usually in the ladies' room behind the Layaway window on the sixth floor . . . when you're in Housewares on the fourth floor. And the escalator near you is going the wrong way. And it's the last day of the month and there's a line halfway out into Credit to pick up the layaways, and you can see at one glance that those people shouldn't be wasting their hard-earned money on poly-filled Rambo comforters with matching pillow shams anyway. Which means you get to cart a bunch of dirty dishes through the store, past the toasters and the books and the lamps and the drapes and through the layaway line into the bathroom to wash them. And usually, with my luck, the person in there just before me threw up. Well, try doing all this with sticky hands. I'm telling you, it will give you a runaway. I thought if I ever saw a glacéed cherry again, I would kill somebody. But sure enough, I was inundated with fruitcakes to try for this book. Trust me.

These are the only ones I could endure, and I have—as you can hear—a good deal of resistance to the whole idea.

There are interesting regional differences in fruitcakes. The Boston Society Bakery cake is Italian in origin and exotic with figs. From Connecticut comes the Matthews 1812, positively orange with apricots. The Nebraska cake and the Kentucky Trappists' cakes are both heavy with brandy and bourbon. The Texas cakes list pecans as the first ingredient and are what we used to refer to delicately as "Methodist" cakes—meaning no booze. But all of these cakes are made with top-quality ingredients, have no artificial preservatives (I would hope not, with all the natural preservatives inherent in sugar, fruit acid, and liquor), keep for months in a tin, and are nice to have on hand for late-afternoon tea.

BEST FRUITCAKE YOU COULD ASK FOR

Mary of Puddin Hill   phone orders: yes
PO Box 241   214-455-2651
Greenville, TX 75401   ae/visa/mc

Mary Horton Lauderdale's pecan fruitcake, baked by following her great-grandmother's recipe, was the hands-down winner with our taste panel for the best fruitcake. The first ingredient is the famous Texas pecan, a small, oil-rich, taste-packed variety. Pineapple, cherries, and dates are held together with a little egg batter. This fruitcake, in a 1¾-pound or 2¾-pound loaf or giant 4½-pound ring, is so rich and moist, it's more confection than cake.

Mary first made this cake for sale one Christmas to raise some extra money. The first year she sold 500 pounds of it, using cases of cherries, dates, and pineapples her parents had donated to the cause, and pecans that she and her husband, Sam, bought and cracked themselves. They hand-mixed the cakes in dishpans, 22½ pounds at a time. That was 1948. Today, lots of things have changed, but they still haul out the dishpans for the ladies they employ every September to brace for the Christmas onslaught. Snapping on rubber gloves, these ladies hand-mix and visit, turning their dishpans full of sticky batter until it's well blended, then hand-packing it into baking pans.

Besides fruitcake, they make other mouth-watering baked goods and candies. Call for a catalog. We adored the pecan praline pie, which is too rich to serve in pie wedges but so delicious that just a sliver will be enough. It's made with a full quart of native pecans in a chewy praline made with real butter and sugar, all packed into an old-fashioned pie crust. This is a good keeper and would be smashing with a cup of Earl Grey.

GERMAN-STYLE FRUITCAKE

Eilenberger's Butter Nut Baking Co.
PO Box 710
Palestine, TX 75801

phone orders: yes
214-SAY-CAKE
(729-2253)
ae/visa/mc

Fred Eilenberger began making a style of fruitcake that originated in medieval Germany and traveled to the New World in the flour-spotted recipe box of Fred's German mother. This butter cake is a light yellow color, loaded with Texas pecans, cherries, pineapple, and raisins. A real cake, not a confection, it will age and mellow into an even better product over time. The Eilenbergers also make a pecan cake that is a full one-third pecans, blended with dates, pineapple, cherries, and a light honey batter. This fruitcake is of the confection type. Perhaps the best cake they make is a bundt ring called Australian apricot. A light yellow butter cake laced with apricots and pineapple and flavored with brandy, it's what they call their "springtime" cake. Tart, well seasoned, and not too sweet, this is the best.

CZECH-STYLE FRUITCAKE

Gladys Cookie Shop
Rte. 1, Box 281-A
Flatonia, TX 78941

phone orders: yes
512-865-3682
visa/mc

The Texas Czechs came with their own version of fruitcake, which is still being made in the farming community of Cistern by Gladys Farek, who started selling the cakes

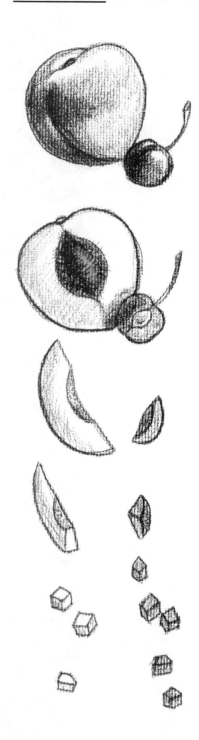

from her home after she'd retired from running a general store. She'd retired to have her sixth daughter and she was, she says, "bored". By anyone else's estimation, Gladys is a human dynamo, and her fruitcakes, sold in loaves, rings, Christmas tree and Texas shapes (from a pound up to a 25-pound Texas) are in such demand that this seven-year-old business takes up not only Gladys's time but the time of her daughters and her husband, Franklin, as well.

Using a 140-year-old Czech recipe, Gladys tosses into a red cement mixer (real efficient, she says, and she got it real cheap besides) 50 percent pecans, followed by pineapple and cherries. No raisins, citron, or spice, Gladys assures you, and just enough batter to hold it together. What usually happens with Gladys is that people just send her their Christmas list and she bakes the cakes and sends them on.

Gladys also makes jalapeño jelly, Texas-sized cookies, cinnamon-coated nuts, and bite-sized party cookies that she'll mail out. Go into her little home bakery and you can buy melt-in-your-mouth strudel, cheesecake, or pecan pie. Somehow, dealing with Gladys isn't like doing business at all. It's more like you asked your good-cook cousin to do your Christmas baking for you and you just gave her some money to pay for the ingredients.

ITALIAN-STYLE FRUITCAKE

The Society Bakery phone orders: yes
Box 877 617-648-4695
Boston, MA 02114 visa/mc

Lillian and Charles Coltin operated Boston's premier Northern Italian restaurant, Allegro, when they began hand-mixing classic fruitcake and an Italian version they call sun-dried apricot cake for use in the restaurant and for sale or gift to a few select customers. The fruitcake is figgy, moist, a medium-caramel color, made with pecans, butter, figs, raisins, apricots, cherries, and pineapple in a light egg batter. The apricot cake is equally interesting, made with 27 percent apricots, dates, raisins, butter, flour, eggs, rum, apricot syrup, pecans, sugar, lemon juice, honey, and salt. As you can see, this is more confection than cake. Being more tart and more orange colored, it is to my mind the more desirable of the two. The Coltins also make beautiful shortbreads that are molded into 8-inch coins embossed with their initials.

Each spring, they make a limited number of classic fruitcakes that they set aside to age for six months, dousing them monthly with rum. Known as Limited-Edition Classic Fruitcakes, these are among the best of the hand-tailored spirited cakes. If you want one of these, order early—they are in short supply. In just three years, the Coltins have moved from the frenetic pace of operating a restaurant and making and dousing the languishing heady cakes to simply being bakers. Now they spend the entire year making "proper" fruitcakes, apricot cakes, and monograms of shortbread.

TRAPPIST FRUITCAKE

See also: Gethsemani Farms.

The monks who made their reputation with cheese also sell a Kentucky bourbon-laced dark fruitcake to accompany the cheese. Made of raisins, cherries, mixed fruit, pecans, pineapple, dates, walnuts, orange and lemon peel in a wine and honey-sweetened batter, this is a solid, dense, not-too-sweet cake that perfectly accompanies their cheese. One of the best gift ideas they have is half a wheel of cheese and half a fruitcake. Considering that this costs in the neighborhood of $12 postpaid, I think that's quite a deal.

WORKING AT HOME A PIECE OF CAKE

Matthews 1812 House
15 Whitcomb Hill Rd.
Cornwall Bridge, CT
  06754

phone orders: yes
203-672-6449
ae/visa/mc

When Blaine and Deanna Matthews bought an old house and started their family, they loved both so much they didn't ever want to leave. So, starting with old family recipes, they began making fruitcakes in their kitchen. Blaine runs the mixer and Deanna hand-mixes the fruits and nuts. On a typical day their house is permeated with the wonderful aroma from 216 pounds of baking cakes.

If you order by phone, you're likely to hear their children, Marianna, 8, and Cynthia, 6, chirping in the background, for the Matthewses believe in working together as a family. Their fruitcakes are as honest as they are. Crisp pecans, apricots, dates, and raisins, real butter, cream, and fresh eggs. No peels, rinds, candied fruits, or preservatives. You'll find them more tart than sweet. We're especially fond of the Lemon-Rum Sunshine Cake, a sharply sweet pound cake made with real lemon, rum, butter, and eggs. Marian Burros found it to be ''moist and deliciously spirited,'' and we agree; it well deserves its name, Sunshine. The Matthewses have expanded their line to include other locally made products. Call or write for a catalog.

SAN FRANCISCO'S FRUIT AND NUT PÂTÉ

The Flour Arts Pantry   phone orders: yes
5668 Oak Grove   415-652-7044
Oakland, CA 94618

If I had to choose just one product that best represents the current trend in specialty foods, it would be Barbara Srulovitz's fruit and nut pâté. Barbara, who worked for a publisher for nearly 14 years as foreign rights manager and sales rep, took the plunge into the food business with just one product. Even though something that quacks like a duck usually is a duck, this product looks like your standard fruitcake but is not. Far from it.

The fruit and nut pâté has no sugar, honey, citron, candied fruits, or chemicals. A 2-pound loaf has less than two tablespoons of flour, less than one egg, a dash of vanilla, and—after baking—a quick misting of amaretto. Turkish and California apricots, prunes, dates, gold and black raisins, figs, almonds, walnuts, pecans. In short, it is composed of entirely natural ingredients, all of which are listed on the label, is full of fiber, low in calories, and compatible with most diets. Gourmands love it, fitness folks love it, diabetics, weight watchers, and people restricted to low-cholesterol foods love it. I love it.

You can order everything from a miniloaf of 12 ounces up to a banquet block—100 ounces and foil-wrapped. The savarin cakes, 40 ounces in a ring, make memorable wedding cakes. For special occasions, Barbara decorates the tops with seasonal dressings: plum jam, cranberry relish, chocolate drizzle, fresh fruit of the season—kumquats and kiwis for Christmas, red flame grapes and lemoned bananas for summer.

I still can't get over it. A 1-ounce piece of this unbelievably rich-tasting cake has only 95 calories and 15 grams of carbohydrates. Incredible. Better than the fat farm!

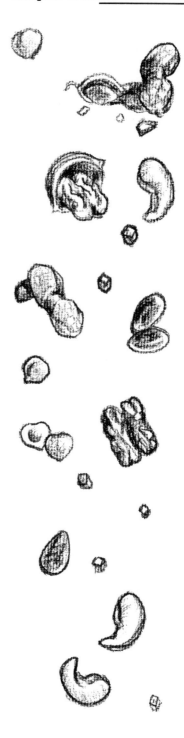

OTHER SUMPTUOUS CAKES

The high point of teatime is really the cake. Fortunately, there are bakeries around that send out sumptuous cakes, ones that are at least as good as, and often superior to, cakes home-baked after three or four hours of hard labor. We have limited our choices to cakes that are really outstanding and that ship well. Out of the running are those that are too dry, too simpering, or too lazy to keep up their reputation. We did order every cake we could find in the back-of-the-magazine ads; those that didn't pass muster shall mercifully remain nameless.

DARK VICTORY

Desserts by David Glass   phone orders: yes
140-150 Huyshope Ave.   212-755-3316
Hartford, CT 06106   ae/visa/mc/dc/cb
                         (Maison E. H. Glass, Inc.)

The New York foodies are right to call this Dark Victory. David Glass's chocolate mousse cake—a flourless cake made only from bittersweet chocolate, butter, sugar,

Oregon Riesling Eggnog

Here's a splendid drink to accompany David's cake.

Serves 8 in 15 minutes

- 3 eggs, separated
  Pinch of salt
- 1 pint whipping cream
- 1 bottle Oregon Riesling
- ¼ cup maraschino cherry juice
- 8 cherries for garnish

Beat egg whites with a pinch of salt until stiff but not dry. Whip cream lightly, then stir in egg yolks and Riesling. Fold egg whites into this mixture along with maraschino juice. Ladle into punch cups and add a stemmed cherry to each cup.

eggs, and cocoa—looks, feels, and tastes like the result of a love affair between a brownie and a truffle, with the intense chocolate mousse resting on a crusty, crunchy bottom. David Glass apprenticed in France and claims he extracted the recipe from a French chef who was on her deathbed. She got well but not before he got the recipe. A likely story with a happy ending.

For five years now, David has been shipping these cakes out to a growing number of chocoholic devotees. Recently he added golf ball-sized chocolate mousse balls that he rolls in hazelnut praline. Both cakes and balls are shipped overnight air and should be kept in the freezer. Choose from original chocolate, espresso chocolate, or orange chocolate cakes. The mousse balls come in all of these flavors plus peanut butter. The cakes come in 6-, 8-, and 10-inch sizes; the mousse balls weigh in at about ¾ of an ounce each and are sold by the pound.

For the ultimate chocolate experience, you can douse the cake slivers with fruit puree—apricot, raspberry, or kiwi—and a dollop of whipped cream. David's favorite is a chocolate mousse sundae made by heating the cake until it runs, then spooning the hot cake over the best ice cream you can lay hands on. Take it from me. Even the most jaded voluptuary will sit up and take notice when served a piece of David Glass's cake.

A BOOZED BUNDT

Dinkel's Bakery   phone orders: yes
3329 N. Lincoln   312-281-7300
Chicago, IL 60657   ae/visa/mc

Here comes a tongue twister. When Joseph Dinkel met George Dickel, guess what happened? Dinkel, who baked in Chicago, was taken with the whiskey that Dickel made in Tennessee and went home determined to make a Dinkel-Dickel cake that could be doused in this fine Tennessee sour mash. This idea kicked around, just talk really, and became part of the family legend. Years and years later, Dinkel's grandson Norm, Jr., perfected the bundt cake that is now shipped from the bakery and is known, ignominiously, as The Sip'n Whiskey Cake. Made from whole wheat flour, raisins, pecans, eggs, and milk, this cake is moist, mellow, not too sweet, and has enough sour mash in it to make you get up and try a Tennessee two-step. We kept trying to be circumspect about it—to only eat it in thin slivers. The cake sent to us lasted about three days. We liked it a lot.

CRUSADERS' CONFECTION

Cafe Beaujolais phone orders: yes
PO Box 730   707-964-0292
Mendocino, CA 95460 ae/visa/mc

In my own crusade for the perfect cake to keep on hand, I'd have to rank Margaret Fox's Panforte di Mendocino right up at the top. And it's not even really accurate to call it a cake. A traditional Italian confection, this dark, dense, aromatic 22-ounce wheel, dusted with powdered sugar and solid with nuts, is more satisfying than candy, more nutritious than cake. Panforte was created in Siena and sold to the Crusaders, who found it a high-energy food that gave them the strength to carry forth into Middle Eastern deserts simply crawling with infidels. Margaret Fox's version is made with only natural ingredients, beginning with nuts, then candied citrus peels, flour, sugar, honey, butter, and spices. Margaret makes four varieties: almond, hazelnut, walnut, and macadamia. The cake will keep longer than any crusade you can muster and tastes so good you likely will never get to find out how long it can last.

Margaret also makes English-style fruitcake, a 24-ounce loaf soaked in brandy, either plain or chocolate. Both cakes are marvelous with tea or port, sherry, liqueur, or brandy. If you're in San Francisco, turn your own crusade north and visit Margaret's Cafe Beaujolais in picture-postcard Mendocino. She serves what's been called the best breakfast in California and a mighty fine lunch as well. Dinner in the summer, with the right chef, can be well worth the trip.

Anchovy Cheese Fingers

In keeping with Margaret Fox's crusade, here's a salty savory to serve alongside the panforte.

In hot butter, sauté some thick slices of French bread, then cut into fingers. Place side by side in an ovenproof dish. Lay an anchovy fillet atop each. Mix some fresh grated Parmesan with equal parts Italian parsley and spread thickly over this. Sprinkle with melted butter, dust lightly with cayenne pepper, and run them under the broiler until they are brown and bubbly.

NEW YORK AT YOUR DOORSTEP

Arnold Reuben Jr's.   phone orders: yes
  Cheesecakes   516-466-3685
15 Hillpark Ave.   visa/mc
Great Neck, NY 11021

This is no New York–"style" cheesecake. This *is* New York. On a plate. For you. From Arnold Reuben, Jr. It comes second-day air. Dense, subtle and sweet, no graham cracker crust, no gloppy fruit, no puffed-up Jello consistency. Just solid, high-fat cream cheese in a sweet family-secret recipe. A little sliver will do. Arnold calls this a slice of New York. I believe him.

He invented this cake, along with the Reuben sandwich, in his restaurant called Reuben's—which is no longer, as he says, "with us." When you order a cheesecake, he'll send along a souvenir menu from Reuben's. Even as far back as 1929, he was encouraging his restaurant customers to "mail home our delicious cheesecakes." Home being, one could tell, some place other than New York. It's fun to look at the old menu, when broiled shad roe was $1.25 and you could get the special dinner, which included a puree of green peas, consommé vermicelli, and a whole broiled live lobster with drawn butter and fresh asparagus, for $1.50. You also got a piece of cheesecake to go with the coffee that was included at that price, too.

Arnold's cheesecake comes large, which serves 20, and small, which serves 8, in plain, amaretto chocolate, marble chocolate chip, or Black Forest flavors. You can freeze this cake with good results.

VISIONS OF SUGAR PLUMS

The Final Blessing   phone orders: yes
PO Box 7533   503-388-1079
Bend, OR 97708   visa/mc

When Joan Batson moved two years ago from Arizona—where she'd been teaching home ec.—to Bend, located in the dead center of Oregon, she decided to change jobs. She built a kitchen beside her house and began turning out the Sugar Plum Cake, a 28-ounce bundt cake she'd made for years from a Bohemian recipe that had been in her family. She'll bake it to order for you, sending it out within a couple of days of receipt of order. This cake is soft, redolent with spices, loaded with sweet plums and walnuts, and glazed to stay moist at least 60 days. At the moment, Joan only ships this cake from September through April, but once people have received one, she'll soon be pressed into working year-round.

DOUBLE-CHOCOLATE BROWNIES AND TORTES

Gwetzli	phone orders: yes
5832 Presley Way	415-655-5621
Oakland, CA 94618	visa/mc

Barbara Hack started making brownies in San Francisco in 1975. Then she moved to Zurich, where she perfected the recipe, taking advantage of the fine chocolate and dairy products she found there. She began to sell the brownies in Switzerland and named them *Gwetzli* (g'wet'-slee), which means "little goodie" to the Swiss. But Barbara got homesick for California and came back, bringing the little goodie with her.

Now made in Oakland, Barbara's brownies are dense as a candy bar, rich and moist. They are made without baking powder and contain pure creamery butter, chocolate liquor, real chocolate chips, and pure vanilla. No preservatives, and they freeze beautifully for months (if you can leave them alone). You can choose from four flavors: double-chocolate with toasted almonds, chocolate mint, chocolate espresso, and peanut butter. All but the peanut butter can be had in torte shape as well as brownies. Barbara Hack isn't kidding when she says her brownies are a cross between a truffle and a brownie. Even though the name *Gwetzli* may sound like some variety of giraffe rather than something to eat, these may be the best chocolate bites for sale on the West Coast.

Roasted Cheese

If you wish to enchant your guests, a sweet Comice pear, roasted cheese, and the Sugar Plum Cake is all you'll need.

Serves 4 in 10 minutes

½	cup sweet butter
½	cup grated Vermont cheddar
	Dusting of cayenne pepper
½	teaspoon prepared mustard
4	English muffins, split and lightly toasted

Blend butter and cheddar into a paste. Season with cayenne and mustard, then pile onto split and toasted English muffins. Run under the broiler until cheese is bubbly and brown. Serve immediately.

OTHER TEATIME SWEETS

Besides the expected biscuits, cookies, and cakes, there are other sweets that are delectable for tea or for dessert. We've found a half dozen that make dazzling dishes a cinch.

Sherry Cheese Pâté

Here's a really splendid savory to counterbalance the heavenly sweetness of a flaming crêpe.

Serves 6 in 1 hour

- 6 ounces soft cream cheese
- 1 cup sharp grated cheddar
- 2 tablespoons dry sherry
- ¼ teaspoon curry powder
  Salt to taste
- ½ cup Polly's Chutney
- 2 green onions and tops, chopped
  Assorted crackers

Process cheeses, sherry, curry powder, and salt to taste. Pour into small serving bowl, cover, and chill until firm. One-half hour before serving, remove from refrigerator and top with chutney and green onions. Serve with crackers.

Polly Jean's Crêpes Suzette

Serves 4 in 20 minutes

Make ahead at your leisure: *crêpes:* Sift together ⅔ cup of flour, 1 tablespoon sugar, and a pinch of salt. Beat together 2 whole eggs and 2 egg yolks and

CONTINUED ON PAGE 223

SAUCY SWEETS

Polly Jean's Pantry
4561 Mission Gorge Pl., Ste. K
San Diego, CA 92120

phone orders: yes
800-621-0852
visa/mc

Five years ago, Johanna Seignious set out to make the best chutney money could buy. She cut all the fruits by hand, and that was no small matter seeing as how her chutney has the longest list of ingredients I've ever encountered for a product of this type—29 fruits, rinds, spices, and honey. But by careful blending and by following a recipe she invented herself, she's created a tart, sweet chutney that is particularly nice at tea. She then went on to create blueberries cassis, cherries jubilee, and sauce à l'orange, all of which can be used for instant flambés. Flame the cherries over cheesecake, the blueberries cassis over vanilla gelato, and the sauce a l'orange over crêpes. Who can ever forget it?

RISING TO THE OCCASION

Soufflé de Paris
PO Box 1833
Laguna Beach, CA 92652

phone orders: yes
C'est Gourmet
714-581-6379
visa/mc

Wendy Edgren was giving French cooking lessons in Southern California when she met up with Parisian Hubert Segard. The two of them have cooked up something that is almost too good to be true: a pure soufflé that comes in its own individual cooking/serving dish nestled in a shiny, varnished basket. All you have to do is take it out of the box, remove the lid, pop it in a hot oven, and in 20 minutes you have a perfectly raised soufflé. Can you imagine that? Wonder of wonders, this all-natural-ingredient product, with no preservatives, can languish on your pantry shelf up to four years—waiting for the moment you choose for it to rise to the occasion. The taste is as good as any I ever made from scratch out of Julia Child, and best of all: like Everest, in my pantry it is *there*. Flavors are Cointreau, hazelnut, chocolate, smoked salmon, Roquefort. This 4½-ounce soufflé is as costly as a fine truffle, but worth it.

FRUIT COMPOTES

The Postilion phone orders: yes
615 Old Pioneer Rd. 414-922-4170
Fond du Lac, WI 54935

Thirty-five years ago, Madame Kuony and her husband established a restaurant in Fond du Lac in a Victorian homestead. Their customers adored the small-batch compotes, sauces, mincemeats, marinades, vinaigrettes, and hazelnut pralines that were served in the restaurant. After tiring of seeing customers on their knees, begging, the good Madame began bottling the products to take home. Today, every bottle that leaves her kitchen is still made, labeled, and tied by hand. This is cooking at its finest. I found Madame at a food show, where even the most jaded buyers were eagerly crowded around her tasting everything in sight and hanging on her every word. She looks like Dr. Ruth and dispenses cooking information with the same kind of Munchkin authority.

Besides the plum puddings, Yule logs, basting sauces, marinades, and vinaigrettes that she carefully makes and sends, her great mounds of fruit compote in crystal compotiers are a feast for eyes and nose as well as taste buds. All are made with imported liqueur and all are equally delicious. You can order them in pairs and in quartet, if you can't choose just one. Who could? Madame suggests apricot-prune blended with tart, fresh limes and rum for use in a flamed omelet. The apple-kirsch liqueur is made with whole almonds, spices, and limes. Try the cherry-pineapple, laced with French cognac and excel-

CONTINUED FROM PAGE 222

then add to dry ingredients. Add 1¾ cups milk and blend until smooth (easiest in a processor or blender). Add 2 tablespoons melted butter and 1 tablespoon rum or cognac. Let batter stand 2 hours in refrigerator before cooking crepes. Cook crepes in 8-inch crêpe pan, removing to sheets of waxed paper to separate them until you're ready to serve.

Crêpes Suzette Polly Jean: Heat sauce à l'orange in finishing pan or chafing dish. Take crêpes one at a time, dip in sauce, fold in quarters, and arrange in pan. Sprinkle 3 tablespoons heated cognac over all and ignite the spirit. Spoon more sauce over each crêpe while still flaming, and serve.

Postilion Coupe Royale

Madame serves this dessert in her restaurant. To make it you need hazelnut praline, which she offers in a jar; Chantilly cream, which you can make in a flash; chocolate sauce; and fine vanilla or coffee ice cream. Envision a fluted dish with mounded coffee ice cream, blanketed under chocolate sauce and lush Chantilly cream, then sprinkled with hazelnut praline. Ultimate pleasure. (Note: Chantilly cream is nothing more than heavy cream whipped to soft peaks and sweetened with confectioners' sugar and pure vanilla.)

lent over vanilla ice cream. Pear ginger, the most exotic, is flavored with angelica, Cointreau, and raisins and can be folded into a crêpe or served with thin slivers of baked ham. Delicious.

ULTIMATE COMFORT FOOD

Wick's Pies	phone orders: yes
PO Box 268	317-584-8401
Winchester, IN 47394	visa/mc

At the polar opposite from the fancy European entries into the sweets sweepstakes stands Wick's old-fashioned sugar cream pie. Wick remembers his granny putting an unfilled pie shell in the oven, pouring sugar cream filling inside, then sitting on a stool in front of the oven and stirring the filling with her finger until the mixture became warm. Wick can't stir all the pies he makes today, but he decided people didn't mind the fact that the filling is thicker on the bottom than on the top. The crust is just like homemade, the filling as sweet and bland and delicious as something your Great-Aunt Susie sent over for Sunday dinner. Wick sends these out six at a time, frozen, by second-day air, and you can keep them in the freezer awaiting the right moment. After a heavy winter dinner, say Thanksgiving or Christmas, this pie is perfect. Wick's pie says one thing: Home at Last.

THE PROOF IS IN THE PUDDING

Mother Sperry's Plum	phone orders: yes
Pudding	206-329-8631
1416 E. Aloha St.	
Seattle, WA 98112	

Yes, there is a Mother Sperry. In fact, there are two mothers, who live across the street from each other and have joined up to make a good old-fashioned pudding, balancing fruits and spices with brandy. When you cut into this dark brown blob, it simply drips with butter. As Mother says herself, this is the great leap backward. And even though this weighs only 26 ounces and comes in a slick red box, it will easily serve six and maybe eight anytime within the next couple of years. Between the booze and the butter, this cake may have a longer life than the rest of us.

THE DANISH SMORGASBORD

Lehmann's Bakery   phone orders: yes
2210 Sixteenth St.   414-632-2359
Racine, WI 53405   visa/mc

There was a time, not so long ago, when if you didn't have a Danish bakery in your neighborhood, you could just forget it. We needn't even comment on those son-of-a-bakery versions of so-called Danish sold in the grocery store. But now, with air shipment, the Lehmanns guarantee you fresh, luscious Danish, delivered quickly in 14 flavors: pecan, almond, walnut, raspberry, apricot, prune, date, cherry, apple, strawberry, pineapple, blueberry, cheese, and chocolate. Made with all natural ingredients, no preservatives, the Lehmann Kringles we got were flaky, delicate, and heady with the aroma of butter. For some reason that I can't explain, we received three of these delectable wreaths, and even the last piece of the last one didn't taste old or dry. Could it be that Danish has gotten a bad rap all these years by virtue of "shortcuts" that simply short-circuited the entire product? You can also order cookies, cheesecake, or a Danish apple cake from Lehmann's.

CHOCOLATE PÂTÉ

True Confections/   phone orders: yes
   MacKenzie, Ltd.   800-858-7100
3522 12th St. NE   ae/visa/mc
Washington, DC 20017

This preposterously smooth, dense, rich, dark chocolate pâté is log shaped, 12 by 4 by 2 inches, and is stuffed with roasted hazelnuts and islands of meringue. Serve it to 18

Mother Sperry's Easy Hard Sauce

And I quote:
   Cream 1 stick soft butter with ½ cup powdered sugar. Whip until light. Add 2 tablespoons good brandy. Beat until fluffy. Chill. Bother to make this. You won't regret it. And keep in mind that this sauce is mostly an excuse for Mother to swig brandy while she works. Remember, idle hands are happy hands.

devotees either pure, as is, or lying in a pool of raspberry puree with just a cloud of rum-laced whipped cream beside it. This Washington bakery will ship it out to you via overnight air, safely blanketed in gel ice and stryofoam. Delicate and divine, it costs less than $40 postpaid. For a big tea or a big dinner party, this is luxe ultimatum.

CHAPTER 7

GIFTS FROM THE KITCHEN

There's nothing quite so welcome as a gift from the kitchen. In my search I found a few items that can help you make memorable gifts from your own kitchen. A few of these, you may just decide you want for yourself. Because these things are handmade, it's best if you call to check on prices, details such as color, and availability. Things change.

HANDMADE TERRA-COTTA BAKING DISHES

Planned Pottery　　　　phone orders: yes
PO Box 5045　　　　　　503-345-2471
Eugene, OR 97405　　　　visa/mc: yes

When expert baker and potter June Knori began experimenting with bread loaf pans, she discovered a new-old secret: The European brick oven flavor can be achieved without a baker's oven. June discovered that her own handmade unglazed terra-cotta bread loaf pans helped her make bread with a crustier crust and a moist, tender interior. And to top it all off, there's a significant energy savings. I love this bread pan and use it every week. You can buy the regular bread baker, the just-for-one baker, a pie and a pizza baker, a French bread baker—a flat tile with native Oregon foliage impressed on the surface makes it too beautiful to leave in the kitchen—and squares she calls bun warmers, which are unglazed tiles you put in the oven, then inside the napkin-lined basket to keep rolls hot at the table. All are handcrafted, unglazed stoneware with no lead, safe in ovens and dishwashers. Her friend Suzanne Ali wrote a 33-page book on brick oven baking that's a must. Ask for it.

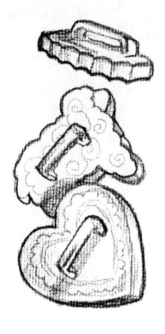

TERRA-COTTA COOKIE MOLDS

Brown Bag Cookie Art
  A Hill Design Company
Hill, NH 03243

phone orders: yes
603-934-2650

Twenty molds to choose from, these unglazed 4-by-6-inch stoneware designs are wonderfully intricate and transfer patterns in relief to the finished cookies. Designs include a splendid woolly lamb, a lacy Victorian heart, and an elegant swan. If you want to start a great family tradition, buy a different mold every year and make cookies for your Christmas tree. They'll even supply you with a cookie recipe booklet offering choices including lemon cardamom cookies, ginger and orange cookies, and, of course, the traditional favorite—plain old sugar cookies. These molds are gorgeous. I want all 20.

ANTIQUE CHOCOLATE MOLDS

Holland Handicrafts
PO Box 792
Davis, CA 95616

phone orders: yes
916-756-3023

When Adrienne Trouw lived in Holland, she was enchanted with the antique chocolate molds she kept seeing. Made of tin, with both front and back designs, they come in everything from the familiar lamb pattern to rabbits, musical instruments, and a real Dutch-looking Santa. One of her favorites, from her private collection, is 17 inches tall and 9 inches wide and features St. Nicholas standing beside three children in a tub. As the Dutch story goes, a butcher had cut up the children, salted them, and put them in a tub, but St. Nicholas rescued them and restored them to life. And we thought American children were exposed to too much violence. . . . Well, anyway, Adrienne collected as many antique molds as she could find. Then, to her good fortune, her husband located an entire warehouse full of them. Now, back home in Davis, she offers chocolate molds made in Holland from original antique casts, in more than 50 designs. Write for a brochure.

PIE CRUST SHIELDS

Terrell International Co.   phone orders: yes
1517 Vine Hill Rd.   408-438-1731
Santa Cruz, CA 95065

Despite the company name, this is actually Jerry Terrell out in his garage trying to help his wife out with the pies. He stamps out things he calls pie crust shields, made of tin, which you lay over the crust's fluted edge to protect it from burning. You can make a big, fancy edge on a pie using these and have it come out picture perfect. These are good little gizmos.

HOMEMADE LIQUEURS

Steve Bragg   phone orders: yes
3711 Coffey Lane   503-684-3363/
Newberg, OR 97132   538-3914

The name of his street aside, Steve Bragg has been interested in coffee liqueur for a good while and has been making it for friends. Now he's put together a kit that provides you with a recipe, bottles, labels, sleeves, and vanilla bean. You, too, can make coffee liqueur.

TOOLS OF THE TRADE

Lieba, Inc.   phone orders: yes
405 W. Franklin St.   301-727-7333
Baltimore, MD 21201   visa/mc

Elaine Latham has built a better mousetrap. Consulting with specialty chefs, she's combined professional-quality tools with the proper instructions to help home cooks do three things. For making fancy chocolates, she provides an instruction book and chef's-quality palette knife, spatula, serrated knife, and three colorants for chocolate: yellow, red, and blue. For making fancy garnishes, including apple birds and beet roses, you get a how-to-book and five tools of the trade. Finally, she offers a "grate-garnishing" machine that reminds me of the infamous Veg-o-matic of late-night TV ads, is sharp as a razor and quick as a wink. It has four grating, slicing, and shredding blades. The slicer works better for chocolate curls than the Cuisinart.

HAND-STENCILED KITCHEN ACCESSORIES

The Barleystock	phone orders: yes
121 Pleasant St.	617-249-6628
Athol, MA 01331	visa/mc

Jayma Wilkins-Elmer and Ken Elmer create traditional stencil designs by hand using hand-mixed paints. Among their interpretations of these designs are the Amish bird, the pineapple, and the pig and the apple—the poor little pig gazing longingly at the one apple on the tree. They stencil these lovely naïf designs onto 100 percent cotton goods: kitchen towels, potholders, place mats, napkins, aprons, and hot pads. They also transfer carefully stenciled geese and heart patterns to wooden country benches.

OLD-FASHIONED PUNCHED TIN

Country Accents	phone orders: yes
RD 2, Box 293	201-996-2885
Stockton, NJ 08559	

In the old days, before refrigeration, perishable foods were kept in food safes. They were sometimes decorated with punched tin, with the sharp sides facing outward to keep the flies at bay. Now the Palotas, James and Marie, have revived this nearly lost craft. They offer custom tin for that old safe you picked up at a garage sale, and a thing they call "ready-punch," a kit that lets you do it yourself. You will get museum-quality tinworks from the Palotas in traditional and contemporary motifs.

DECORATIVE ART TILES FOR THE KITCHEN

Basheer Studios   phone orders: yes
PO Box 6   603-886-1701
Hudson, NJ 03051   visa/mc

Ken and Jackie Basheer create brilliant kitchen tiles inspired by familiar comestibles: eggplants, peas, pears, and peppers—at least 25 fruit and vegetable designs. They'll make up some just for you, using a background color of your choice. Here's the place to call when you want to redo your kitchen.

OLD-FASHIONED KITCHEN SOAPS

Sappo Hill Co.   phone orders: no
654 Tolman Creek Rd.   503-482-4485
Ashland, OR 97520

This is not as ugly as homemade soap, but it's handmade from all-vegetable oil and glycerine, poured into ordinary plastic pipe to cool, then hand-cut into discs. You'll never get dishpan hands (or any other exposed parts) using any of the 20 or so scents: lemon, almond, cinnamon, Oregon berry, and others. Use this soap once and you'll never want any other kind. Write for a brochure. As owner John Toso reminds us: "Soap and education are not as sudden as a massacre, but they are more deadly in the long run . . ." (Mark Twain).

CHAPTER 8

MAIL-ORDER MENUS

I. Can you boil water?
II. Tea for two and other delights
III. Interested in ethnic cooking?
IV. The "You look as if you slaved over a hot stove"—but you didn't—dinner parties

M.O.M. is the answer to the question often asked around our house: Who's cooking tonight? It's our own personal acronym for Mail-Order Menus, meals that are so simple to get together, the cook may not need to know much more than how to boil water and how to set the table.

Discovering the better-than-homemade items available by mail, all over the country, has changed entirely my attitude toward entertaining. I don't have to wait until I have half a day to do the cooking. I don't demand of myself that I make the bread, the entrée, the dessert, and the table arrangement. Now, more than likely, I will make one dish from scratch—something I really enjoy cooking—and fill in the rest with fine foods made by other people. Buy the bread. Buy the dessert. Skip the alternate side dishes. Now, I can have company over with no more than an hour's preparation.

And I have discovered that offering some special cheese, a cake, or a piece of meat that I had shipped in just for them is an honor to the guests that goes beyond taking them out to the fanciest restaurant in town. It says: "I thought about you and I care." It's really fun to call somebody and say, "When can you come to dinner? I'd like to order a live lobster. Tell me when you can come and I'll have it shipped to arrive that day." Let me tell you—the tone of the party is set before the guests ever get there.

I've divided this chapter into four parts. The first seven menus can be presented by anyone who can boil water, melt butter, and set the table. These dinners require no recipes. What few directions you might need arrive with the food. Here's where that live lobster comes in. And pasta specialties. Even 50 pounds of crawfish.

Second are a group of just-for-two-parties—with food —that require little more of you than placing an order or two. Tea for two. A real American breakfast. A cheese and pâté picnic. A midnight supper. These are tête-à-tête get-togethers where the food says: you count.

Third, are you interested in ethnic cooking? Want to try but don't know where to get the stuff or what to do with it once you've got it? Thai, Indian, Indonesian, Cajun, even good old Tex-Mex. Here's how.

And finally, I offer you seven dinner parties you can throw that will make it look as if you slaved over a hot stove for a week just getting ready, but you didn't. Here are the dinners to make your reputation.

With each menu you'll find a Mail-Order Pantry list that shows where you can get the foods by mail. Practically speaking, you'll probably be offering these menus with just one or two items sent in. The idea is to make it easy on yourself. So substitute from the fine food specialists in your area to fill in, and have a wonderful party that you can enjoy yourself. If the recipe is in this book, you'll find that noted beside the food purveyor's name in your pantry list; the recipe will appear beside the purveyor's listing in the foregoing chapters of the book. Once again, you'll find that there aren't a lot of recipes required to get these dinners together. Remember, that's the whole point. It's home cooking—but mostly, you don't have to do it.

SECTION I: Can You Boil Water?

THE FOUR-STAR RESTAURANT DOOR-TO-DOOR DINNER

Gerard Rubaud has solved the problem of what to do if you want to offer a complete haute cuisine dinner but don't want to cook it and don't want to go out for it either. Working in a renovated supermarket, he and his classically trained chefs prepare classic French dishes and put them fresh—are you ready for this?—in boil-a-bags. They send these lavish dinners out by overnight air express, so like magic you can have a full-blown dinner, created by classically trained chefs, never frozen, sent to you. All you have to do is warm the plates, buy the wine and flowers, get a loaf of decent bread and your guest or guests. Servings are from 2 to 200. Call for a menu. It looks as inviting as Maxim's.

Here's a sample. For two, this dinner would run you about $55. You'll soon see what Gerard means—fresh from his kitchen to your table. Just think: You can do all this with one phone call. You won't need any recipes here. Just know how to boil water, that's it.

GERARD'S DIAL-A-DINNER

Mosaic of Vegetables Pâté
(assortment of fresh vegetables
cooked in a light mousse,
served with a tomato/basil sauce)

Chicken and Crayfish Consommé
(crayfish with diced carrots, peas, and zucchini)

Seafood Pasta
(fresh sea scallops, mussels, monkfish,
and fresh pasta in a lobster sauce)

Lamb Navarin
(leg of lamb, diced and sautéed
in white wine and tomatoes,
served with baby vegetables)

Pear Charlotte
(fresh pear in a Bavarian custard
surrounded with ladyfingers
and served with raspberry sauce)

The Mail-Order Pantry

Gerard's Haute Cuisine
PO Box 203
Fairfax, VT 05454
phone orders: yes
802-849-6141

THE FIFTEEN-MINUTE MENU

Flown in live from Malaysia, the tiger prawns are almost a quarter pound apiece, and so striking with their black-ribbed shells that to rest one atop a bed of fresh pasta, dressed with this most arresting Pasta Plus sauce, would make a dinner to remember. And it won't take longer than 15 minutes to prepare. The pasta sauce is so delicious that you can make this meal vegetarian, without the prawns, and no one will complain.

Malaysian Tiger Prawns on a Bed of Fresh Pasta
with California Almond with Leeks and
Capers Pasta Plus Sauce
Hearts of Romaine with Raspberry/Walnut Dressing
Crisp White Wine   Truffles for Dessert

CAPE COD IN A CAN: THE TRADITIONAL CLAMBAKE

This is almost more fun than a trip to the beach. Figure out how many you want to serve—up to 10 from one can—then call up the clambakers and they'll get it all together for you. All you have to do is pop the lid off the can, place the can on the stove, pour beer or wine over contents, and boil. In 30 minutes you have it: Cape Cod. The accompaniments are traditional.

Steamed Chicken Lobster
Steamer Clams   Blue Mussels   Dill-Seasoned Codfish
Corn on the Cob   Spanish Onions   Red Bliss Potatoes
Italian Sweet Sausages
French Bread and Sweet Butter   Beer
Ice-Cold Watermelon

THE GREAT LOBSTER DEBAUCH

Rome could have burned for all we cared the night we boiled the lobsters. Placing a big, clear salad bowl in the middle of the table to catch the lobster and clam shells, providing double napkins for all, melting enough butter to make a cardiologist cringe, and serving nothing beyond boiled or uncooked accompaniments, this dinner had more impact for less effort than any I ever prepared in my whole life. This big, impressive meal is like a trip across America. Almost every region is represented by the best foods you could ask for.

Three Cheeses and Crackers
(Oregon blue, Kentucky Trappist, and Vermont cheddar with California Lahvosh heart crackers)

Atlantic Clams Steamed in Sonoma White Wine
Elephant Garlic/Italian Parsley

Live Maine Lobster with Drawn Butter

San Francisco Sourdough Bread
and Sadie Kendall's Sweet Butter
California Wild and Brown Rice
Carrots with Fresh Clipped Mint
Limestone Lettuce with Assorted Vinaigrettes

Chicago's Sip'n Whiskey Cake
with Crème Fraîche and Tennessee Whiskey
Upper Canada Coffee   Tikal Liqueur (or Kahlua)

The Mail-Order Pantry

Oregon blue cheese: Rogue River Valley Creamery
Trappist cheese: Gethsemani Farms
Vermont Cheddar: Shelburne Farms
live lobster and steamer clams: Marblehead Lobster Co.
garlic, parsley, and mint: Herb Gathering, Inc.
sourdough bread: Boudin Bakery
sweet butter and crème fraîche: Kendall Cheese Co.
wild rice: Deer Creek Wild Rice
vinaigrettes: Beautiful Food
cake: Dinkel's Bakery
coffee: Upper Canada Coffee Works & Tea Mill
Tikal liqueur: Steve Bragg

TEXAS CRAWFISH BOIL

These farm-raised crawfish, looking for all the world like baby lobsters, bright red, just about one good bite in the tail of each one, are startling when they arrive: 50 pounds squirming and crawling all over themselves. But set up a backyard party, boil them outside in shrimp boil, make your favorite recipes for potato salad and baked beans, order a pony of local beer, chill a watermelon in a washtub, play some Willie Nelson music, use nothing but forks and paper plates, and you'll have a party for 25–35 people they won't soon forget.

Boiled Crawfish
Potato Salad
French Bread and Sweet Butter
Watermelon
Baked Beans
Beer

The Mail-Order Pantry

crawfish: Texas Crawfish Farms
crawfish/shrimp boil: Gazin's
New Orleans French bread: Gazin's

KEY WEST CUISINE

For the longest time, Florida kept its stone crab legs a secret, but now that the fast shippers have gotten hold of them, you can have them, along with other delectable Florida seafood, anytime you want. For a first course, make an ad-lib salad from the scooped-out flesh of juicy Florida oranges, coconut, and walnut pieces, stuffed into the orange halves.

Cold Tropical Orange Cup
Giant Shrimp Stuffed with Stone Crabmeat
Confetti Pasta and Cream
Marinated Red Pepper Strips
Emmanuel Roux's Pralines
Black Coffee with Chicory

THE OHIO ITALIAN EMERGENCY DINNER

Everything for this dinner except the salad greens can rest safely on your emergency shelves: the dried pasta, the canned sauce, the soufflé in a jar. Then, should you need to turn to it in a hurry, here it is. You can enjoy it vegetarian or, to make it really memorable, make Mama Schiavone's meatballs using half lamb and half beef. The bright red marinara sauce with onion and garlic will make this dish seem as if you'd stirred it up from scratch and spent all day doing it.

Schiavone's Spaghetti and Meatballs in Sauce
Hearts of Romaine with Classic Caesar Dressing
Robust Red Wine
French Bread and Butter
Hazelnut Soufflé de Paris

SECTION II: Tea for Two and Other Delights

THE THREE LITTLE PIGS' PICNIC

Le Trois Petits Cochons will send you a group of three fresh pâtés along with a jar of cornichons that will make the beginnings of a dazzling picnic. Use a great-looking basket and pack it with a table cloth, stemmed glasses, a bottle of wine (don't forget the corkscrew), real china plates, all the utensils, fruit, cheese, and a baguette of French bread. This is a picnic.

Three Pâtés
(venison with juniper berries and cognac;
goose liver/Sauterne mousse;
pork and chicken livers with cèpes and Madeira)
Garlic Mayonnaise and Mustard
Cornichons
Blue Heron Brie   French Baguette
Perfect Pears
Oregon Pinot Noir

> **The Mail-Order Pantry**
>
> pâtés and cornichons: Les Trois Petits Cochons
> brie: Blue Heron French Cheese Co.
> bread: Boudin Bakery
> pears: Pinnacle Orchards

TEA FOR TWO

Four o'clock in the afternoon. A china teapot at the ready. Merrily boiling water. Tea leaves left loose for reading. (I know you don't know how to read tea leaves—make something up.) A fine cake on a footed stand. A few fine cheeses. A vegetable pâté. Crackers. Here's a grand old tradition worth hauling out of the attic. Get brewing.

The Queen's Tea
Blue Corn Crêpes with Lemon Curd
Port Cheese Rolled in Walnuts
Vermont Common Crackers
Cowboy Caviar
Lemon Sunshine Cake

> **The Mail-Order Pantry**
>
> tea: Upper Canada Coffee Works & Tea Mill
> blue corn: Blue Corn Connection (with crêpes recipe)
> lemon curd: Thatched Cottage
> cheese ball: Herkimer Family Treasure House
> Vermont crackers: Harman's Cheese & Country Store
> vegetable pâté: Cowboy Caviar
> lemon sponge cake: Matthews 1812 House

THE ALL-AMERICAN BREAKFAST

The one meal that Americans can claim as their own is breakfast. By shopping from the best food purveyors in the U.S. of A. you can make the best of the best. For two

The Mail-Order Pantry

grapefruit: Pittman & Davis
buckwheat cakes: Brumwell
Flour Mill
sausages: Early's Honey Stand
butter: Kendall Cheese Co.
maple syrup: Butternut
Mountain Farm
strawberries and peaches:
Greenbriar Jam Kitchen
cocoa: Rainbow Tea & Spicery
coffee: The Kobos Co.

or twenty. Here are the best examples we could find of the necessities for that fine American convention.

Texas Grapefruit on the Half Shell
Soft Scrambled Eggs
Heart of Iowa Buckwheat Cakes
Tennessee Country Sausage
California Sweet Butter   Vermont Maple Syrup
Massachusetts Sun-Cooked Strawberries
and Brandied Peaches
Oregon Hot Spicy Cocoa and Arabica Coffee

The Mail-Order Pantry

muffins: Wolferman's
lox: Josephson's Smokehouse
and Dock
pears: Pinnacle Orchards
preserves: Deer Mountain
Berry Farm
hazelnut honey butter: Oregon
Apiaries
coffee: The Kobos Co.

NORTHWEST SUNDAY BRUNCH

Salmon come in many forms from the cold waters of the Pacific Northwest. One of the best processors of these versatile fish is Josephson's. Using their moist, bright red, cold smoked lox with poached eggs and your favorite recipe for hollandaise, sprinkle a few capers on top and you'll have a Northwest breakfast that will carry you through the day.

Poached Egg on a Toasted English Muffin
with Strips of Cold Smoked Lox
Hollandaise and Capers
Poached Pear   Fried Potatoes
Red Raspberry Preserves   Hazelnut Honey Butter
Coffee

The Mail-Order Pantry

lemon vinaigrette: Beautiful
Food
steak and lobster: Pfaelzer
Brothers (with recipe for filet
flambé)

CONTINUED ON PAGE 241

PFAELZER'S MIDNIGHT SUPPER FOR TWO

When Pfaelzer sends you a box containing two perfect steaks and lobster tails, you have the heart of a fine dinner. After allowing time for thawing, you then need no more than a half hour to prepare this simple but sublime meal.

Limestone Lettuce with Lemon Vinaigrette
Bourbon Pepper Filet Flambé

(Kentucky bourbon flamed filet mignon
studded with peppercorns)
Broiled Rock Lobster Tails with Lime Butter
First-Quality French Bread and Sweet Butter
Gamay Beaujolais   French Roast Coffee
Ported Figs Stuffed with Whole Almonds

CONTINUED FROM PAGE 240

figs: Timbercrest Farms (with
recipe)
almonds: Nunes Farms
Almonds

SECTION III: Interested in Ethnic Cooking?

Starter packages of ethnic specialties make the plunge
into exotic cuisine easy and pleasant. Here are a few of
the best ones we discovered.

COMPLETE THAI DINNER PANTRY

The Ethnic Pantry provides this four-course dinner for six
to eight people, complete with recipes and special ingredients. For every dish, you get the recipe, complete
instructions, necessary ethnic ingredients, and a list of
what you need to buy fresh from the grocery store.

Rich Mushroom and Shrimp Soup
Sweet and Spicy Beef Curry
Curried Shrimp and Cucumbers
Apple (or mango) Salad
Thai Sweet Sticky Rice   Krupuk (shrimp chips)
Fish Sauce   Thai Chili Paste

The Mail-Order Pantry

complete Thai dinner: The
Ethnic Pantry

FESTIVAL OF LIGHTS BOMBAY DINNER FOR EIGHT

If you're intrigued by Indian cuisine but need help with
the spice blends, here's one answer. Combine the basic
imported spice blends with Rumi Engineer's special carrot chutney, and you'll have an Indian feast suitable for
their Festival of Lights—a combination of our Christmas,
Thanksgiving, and New Year's celebrations, all rolled into
one. If you want to create your own festival, fill kid's lunch-
sized paper bags halfway with sand, insert candles inside,
and line your driveway and entrance with these Indian-

The Mail-Order Pantry

basic Bombay dinner kit:
Maison E. H. Glass, Inc.
chutneys: Rumi Corporation

style luminarias. Come sundown, light the candles and your guests will feel in a festive mood before they set foot in the house.

Basmati Rice Curry
Major Grey's Chutney   Rumi's Carrot Chutney
Bombay Duck (a fish condiment)   Chicken Tandoori
Pappadoms (lentil wafers)
Condiments: riced hard-cooked eggs, diced green
onions, raisins, sliced bananas, cucumber slices
in yogurt, salted peanuts, sliced raw onion rings,
and bell pepper rings

INDONESIAN RIJSTTAFEL

The Mail-Order Pantry

complete Indonesian dinner:
The Ethnic Pantry

From The Ethnic Pantry again, here is a complete four-course dinner designed to serve six to eight people. You simply fill in the fresh ingredients, follow the instructions, and you'll have your own Indonesian rijsttafel in America.

Meat Satay with Peanut Sauce
Aromatic Lamb Curry
Chicken with Indonesian Soy Sauce
Vegetables in Spiced Sauce
Asian Jasmine Rice   Krupuk (shrimp chips)
Fried Coconut and Peanut Condiment
Indonesian Soy Sauce
Sambal Oelek and Sambal Badjak
(red pepper and tamarind paste condiments)

THE CAJUN FEAST

The Mail-Order Pantry

all the Cajun fixins: Gazin's

Let the good times roll, say the Cajuns, and one of the easiest ways to do this is to rely on Gazin's in New Orleans. They'll send you everything from freshly made New Orleans–style French bread, to soups and sauces, to just-made fish dishes that they have made up in Pierre Port and ship frozen, looking just like what you'd get if you were there eating in one of South Louisiana's chrome-stool diners. One call to Gazin's and you'll get this whole dinner. If you ask, they'll even send you a Justin Wilson record so you can play some Cajun music. Whhoo-eee. *Jolee Blon.*

Crayfish Bisque

Oysters Rockefeller

Stuffed Crab   Stuffed Shrimp

Stuffed Oysters   Stuffed Jalapeños

Baked Potato with Shrimp

New Orleans French Bread

Cafe du Monde Coffee and Chicory

New Orleans Sundae with Elmer's Gold Brick Sauce

TEX-MEX FAJITA FIESTA

Around San Antonio, this outdoor style of cooking is popular. You can get everything you need for this meal (except the guacamole, rice, and pralines) from El Paso Chile Co. Oh, you'll have to get your own beer, too. The beer of choice for this meal is Pearl, just in case you're a demon for authenticity. The way this works is this: You grill marinated strips of skirt steak over hot charcoal, then fold into hot flour tortillas and top with salsa and guacamole. Use paper plates, lots of paper napkins. This is meant to be mostly for fun and not much trouble.

The Mail-Order Pantry

chili powder, fajita marinade, and salsa: The El Paso Chile Co.
rice: Farms of Texas Co.
pralines: Lamme's Candies

Chili con Carne with Beans

(garnished with slices of fresh lime

and grated cheddar)

Just-Steamed Corn Tortillas

Fajitas in Flour Tortillas

(with guacamole, fresh tomato salsa,

green onion, and jalapeño)

Texmati Rice

Beer Without Measure

Lamme's Austin Praline and Vanilla Ice Cream

SECTION IV: The "You Look as if You Slaved over a Hot Stove"—But You Didn't—Dinner Parties

The Mail-Order Pantry

escargots: Enfant Riant (with recipe)
Chateaubriand: Certified Prime (with recipe)
Oregon Blue cheese: Rogue River Valley Creamery
California almonds: Nunes Farms Almonds
olives: Santa Barbara Olive Co.
sun-dried tomatoes: Timbercrest Farms
tomatilloes: Frieda's Finest (with recipe)
ice cream topping: Grand Finale

CERTIFIED PRIME DINNER

Using California escargots for an appetizer and a Chateaubriand cooked in the most foolproof way—by roasting—you can create a dinner that you'll want to do again and again.

Escargots Mendocino with Sourdough French Bread
Roast Chateaubriand with Oregon Blue Cheese,
California Almonds, and Green Olives
Butter Lettuce and Sun-Dried Tomatoes with Vinaigrette
Lima Beans Santa Barbara with Tomatilloes
French Bread and Butter
A Robust Red Wine: Cabernet or Pinot Noir
Vanilla Ice Cream and Grand Finale
Triple Chocolate Sauce

The Mail-Order Pantry

pistachios: CIF Nut Ranch (with sweetbreads recipe)
rice and coffee: Community Coffee (with rice recipe)
lemon Chardonnay dressing: Cuisine Perel
brownies: Gwetzli

CALIFORNIA CUISINE

Based on French principles and California's provender, here's a dinner that's easier to prepare than you ever thought possible. Popcorn rice is white and smells while cooking like you-know-what. A nuttier taste than plain long-grained.

Sweetbreads in Pistachio Sauce
(with cherry tomatoes, avocado slices, and pistachios)
Popcorn Rice Picante   Ugli Fruit and Banana Slices
with Lemon Chardonnay Dressing
French Bread and Sweet Butter
California Chardonnay
Double-Chocolate Brownies   French Roast Coffee

THE FRENCH FARMER'S SUPPER

Back when ducks were as common to the kitchen as chickens, this was considered the most practical way to get supper on the table. Now we call it a delicacy. Just sautéed duck breast still pink in the middle and sliced paper-thin, with a side dish of red boiled potatoes and sautéed vegetables. Seems like a feast these days.

Sautéed Duck Breast in Peppercorns
Boiled Red Potatoes   Sautéed Baby Zucchini
Bibb Lettuce and Chicory with Lemon Vinaigrette
Company-Best Whole Wheat Rolls and Sweet Butter
Prunes and Walnuts with Crème Fraîche

The Mail-Order Pantry

duck breasts: Wellington Farms (with recipe) or D'Artagnan
zucchini: California Sunshine Fine Foods
vinaigrette: Beautiful Food
rolls: Butte Creek Mill (with recipe)
prunes and walnuts: Timbercrest Farms
crème fraîche: Kendall Cheese Co.

UPPER MICHIGAN WOODS DINNER

From up in the cold North Woods come the mushrooms and cherries to create a fine American dinner.

Pâté Morel
Grilled Pork Tenderloin
with Michigan Dried Tart Cherries
Minnesota Wild Rice
Steamed Broccoli with Lemon Butter
Cabernet Sauvignon
French Roast Coffee
Simply Shortbreads and Gelato

The Mail-Order Pantry

morels: American Spoon Foods (with recipe) and Forest Foods, Inc.
cherries: American Spoon (with recipe)
rice: Community Coffee
shortbreads: Simply Shortbread

THE VIRTUES OF VEAL

Here is the simplest, most elegant presentation I can think of for veal as good as Rachel Nicoll's. Pipe the mashed potatoes around the serving platter's edge. Steam some fresh peas and you've practically got it made.

Ruth Robinson's Marinated Mushrooms
Rachel Nicoll's Quenelles de Veau
Mashed Potatoes
Fresh Buttered Peas
Limestone Lettuce and Papaya
with Brandy Honey Dressing
Merlot
Chocolate Mousse Cake

The Mail-Order Pantry

mushroom marinade: Kimberley Wine Vinegar Works (with recipe)
veal: Summerfield Farm (with recipe)
brandy honey dressing: Victorian Pantry
chocolate mousse cake: Desserts by David Glass

The Mail-Order Pantry

lamb or lamb stew: Jamison
Farms (with recipe)
curry-almond salad dressing:
Cook's Classics, Ltd.
sourdough starter: Goldrush
Enterprises
apricot cake: Matthews 1812
House

THE PENNSYLVANIA SPRING LAMB STEW SUPPER

Sukey Jamison and I both think the shanks are about the best-tasting part of a lamb. She makes this stew and will send it to you, frozen, in quarts, or you can make it yourself. It makes a heartwarming midwinter meal.

Sukey Jamison's Lamb Shank Stew
Pomegranate and Grapefruit Salad
with Curry-Almond Dressing
Sourdough Biscuits and Sweet Butter
Apricot Fruitcake and Coffee

The Mail-Order Pantry

beef: Omaha Steaks
International (with recipe)
rice: Maison E. H. Glass, Inc.
tea: Ten Ren Tea Co.
pecan praline pie: Mary of
Puddin Hill

OMAHA'S KOREAN BARBECUE

When you have first-class meat, you don't need much else. Here is a recipe from Omaha Steaks that showcases their first-quality beef. As simple to prepare as anything here.

Omaha Steaks' Korean Barbecue Beef
Stir-Fried Snow Peas and Cashews
Basmati Rice
Chinese Green Tea
Pecan Praline Pie

MAIL-ORDER GROCERY STORES

Here are 27 of the best mail-order grocery stores I could find. Notice particularly that they offer regional specialties grouped together under one umbrella, making shopping for something as specific as, say, Cajun foods a snap.

1. Bayou Buffet
PO Box 791127
New Orleans, LA 70179

phone orders: yes
504-482-3752
visa/mc

Creole and Cajun foods, Crab boil, Rotel tomatoes, Peychaud's bitters, Steens syrup, Camellia kidney beans, wild pecan rice, even Pat O'Brien's hurricane mix.

2. The Chef's Catalog
3915 Commercial Ave.
Northbrook, IL 60062

phone orders: yes
312-480-9400
ae/visa/mc/dc/cb

Kitchen hardware, professional restaurant quality. I want one of everything I see! A jumbo fish and veggie basket for the grill, automatic cherry stoner, a Cantina chili pot.

3. The Chocolate
Collection
PO Box 217
Paradise, PA 17562

phone orders: yes
800-342-5322
visa/mc

Want anything in chocolate? From Geneva, Paris, Brussels, or Madrid? Truffles, candy bars, baking chocolate. The works.

4. Community Coffee   phone orders: yes
PO Box 3778   800-535-9901
Baton Rouge, LA 70821   ae/visa/mc

American regional foods. South Louisiana specialties, good jams, pasta sauces and salad dressings.

5. DeLaurenti   phone orders: yes
1435 First Ave.   206-622-0141
Seattle, WA 98101

More foodstuffs packed into less space than I've ever seen. A vast assortment of everything from mustards to jams to cheeses to mushrooms to meats, you name it.

6. Gazin's   phone orders: yes
PO Box 19221   504-482-0302
New Orleans, LA 70119   ae/visa/mc

Everything from Cajun Power Chili Sauce, their own spice blends, a Creole Feast assortment that includes delicious wild pecan rice, turtle soup, creole mustard, remoulaude sauce, and a New Orleans cookbook.

7. F. H. Gillingham & Co.   phone orders: yes
16 Elm St.   802-457-2100 ext. 83
Woodstock, VT 05091   visa/mc

Established in 1886, they still send fresh MacIntosh apples in season, maple syrups, cheddars, mustards and local preserves.

8. Latta's of Oregon   phone orders: yes
PO Box 1377   503-265-3238
Newport, OR 97365   ae/visa/mc

Northwest regional specialties: Indian fry bread, huckleberry preserves, filberts, dried peaches, and a vast array of jams, spices, syrups, and herbs.

9. Maison E. H. Glass, Inc. phone orders: yes
52 East 58th St.   212-755-3316
New York, NY 10022   visa/mc

3,500 domestic and imported foods. Everything from Caspian caviar to rattlesnake, from lebkuchen to their famous fig pudding.

10. Made in Montana   phone orders: no
300 Buffalo Jump Rd.   visa/mc
Three Forks, MT 59752

A cooperative venture among Montana craftspeople and cottage kitchen operators. Turkey tamales to handmade green willow furniture.

11. Made in New York   phone orders: yes
Store   607-272-2125

PO Box 2000   ae/visa/mc/dc/cb
Ithaca, NY 14851

Everything to eat, that's fit to eat, that's made in New York from Broadway to Buffalo. Smada Farms maple syrup, chicken wing sauce, famous Red Wing peanut butter, Ithaca soap.

12. Napa Valley   phone orders: yes
Connection   800-422-1111
1121 Hunt Ave.   visa/mc
St. Helena, CA 94574

Live in California? You can mail-order a staggering selection of local wines. Out of state, you'll have to settle for wine vinegars, and jellies.

13. Norm Thompson   phone orders: yes
PO Box 3999   800-547-1160
Portland, OR 97208   ae/visa/mc/dc/cb

The Northwest's answer to L. L. Bean, Norm Thompson also carries a valuable group of locally made Northwest food products: smoked salmon, Cougar Gold cheese, raspberry preserves, beer bread, pickled asparagus, wine cookies.

14. Oakville Grocery   phone orders: yes
7856 St. Helena Hwy.   707-944-8802
Oakville, CA 94562   ae/visa/mc

The original West Coast regional gourmet grocery store. The very best from the Garden of Eden that is California.

15. Panhandle Popcorn   phone orders: yes
PO Drawer 878   800-255-7000 (national)
Plainview, TX 79093   800-692-1365 (TX)
                             visa/mc

Besides the predictable popcorn, popped and un-, you can also get a good barbecue kit or Tex-Mex package.

16. Paprikas Weiss   phone orders: yes
1546 Second Ave.   212-288-6117
New York, NY 10028   visa/mc

Carrying thousands of items, from Hungarian salami to Australian glacéed fruits, this New York fixture has been importing foods most of this century. Peppers, cheeses, spice grinders.

17. G. B. Ratto,   phone orders: yes
International Grocers   415-832-6503
821 Washington St.   visa/mc
Oakland, CA 94607

A good selection of imported olive oils and all Mediterranean type foods as well as grains and meals, beans, seeds, and glacéed fruits. They have an enormous catalog that lists everything from soup to nuts. Specialties from Indonesia, the British Isles, Israel, Argentina, Brazil, India, West Africa, and Italy. Pomegranate juice, red palm oil, vinadloo paste, cassava meal, and treacle drops.

18. H. Roth & Son   phone orders: yes
1577 First Ave., PO Box F   212-734-1111
New York, NY 10028   visa/mc

Everything for bakers, from a variety of flours to special sugars, to exotic cookie cutters and confectionary molds. On one page, 15 hand graters to choose from.

19. S. E. Rykoff & Co.   phone orders: yes
PO Box 21467   800-421-9873
Market Street Station   visa/mc
Los Angeles, CA 90021

Delicious sweet pickled cherries, asparagus spears vinaigrette, *olives de Nice,* and *picholines du gard,* quail eggs, even a French bean slicer and first-quality imported Belgian chocolates for couvertures: dark, milk, white, and hazelnut filling, balsamic vinegar, and various nut oils.

20. Select Origins   phone orders: yes
Box N   516-288-1382
Southampton, NY 11968   ae/visa/mc

Arizona medjool dates, California monukka raisins, Brittany France shallots, Bordeaux wine marinade, Cochon et Co. mustard, oils, vinegars, pastas, mushrooms. And the spices and herbs, just to name a few —Madagascar cloves, Sumatran cinnamon sticks, Jamaican allspice, saffron from Murcia, Spain.

21. The Silver Palate   phone orders: yes
274 Columbus Ave.   212-799-6340
New York, NY 10023   ae/visa/mc

Good preserves, fruitcakes and sauces, fruits in liqueur (oh, those vanilla rum clementines!), chutneys, barbecue sauces, vinegars, oils, mustards, sweet sauces.

22. Sir Thomas Lipton's phone orders: yes
Trading Co.   800-932-0488 (national)
PO Box 2005   800-325-1035 (NH)
Nashua, NH 03061   visa/mc

For tea shippers everywhere, the works.

23. A Taste of Texas   phone orders: no
Texas Dept. of Agriculture 512-462-7624
PO Box 12847
Austin, TX 78711

Where to find the original maker of everything from Arbuckles pickles to Shotgun Willie's chili.

24. Todaro Bros.   phone orders: yes
557 Second Ave.   212-679-7766
New York, NY 10016   ae/visa/mc

Fifty varieties of pasta, from conchiglie to tortellini to ziti. Balsamic vinegar, unfiltered olive oils, panettone and *pandoro,* prosciutto and *salsiccia abruzesa.* Cheeses and lots of mushrooms. This is little Italy.

25. To Market to Market   phone orders: yes
PO Box 492   503-657-9192
West Linn, OR 97068   visa/mc

Kathy Parson is rare—a cook with a sense of design. She creates custom gift baskets, combining fine foods in original theme presentations that are then packaged in luxurious containers.

Kathy's latest design is *The Satisfaction Guaranteed Tote Bag,* a handsome buff canvas shopping bag, sturdily bound by black handles. We've chosen the very best food items and stuffed the tote with goodies, a copy of this book, and an apron stamped "Satisfaction Guaranteed."

26. The Vermont Country   phone orders: yes
Store   802-362-2400
PO Box 3000   visa/mc
Manchester Center, VT
  05255

Vrest Orton calls his catalog the "Voice of the Mountains . . . The Strength of the Hills Is in the People." For a commercial presentation, this is one of the most revealing documents about a region I ever saw. Anthropologists, take note. Cider jelly, Vermont cheddar. Pure cotton and wool *totally sensible* garments and bedclothes. Canned New England foods including dandelion greens and fiddleheads. A folding rocker, a whole raft of books written by Vrest Orton himself, toenail clippers and pine soap, roller skates and rubber boots. God, I love the variety you find in America.

27. Williams-Sonoma   phone orders: yes
PO Box 7456   415-652-9007
San Francisco, CA 94120   ae/visa/mc

Chuck Williams calls this simply "A catalog for cooks," and unless you have been cooking for the past several years on a cruise ship that never came into port, you know that this catalog—above all others— is the one to have. Foodstuffs, gear, recipes, and tabletop ware that I would rob banks to lay hands on. Chuck Williams makes you want to cook. And to that end, I am getting up from here right this very moment and going to make this tomato asparagus pasta sauce recipe I see in his catalog. Good-bye.

COMPANIES

A&B Nut Basket, 80
Adrienne's, 188
Alaska Wild Berry Products, 34
American Spoon Foods, 77
Andre Bollier, Ltd., 186
Apple Attractions, 76
Arnold Reuben's Cheesecakes, 220
Australian Seafood Products, 120

Bainbridge Co., 43
Baldwin Hill Bakery, 23
Barleystock, The, 230
Basheer Studios, 231
Bayou Buffet, 247
Beautiful Food, 166
Beginnings, Endings, Etc., 38
Bent, G.H. Co., 204
Berry Best Farms, 36
Blanchard and Blanchard, 157
Bland Farms, 66
Bliss, George, Avocados, 74
Blue Corn Connection, 27
Blue Heron French Cheese Co., 20
Boetje Foods Inc., 170
Bon Melange, 145
Boudin Bakery, 28
Bragg, Steve, 229
Briar Hills Dairy, Inc., 5
Briggintine Monks, 174
Brown Bag Cookie Art, 228
Brown's, C.C. of Hollywood, 192
Brumwell Flour Mill, 30
Buckley's English Toffee, 176
Burger's Ozark Cured Hams, 110
Butte Creek Mill, 31
Butternut Mountain Farm, 52

C.H.S., 64
CIF, 82
Cabot Farmers Co-op Creamery, 10
Cafe Beaujolais, 219
California Sunshine Foods, 60
Callaway Gardens Store, 83
Campbell's Farm, 105
Captain's Pride, 124

Carrol-Norman, 169
Cascados Farms, 141
Cavanaugh Lakeview Farms, 101
Caviarteria Inc., 127
Certified Prime, 112
Chapin's Fudge, 174
Chef Allen, Inc., 118
Chef's Catalog, The, 247
Chenel, Laura, 6
Chinese Kitchen, The, 144
Chocolate Collection, The, 247
Chocolate Lace, 177
Circle K Enterprises, 124
Clambake Co., The, 114
Clearview Farms Cannery, 151
Community Coffee, 25, 248
Confidence Co., 102
Conner Farms, Inc., 65
Conrad Rice Mill, 71
Cook's Classics, 165
Corti Bros., 41, 134
Costello Farms, 68
Cotuit Oyster Co., 116
Country Accents, 231
Cowboy Caviar, 153
Cranberry Sweets Co., 185
Crand's Candy Castle, 189
Creole Delicacies Co., Inc., 181
Crowley Cheese, 10
Cuisine Perel, 165
Curling Iron Beef Co., 113

Daniel Weaver Co., The, 91
D'Artagnan, 98
Dearborn, 195
Deer Creek Wild Rice, 69
Deer Mountain Berry Farm, 36
DeLaurenti, 248
Desert Rose Salsa, 153
Desserts by David Glass, 217
DeWildt, Mrs., 143
Di Camillo Baking Co., Inc., 210
Dickie Davis, 150
Dinkel's Bakery, 218
Dundee Orchards, 79
Dupre, Gaston, Inc., 180

Early's Honey Stand, 110
Edwards, S. Wallace & Sons, 105
Eilenberger's Baking Co., 213

Eisenhower Candies, Inc., 177
Ekone Oyster Co., 116
El Paso Chile Co., The, 142
Enfant Riant, 128
English Tea Shop, The, 26
Enstrom Candies, Inc., 176
Estus Gourmet, 70
Ethnic Pantry, The, 144
Evangeline Pepper Products, 177

Falling Waters Flours, 32
Farms of Texas, 70
Final Blessing, The, 220
Fisher Brothers Fishery, 119
Flour Arts Pantry, The, 216
Flying Foods International, 96
Forest Foods, Inc., 54
Fran's Patisserie, 188
Fresh Northwest, 61
Frieda's, 60
Full Moon Mushroom Co., 55

Gaspar's Sausage Co., Inc., 92
Gazin's, 30, 248
Genovesi Food Co., 139
Gethsemani Farms, 18, 215
Gillingham, F.H. & Co., 248
Gilroy Farms Garlic, 68
Gladys Cookie Shop, 213
Glie Farms, 58
Golden Gulf, 118
Golden Valley Nut, 81
Golden Whisk, 133
Goldrush Enterprises, 29
Gordon-Thompson, Ltd., 95
Grand Finale, 191
Grandpa Buswell's Candy, 185
Great Western Buffalo Co., 102
Greenbriar Jam Kitchen, 35
Guilford Cheese Co., The, 17
Gwaltney of Smithfield, 106
Gwetzli, 221

Hachar Imports, 145
Halcyon Gardens, Inc., 63
Hanes, Mrs. Travis F., 208
Hansen Caviar Co., 126
Harbor Sweets, 190
Harman's Cheese & Country Store, 11
Harrington's, 107
Harry & David, 72

PRODUCTS

Español, 41
Picante, 155
Tex Mex, 142, 150, 155
Salts, herbal, 151
San Francisco sourdough:
    bread, 28
    starter and mixes, 29
Sauces, see also: barbecue,
        butter, Cajun, Creole,
        curry, fajita, herb, hot,
        Indonesian, pasta, picante,
        salsa, spaghetti, teriyaki,
        tomato
Sausage:
    andouille, 93
    baloney (bologna), 91
    East European, 90, 91
    French style, 87, 89, 98
    German style, 90, 91
    goose liver, Israel, 96
    Louisiana, 93
    Portuguese, 89
    reindeer, 45
    salami, 72, 73
    smoked, 108, 110
    summer, 91, 108
    Tasso, 93
    venison, 95
Scallops, Cape Cod, 122
Scrapple, Philadelphia, 91
Scrod, 122
Seasoning mixes:
    Brazil, 144
    Cajun, 93, 145
    Chinese, 144
    herbal, 151
    India, 144, 147
    Indonesian, 143, 144
    New Mexico, 141
    North and East Africa, 144
    Thailand, 144
Seeds, flower, herb, and
        vegetable, 61
Shad, fresh, 122
    smoked, 122
Sheep, wild Corsican, 98
Shortbreads, 207, 208
Shrimp:
    jumbo, 120
    smoked, 122
Snails, 128
Snapper, 121, 123

Soap, handmade, 231
Soldier beans, 11
Sole, Dover, 96
Souffles in a jar, 222
Sourdough sauce, 34
Spaghetti sauces, 133, 134
Spices:
    Brazil, 144
    Cajun, 145
    Chinese, 144
    general, 203
    India, 144, 147
    Indonesian, 143, 144
    Mexican, 144
    Mid Eastern, 144
    New Mexican, 141
    North and East African, 144
    Tex Mex, 141, 142
    Thailand, 144
Squab, 60, 96, 98
    eggs, 60
Squid ink, 96
Steaks, 111, 113, 115
Stencilled kitchen accessories,
    230
Sturgeon, fresh, 123
    smoked, 122
Sugarplum cake, 220
Sun-dried tomatoes, 74, 139
Sweet and Hot Sauce, 150
Swordfish, 121, 122
Syrups, fruit, 39

Taffy, 178, 179, 181, 183
Tasso sausage, 93
Teas:
    Chinese style, 201
    English style, 200
    Hawaiian, 65
    herbal, 151, 203
Teriyaki sauce, 140
Tex-Mex supplies, 142, 145,
    155
Tiles, handpainted, 231
Tillamook cheddar, 20
Tinware, Mexican, 145
Toffees, 176, 177, 183
Tomatoes:
    antipasto, 152
    caviar, 153
    dilly, 150
    marinated, 74, 139

sauce, 133, 141, 153, 157,
    165
sun-dried, 74
Texas, 150
Tools, garnish/grate, 230
Trail mix, 74, 81
Trappist cheese, 18
Trout, smoked, 127
Truffles:
    fresh Italian, 127
    fresh Oregon white, 56
    Périgord, 102
Truffles, chocolate, 174, 183,
    186, 187, 188, 195
    kit, 195
Tuna, fresh, 121, 123
    smoked, 123
Turbot fish, 96
Turkey, 95, 96, 101
    "breast," 109
    smoked, 101
    wild, 98, 100
Tutti Frutti sauce, 148

Valley Lahvosh, 24
Vanilla, 146
Veal, milk fed, 104
Vegetables, gourmet, 55, 60,
    61, 62, 77, 96
Venison, 95, 98
Vermont Farmhouse Cheese, 21
Vermont granular cheese, 12
Vinegar:
    balsamic, 41
    fresh herb, 162, 163
    fruit, 37, 81, 163, 164
    raspberry, 162
    rice wine, 144
    wine, 161

Walnuts:
    black, 78
    farm fresh California, 81
    jumbos, 80
Wild rice, 69, 70
Wreaths:
    bay, 67
    cinnamon stick, 67
    chile, 67
    Christmas fir, 61
    garlic, 67
    Tex Mex, 142

RECIPES

APPETIZERS

Anchovy cheese fingers, 219
Brie with pecans, 20
Chopped catfish, 125
Escargot mendocino, 129
How to eat foie gras, 98
Marinated mushrooms, 161
Roasted cheese, 162
Sherry cheese pâté, 222
Vermont cheese pudding, 13
Vermont cheddar pastries, 14

BREADS

Blue corn crêpes, 27
Pumpernickel bread, 32
Whole wheat rolls, 31

SOUP

Conch chowder, 121
Elephant garlic broth, 67
Portuguese kale soup, 93
Posole, 141
Tasso seafood gumbo, 94
Trappist cheese bisque, 18

SALAD

Classic potato, 165
Fresh salmon, 163
Nasturtium fruit, 59
Sheila Cook's, 165
Smoked capon, 100
Warm duck, 163
West Indies, 66
Winchester herb vinegar/oil, 59

SAUCES

Augusta, 61
Barbecue, 169
Cherry, red tart, 79
Cumberland, 97
Hazelnut butter, 81
Hollandaise, simple, 26
Mustard, 118
Pear glaze, 109
Red eye gravy, 110

Sun-dried tomato/cream, 134
Venison/elk marinade, 96

VEGETABLES

Jerusalem artichokes, 62
Leeks, 62
Lima beans Santa Barbara, 60
Morel pâté, 55
Nasturtium sandwiches, 59
Onion pie supreme, 65
Potatoes, roasted new, 127
Potatoes, with caviar, 19
Rice, popcorn picante, 72
Vegetable pâté, 24
Yellow eye beans, Vermont, 49

MAIN DISHES

Poultry and Rabbit
Chicken breasts/marmalade, 40
Chicken broiled/mustard, 170
Chicken grilled/olivia, 136
Chicken Indian, 137
Chicken Moroccan, 82
Duck breast, sautéed, 102
Pheasant/gjetost cream, 5
Rabbit, grilled, 101
Rock cornish hens, glazed, 164

Fish
Golden crabmeat quiche, 119
Scallops Los Gatos, 132

Red Meat
Barbecue beef, Korean, 110
Bratwurst a la Vern, 90
Chateaubriand/blue cheese, 112
Fajitas, fabulous, 142
Filet flambe, bourbon, 111
Grillades, Evangeline, 171
Ham, how to carve, 106
Ham, how to cook, 107
Lamb shank stew, 103
Meatballs Schiavone, 135
Polish sausage/molasses, 91
Pork tenderloin/cherries, 78
Quenelles de veau, 104

Pasta and Rice
Fettucine with
    mussels/tomatoes, 139
Fresh w/sheep cheese/bacon, 6
Indonesian rijsttafel, 143
Lemon pepper, 157
Linguine/cheese, 20

Sandwiches/Pizza/Eggs
Cracker bread sandwich, 25
Oyster loaf, 30
Pizza, fresh herbed, 63
Scrambled eggs w/feta, 4
Shallot omelet, 61

DESSERT

Benedictine compote, 74
Chocolate fudge sauce, 191
Cracker pudding, 205
Crumpet flambé, 28
Figs, ported w/almonds, 75
Finghi, Sicilian, 160
Ginger fruit kebabs, 44
Ginger papaya, 44
Hard sauce, easy, 225
Huckleberry dumplings, 38
Lemon curd, 29
Maple nut brittle, 50
Maple whiskey cake, 195
Mousse, white chocolate, 194
Paradigm sauces, 194
Pecan pie, real Texas, 84
Pistachio custard, frozen, 209
Plum cake, puckered, 76
Polly Jean's crêpe suzettes, 222
Postillion coupe royale, 223
Ruth Roffer's hot fudge
    brownies, 193
Susan Kobos's dutch baby, 204

DRINKS

Cafe Brulot, 203
How to make a proper pot of
    tea, 200
Oregon Riesling eggnog, 218
Vermont shake, 50